W9-CRF-932

The Collected Wit and Wisdom of Norman Todd

A Publication of
The Victoria Rhododendron Society

The Collected Wit and Wisdom of Norman Todd

ISBN 978-0-9693989-2-9

Copyright ©
2011
Norman Todd

Front Cover: Photos by Garth Wedemire
Back Cover: 'Iona Campangola' Garth Wedemire,
        5 Firwood Nursery photos by Betty Gordon.
Cover Design: alanaparsons.com

Contents

Foreword

I suppose my life can be divided into three parts. The first part was early life and university years; then living in the extremes of Eastern Canada and lastly, coming west and discovering a surfeit of rhododendrons.

Where I grew up there was an uninhabited castle nearby with extensive grounds. It had been taken over by the military at the start of WW II. They abandoned it pretty quickly to a caretaker we called the DOM – the Dirty Old Man – who lived in squalor in one of the hundred or more rooms. We had access by an unsecured window. There were stone-staired turrets and dungeons and extensive heavily treed grounds with an understorey of huge rhododendrons. This was a children's paradise. Then we grew up.

I worked summers in the shipyards and studied naval architecture at Glasgow University in the winters.

After graduation, I decided like so many to emigrate to Canada. There was no difficulty finding a job. I decided on a job in the Design Office of Davie Shipbuilding. I had the best of views out my windows. We worked at ten-foot drawing tables so there were several windows. I was able to watch all the traffic on the St. Lawrence. I looked directly across to Montmorency Falls. Up to the left I could see Quebec City and Ile d'Orleans on the right. We never saw a rhododendron in Quebec.

We spent a year and a bit in La Belle Provence before moving to take a job at the Ship-model Testing Tank at the National Research Council in Ottawa.

I had various other jobs in Ottawa including a stint in the Royal Canadian Navy while completing a Masters degree at Carleton University.

We moved to Victoria in 1972 and bought a house on Rockland Avenue. The garden was full of rhododendrons.

I had come west to look after planning and building the Institute of Ocean Sciences out at Patricia Bay. This was a ten year plus project and after it was completed I was offered the job as Administrator which was much more attractive than going back to Ottawa.

Various site conditions on the land where the institute was to be built required that one of the first consultants we hired was a landscape architect. This was Clive Justice. Clive had just recently returned from a strenuous expedition to Sikkim retracing the 1848-49 steps of Sir Joseph Hooker. I was an attentive audience.

Clive introduced me to the elite of the local rhododendron world – Albert de Mezey, Peggy Abkhazi, Stewart Holland. We joined the Vancouver Island Rock and Alpine Society and met many other experts including Ernie Lythgoe, Rex Murfitt, Ed Lohbrunner and Al Smith.

In 1973 the University was bequeathed the Buchanan Simpson property at Marble Bay on Lake Cowichan. Rex Murfitt and Alan Cook of Stanley Park oversaw the moving of many plants to the University grounds. One half of the University garden was inside the ring road and half outside. The chapel was not then built. I got pressed into service, along with Ernie Lythgoe and thereafter we spent every Saturday morning in the garden. Tony James, head groundskeeper, was very enthusiastic as was Steve Brown of his staff.

With all this new plant material to study, David Ballantyne of the Botany Department and I decided to put on an 8 week course on rhododendrons. This was well attended. The majority went on to found the Victoria Rhododendron Society. The Vancouver Chapter was a hoary old society by this time; we were the newbies on the scene. There then followed a spate of new chapters, with Duncan, Courtney, Nanaimo and Mount Arrowsmith swelling the numbers of the interested on the Island. The mainland was not to be outdone and a number of new chapters were established.

Our new Victoria chapter had a newsletter from the beginning but it was a miserable one-page affair. Alec McCarter volunteered to take on the duties of Editor and it became one of the most readable and technically interesting newsletters in the entire ARS.

We were full of energy and bravado and bid for and won the job of hosting the 1989 spring convention. The preceding winter was a vicious one and many of the blooms were frosted. The convention was the first to be held in the new Convention Centre. Usually these affairs attracted about 600 registrants. We still hold the record for the best-attended convention with 1,100 checking in. We were all exhausted. We held the convention again in 2005. That was our 25th anniversary. Our new editor, James Fuller, published a small book – "A Rhesplendence of Rhododendrons" – to mark the occasion.

The years since the last convention are within the memories of most members so I will say no more.

It is our hope that this present volume, which is due to the sweat and persistence of our current President, Calvin Parsons, will record some of our past activities and perhaps bring a smile to the reader's face.

Norman Todd
June 2011

Second Forward
If I were to sell the reader a barrel of molasses and he, instead of sweetening his substantial dinner with the same judicious intervals, should eat the entire barrel at one sitting and abuse me for making him sick, I would say that he deserved to be made sick for not knowing any better how to use the blessings this world affords. And if I sell to the reader this volume of nonsense and he, instead of seasoning his graver reading with a chapter of it now and then, when his mind demands such relaxation, unwisely overdoses himself with several chapters at a single sitting, he will well deserve to be nauseated, and he will have no one to blame but himself for it.
Mark Twain

Acknowledgements

It is with reverence and honour that we present to you "The Complete Wit and Wisdom of Norman Todd". For over thirty years Norman Todd has entertained us with his humour and knowledge of the genus Rhododendron. Several years ago Norm's faithful computer expired with no backup and all his writings were gone. Through the efforts of many of his rhodoholic fans, a thorough search of the paper and digital archives resulted in collecting 74 of Norm's articles for this book. Many of our members will gladly tell you that they became hooked on rhodos after encountering Norm. "There's always room for one more rhodo," Norm would chirp to anyone willing to listen, and many of us followed his sage advice.

Norman's words in these articles are full of wit and wisdom. His witty comments at our monthly rhodo raffles were experiences not to be missed. The best part of any encounter with Norm was at his Firwood Nursery where he could show a person the better attributes of rhodos. And of course sitting down with Norm over a cup of 'decapitated coffee' was the highlight of any visit.

We wish to thank the many people who sent emails about various articles once folks realized that we were collecting all Norm's articles. Special thanks to Bill and Theresa McMillan, Ann Widdowson, Glen Jamieson, and Linda Gilmore for scanning or typing or submitting various articles from the paper world. Joyce Whittle used her fine editing skills to polish up our efforts. Any errors, omissions or inconsistencies are not a reflection of Norm's command of the English language (although any computer spell-checker would disagree) but our mistakes.
Enjoy.

Calvin Parsons
President, Victoria Rhododendron Society, October 2011

The Ten Best Dwarfs for the Rock Garden
October 1984

Rhododendron is a genus offering the gardener a high range of choice. For the alpine or rock gardener the genus is a gold mine. All rhododendron lovers are promiscuous with their advice and what follows is no exception. I've chosen to define a dwarf as a plant not more than 50 centimeters or 20 inches in height or breadth when 10 years old.

Rhododendrons have a longevity at least equal to humans and will grow larger than our arbitrarily defined size, but by then we treat them as senior citizens and should go to some trouble to accommodate them. By restricting the size we effectively rule out the elepidote (non-scaly) rhododendrons. Most of the really small alpine plants are lepidotes (scaly) as they need the scales to control the high variations in moisture that occur at high altitudes where they grow. Plants not hardy in Victoria are also not considered.

Up near the top I would put 'Rose Elf'. It is a plant which sometimes suffers from the connoisseur's disdain because of its being so easily available – seen in every garden centre. But its popularity is well deserved. It is compact, a bun, tight and even. It buds easily, flowers early, withstands drought better than most and doesn't complain of our coldest Januaries. It shows its *Rhododendron pemakoense* genes in its colour in having some blue in the predominant pink. It's not a great challenge to grow, but pays its rent uncomplainingly.

Also close to the top is another hybrid seen in nearly every garden centre, 'Moerheim's Beauty'. If you don't like mauve leave this one out, but it possesses all of the good qualities of 'Rose Elf'. We might have to mark it down a bit because it is somewhat larger. Some of the recent introductions as described in the ARS Journal evoke interest and envy but this list only considers the plants I've had experience growing. Fairly recent introductions are Peter Cox's 'Chikor' and 'Curlew'. Both are very highly rated. I like 'Chikor' better not just because it is smaller but 'Curlew's' flowers seem to me to be too large for the scale of

1

the plant. Also I admit to a bias of not really liking yellow flowers with red blotches or speckling. I think they remind me of gladiola. 'Chikor' does have some red in its yellow, but it is not too noticeable. It is easy to make it look like a little bonsaied tree and it looks good with dwarf conifers. This brings up two other yellows, both of which I consider really choice. Both are hybrids and both present irrefutable counterattacks on Farrer's hang-up about hybrids having "sold their birthright for a mess of comfort." The first and better is 'Patty Bee' a cross of *R. keiskei* 'Yaku Fairy' and *R. fletcherianum*. The leaves are a clear green of thick substance arranged in neat prostrate sprays. The flowers are a clear true yellow and relatively large but not obtrusively so. The second is 'Princess Anne' a Reuthe hybrid of *hanceanum nanum* and *keiskei*. Its foliage has a bronzy cast in winter. It is a little harder to please but given some protection from the hottest sun should do well in the rock garden. Both 'Patty Bee' and 'Princess Anne' have *keiskei* as a parent and the smallest forms of this have to be ranked as the best yellow of all for the rock garden. There is some confusion as to whether there is only one clone called 'Yaku Fairy' or whether all high altitude plants from the island of Yaku Shima are known by this name. Anyway, it is a tight little bun, as tight as any *armeria*. When grown well not a leaf shows when blooming. For sheer refinement, elegance and finesse the little Japanese azalea *kiusianum* has to be among the best. The small leaves are bright green, the spring leaves being quite a bit larger than the summer ones. Its spreading form and willingness to flower make it rival any alpine plant in desirability. It comes in a range of colours from purple through pink to white. Ed Lohbrunner grew a white one called 'Mt. Fuji', which is very dwarf and one of the best.

A list of the top ten dwarfs in most publications would include *R. impeditum*. I wouldn't contest that. It's a super plant, easy of disposition, usually puts on two or more flushes of growth until reaching the age of discretion. Its blue green leaves, almost cactus like, are interesting at any time of year and it often blooms in the fall, not as profusely as in spring but with assurance that spring will surely follow winter. It's easy to get so no one need be without it but I have a small codicil to insert – I think I like its first cousin *R. tapetiforme* better. It's not easy to describe the reason – little clearer flower colour, a more distinct leaf. Maybe it is only where we have them growing or the form we have that makes the difference which really is not very great. Last, I think we have to include *R. indicum* 'Balsaminiflora', an evergreen azalea with long narrow leaves and fully double pink flowers so tight in the centre that Pierre Trudeau could have worn it as a boutonnière. But for us it is a bit of a disaster as the deer and rabbits think highly of it, as highly as do most rhododendron lovers.

There is not a red on the list. If you really feel "better red than dead" try 'Ruby Hart', somewhat larger than our specifications permit but very fine indeed.

'Mary's Favourite'
1989

One of the first rhododendrons we acquired after arriving in Victoria was 'Mary's Favourite'. Acquired is not a good word as it was a gift from its creator, Albert de Mezey. Albert is one of those people who exert great influence on the way one's interests develop; it was fortunate for us, new arrivals, that we, so quickly, had our interest in rhododendrons encouraged by Albert's knowledge and generosity.

'Mary's Favourite' is a rhododendron which one admires instantly. It is among the most consistently floriferous rhododendrons one can grow. The bell-shaped pink flowers are borne at every growing point – five to six flowers in the truss. They are of appropriate scale for the size of the round *R. williamsianum*-type leaf. It is a cross of *williamsianum* and *R. wardii* (*croceum*) made by Albert in 1953. His sister admired it so much that he decided to name it to reflect her appreciation.

It is at its peak of perfection with some of the flowers fully open. Their lighter pink shade contrasts most effectively with the deeper pink buds. Our plant, which was a layer in Albert's garden is now six feet tall and grows against a wall next to a columnar camellia 'Debutante' which is the same shade of pink. The camellia blooms first but there is a two week's overlap with 'Mary's Favourite', giving a nice continuity.

An elderly neighbour always makes a special trip each spring to see the rhododendron but seldom remarks on the camellia.

Propagation from cuttings is of moderate easiness or difficulty depending on how you view these things. The new wood hardens quite early in the season – it goes from green to brown – so cuttings should be taken in July. One of the problems that I find in taking cuttings is to find a shoot that does not have a flower bud. I hate to cut away next year's bloom. This is merely a psychological deterrent. Just make sure to break out the flower bud. Les Clay is attempting to propagate 'Mary's Favorite' in tissue culture.

Ease of rooting from cuttings bears no relationship to ease of getting meristem growth in a test tube, so there is no guarantee that Clay will be successful. As Les says, he has not yet been able to get 'Elizabeth' going in tissue culture, and 'Elizabeth' is probably the easiest rhododendron to root from cuttings.

I often joke that 'Mary's Favourite' is a "Victoria Cross": it certainly deserves one. It is a rhododendron that always gives one hundred percent performance.

On Fall Blooming Hybrids
1989

Why is it such a sin for a rhododendron to bloom in the fall? I like to show off the odd bloom that appears here and there at this time of year. I was chatting with Mark Nixon, our member from Nanoose Bay, and we agreed that to use the term "precocious" for flowers at this season was pejorative and why, we asked, should it not be encouraged? Few shrubs bloom at this time of year; any new ones would be welcome. It might be a bit of a problem to continue the breeding line if the seed parent were left outside as it might not produce seed, but that could surely be overcome. Some varieties bloom, almost reliably, in the fall – the lepidotes more so than the elepidotes. In our garden, *R. impeditum* always has some bloom, as does *R. fletcherianum*. In the University of Victoria gardens, 'Lady Chamberlain' blooms magnificently each October. 'Sapphire' and *R. russatum* show the odd bloom every year. Enough for a start I'd say.

As stated the elepidotes are less prone to bloom. It may be that fall blooming is induced by summer drought conditions as was advocated in a fairly recent article in the Journal. 'Elizabeth' blooms in the fall more often than not. 'Coral Velvet' which was reputedly raised from *R. yakushimanum* seed seems to me to bloom at anytime it wants. They would be good companions as they have strong indumentum and compatible habit. I saw *R. campylocarpum* in bloom the other day and there's a not-very-good flowered plant of *R. herpesticum* in the University of Victoria garden which seems to like blooming in the fall rather than the spring.

Would you buy a fall blooming rhododendron?

**On Weather Watch
and the Mystery of 'Christmas Cheer'
1989**

The very mild weather we have had in December and January has prompted the earliest bloom I have seen. *R. dauricum* showed colour in our garden on 24 December and was in full bloom on 5 January. Its mauve-violet colour is very welcome at this time of the year – it is less appreciated later in the season. Growing it with the small early narcissus – *N. cyclamineus*, and with the winter blooming cyclamen (*C.*

5

coum) and with the yellow iris (*danfordiae*) would make a very attractive winter scene. One could add a white winter heather like 'Darleyensis', 'Springwood White', 'Silpersmeltze' and have a mass of colour which would rival the shows of April and May.

I note a wide variation in the blooming time of 'Christmas Cheer'. There is a very large plant on Rockland Avenue near Moss Street which generally shows colour by New Year's Day. I have some plants which are supposedly 'Christmas Cheer' – not all from the same source – which don't open until much later. There is bloom (1 Feb) on what I have labeled as 'Rosamundi', a very similar plant. I know of another grouping of so-called 'Christmas Cheer' where there is about five weeks difference in blooming time in plants that are not more than fifteen feet apart.

Are there different clones of 'Christmas Cheer'? Could such small variances in microenvironment cause a gap of ten to twelve weeks blooming time?

On *R. chrysanthum*
1989

I have one truss this year on *R. chrysanthum*. The truss has eight flowers, each one standing up on a long pedicel in a way not unlike the *saluenense* group. It is a light yellow (English primrose) with a slightly deeper yellow ray down each lobe. The flower is, in my opinion, very good. The plant itself is a miserable thing. It must be the slowest growing rhododendron in relation to leaf size. The leaves are definitely high on the list of gourmet food for weevils! It is a plant which is easily overlooked when not in bloom.

Some will recall that this is the rhododendron used by the German, Doctor Koelpin, to treat arthritis. This was in 1776 and he used a tea prepared from the leaves of *chrysanthum*. As David Leach describes it in "The Two Thousand Year Curse of the Rhododendron", Koelpin treated 15 patients and managed to kill two of them. He did not attribute their deaths to the tea and published a book three years later advocating tea for the treatment of arthritis and rheumatism. Countless thousands no doubt suffered and no doubt there were other deaths caused by following Dr. Koelpin's nostrum.

I find I do not now overlook *chrysanthum* when it is not in bloom.

Puzzles in Rhododendron Poison
1989

I always thought popcorn was as North American as Niagara Falls. It is recorded that at the first Thanksgiving dinner hosted by the Pilgrims with ninety-two Indians as guests, the Chief's brother disappeared into the woods and returned with a bushel of popcorn, a startling novelty to the colonists. The Incas used popcorn for funeral decorations and Columbus reported that the West Indians sold popcorn corsages to his crew.

Popcorn is a variety of maize, *Zea mays*, whose only provenance is the Americas.

But popcorn is not quite the exclusive North American phenomenon that many of us assume. Kingdon-Ward and Ludlow and Sheriff, those latter day plant hunters in Burma, Tibet and thereabouts talk about the cultivation of maize and the eating of popcorn. E. H. Wilson in the second volume of "A Naturalist in Western China" writing about his journeys which he undertook about the turn of the century, notes that maize was an important cereal in that area. "This plant is of American origin, but it has been so long cultivated in China that the date of introduction is not ascertainable". Bailey's "New Cyclopedia of American Horticulture" (1906) says very little Sweet Corn was exported and that "the distribution of Sweet Corn into cultivation made little progress prior to the last half of the nineteenth century".

It seems that corn migrated and spread in Asia very rapidly and with it, presumably, went some popcorn. Now

7

Crackerjack must be exclusively American? Listen to what Frank Kingdon-Ward says in "Plant Hunter's Paradise": "..for in spite of Cranbrook's and Mano's alarming experience I still continued to eat the excellent popcorn and honey which the Tibetans brought us". Tibetan Crackerjack!

What was the "alarming experience" Kingdon-Ward was referring to? Earlier in the book he tells of the Tibetans bringing them mead brewed from the local honey which he concluded must have been rhododendron honey. He says, "It had no ill effect other than making us completely drunk". But when whole honey was brought, it was a different story. His travelling companion, Lord Cranbrook, after eating honey "..had hardly gone a quarter of a mile up the river bank when without warning he had collapsed and fallen into the backwater. The water had revived him somewhat and though unable to walk "he had climbed out of the river and shouted for help. By evening (he) was his cheerful self again". Their servant suffered the same symptoms – the cause – rhododendron poisoning. Ludlow and Sheriff recorded similar experiences.

This brings to mind that famous historical coincidence relating to rhododendron poisoning. In 401 B.C. a Greek army led by Xenophon camped near Trebizond on the Black Sea where there were many beehives. They ate the honey and "lost their senses". Their pursuers did not find them. Three hundred and thirty-five years later, Roman armies under Pompey camped at the same place, ate the honey, were found by their pursuers and were massacred.

An excellent account of this and other happenings relating to rhododendron poisoning is given by David Leach in "The Two Thousand Year Curse of the Rhododendron" published in the A. R. S. book "Rhododendron Information".

Leach says the culprit constituent in the Trebizond honey came from the nectar of the yellow-flowered 'Pontic Azalea', *R. luteum*. However in a most comprehensive book "Honey" (Ed. Eva Crane, Crane, Russak and Co. Inc., New York, 1975) one of the authors states, "Bees foraging exclusively on *Rhododendron ponticum*, indigenous to Asia

Minor, produce poisonous honey, a fact known in antiquity and thoroughly investigated in recent years. The active substance, andromedotoxin, acetylandromedol, has been detected in the nectar of several Ericaceae, e.g. *Rhododendron ponticum, Kalmia latifolia, Ledum palustre* and *Tripetaleia paniculata*." So it seems certain that *ponticum* has poisonous nectar. Does *luteum* have poisonous nectar too? Or when combined is the resulting honey more debilitating than when the nectar from only one species predominates? They do bloom at about same time.

Leach's article gives rise to another little puzzle. It concludes with a report on work done at my Alma Mater – The University of Glasgow – on the toxicity of *R. thomsonii* and its hybrids. Among those plants rated highly toxic are *thomsonii* itself, *arboreum, niveum* and *pratti.* Peter Cox, in "The Larger Species of Rhododendron", writing of *thomsonii* says, "Honey from the nectary of this species is said to be non-poisonous and the Tibetans sometimes eat the flowers". Questions remain.

There is evidence of another puzzle about eating rhododendron flowers. In Fletcher's account of the travels of Frank Ludlow and Gordon Sheriff – "A Quest of Flowers" – he writes "..the best they gathered (were) a form of *R. cinnabarinum* (16027) with apricot-red to yellow bells which the local children ate with relish after first plucking away the stamens and ovary." *Cinnabarinum* is one of the few lepidote rhododendrons having nectar. There are several reports – some recent – of its being extremely toxic. To quote Cox again, "Considered universally poisonous to goats and cattle including the wood; even the wood smoke causes the eyes to inflame and cheeks to swell".

Lest you decide to get rid of all your rhododendrons for fear of poisoning yourself and the whole community (a thing you would certainly not do by burning as the smoke might get in your eyes) let me mention some reassuring facts from the honey book previously referred to. Honey from the Alpenrose (*R. ferrugineum*) and *R. hirsutum* is noted as being very light and mild with a high enzyme content. Honey from

Calluna, Erica and *Vaccinium* is also rated very highly. (An interesting aside, the honey from *Eucryphia* is considered by some to be the finest honey of all).

This little survey of rhododendron poisons gives rise to a number of interesting points. How did corn get to Asia and spread so quickly? Is *luteum* poisonous? Is thomsonii or some of its hybrids? Is *cinnabarinum* or are only some *cinnabarinums* poisonous? In areas where *ponticum* is endemic, as in parts of Britain, is honey contaminated? Do other members of the *Pontica Subsection* have poisonous nectar? (The plant known in Britain as *ponticum* is now known to be a hybrid with *catawbiense*.)

A final note: one chapter of the American Cancer Society lists eating popcorn (dry) among its recommendations for noncarcinogenic activities, along with sitting in the shade and having a good laugh.

Rhododendron Classification –
An Attempt to Explain
1989

"Read not the times, read the eternities" said Henry David Thoreau. Having been a bit of a botanist himself, I wonder how Thoreau would apply his own stricture to the rhododendron classification debate that is ongoing. One could certainly argue that the "eternities" are being changed for the "time".

Some members have suggested that a short piece on the question of classification would be useful and, with presumption and trepidation, here goes. (The excuse for a gardener to do this is that as gardeners we have a very real vested interest in that we need to know what to call our plants).

Most of us have learned the names of our rhododendron plants from the old system of classification which was derived by Sir Isaac Bayley Balfour just after the turn of the century. Sir Isaac was Regius Keeper at the Royal

Botanic Garden in Edinburgh, Scotland and it was to that place that collectors like George Forrest were sending a huge volume of new plant material for classification. (It is interesting to note that J. C. Williams of Caerhays in Cornwall paid Forrest a bonus for every new species of rhododendron, as classified by Balfour, that Forrest introduced). Balfour was deluged and could only deal with this in a way which he himself knew was a temporary expedient. Essentially, he used what Cullen has called a "horticulturally-based system". He grouped "species" around a type, usually best known or garden-worthy, into what he called "Series". Thus, there was the Fortunei series, the Triflorum series etc. Unfortunately, he died before he could revise his temporary system and as it met the needs of gardeners, it was accepted and became entrenched.

From a scientific point of view, it is not at all acceptable and the new system as developed by Sleumer, Chamberlain, Cullen, the Philipsons et al., aims to remove the irregularities. It divides the genus into sub-genera, sections, subsections, species, sub-species and to satisfy us gardeners, varieties. (Instead of "variety" some have proposed the word "Group" but that seems awkward to me).

Where we gardeners react to this new system is when the name of what we have considered a distinctive plant disappears. What we know as *R. concatenans* now becomes *cinnabarinum subsp. xanthocodon, var. concatenans*. And poor old *R. rhabdotum*, with its distinctive red line down the middle of each corolla lobe, is now just a variety of *dalhousiae*. Under the new system, the number of species has been reduced to about half the previous number.

I will not try to define what makes a rhododendron a rhododendron i.e., what is included in the genus. It is complicated but for those who wish to pursue this, see Sleumer's paper in "Contributions Towards a Classification of Rhododendron" published by the New York Botanical Garden, 1980, pp 1-8.

The definition of what a species is, is easy enough to write, but still seems a bit arbitrary. To be a species, a plant must differ from others in at least two independent characteristics and have a different geographical or ecological distribution from its nearest allies. (Why two?) We know how easily many species breed with other species to give us the hybrids we all grow. On the face of it, the idea of a species doesn't make much sense to the plants themselves. However, we also know that some within the genus will not cross. This is one good practical test for breaking the genus into sub-genera.

There are eight sub-genera, but we need only concern ourselves with four. These are: Rhododendron, Hymenanthes, Pentanthera and Tsutsutsi and these are fairly easily recognizable.

Sub-genus Rhododendron includes all those with scales – the Lepidotes. A ten-power magnifying glass will show the scales quite easily. For the most part, looking at the underside of the leaves will reveal the scales, but on some when the underside of the leaves have hairs as well as scales, (e.g. *edgeworthii*), you have to scrape the hairs off to see them. Scales also occur on the tops of some leaves, on the flower parts and on the stems. Scales are easiest to see on the new growth.

Sub-genus Hymenanthes does not have scales. They are the elepidotes (e.g. *R. fortunei* and *R. yakushimanum*). Many of these are indumented, (i.e. with a felt-like, or plaster-like coating on the underside of the leaf). Most within these first two sub-genera have ten stamens, although a few have less and quite a few in Hymenanthes have more.

The next sub-genus always has five stamens/anthers and for that reason is called Pentanthera. They are deciduous and are what we know as deciduous azaleas. Most are easily recognized as such, but some species such as *R. mucronulatum* may be mistaken for an azalea. It is a lepidote and has ten stamens.

The Tsutsutsi sub-genus is made up of the evergreen azaleas. These have five stamens, sometimes more, and often different numbers on the same plant, and have hairs lying flat on the upper side of the leaves pointing to the tip (adpressed hairs). Evergreen azaleas are partly deciduous in that they grow two sets of leaves every year – a spring set which fall off and a lasting summer set. Again a ten power magnifying glass will permit seeing these hairs quite clearly.

The other four sub-genera are the exceptions – that prove the rule? They are misfits and evolutionary conundrums. Azaleatrum has two species, *R. ovatum* and *R. staminium*. Our own native *albiflorum* is all alone in Candidastrum.

Semibarbatum and *camtschaticum* are each in their own sub-genus.

As already mentioned, species within one particular sub-genus will generally not cross with plants from another sub-genus. Well-known exceptions are *Broughtonii Aureum* (elepidote x deciduous azalea) and 'Hardijzer's Beauty' (lepidote x evergreen azalea). Crosses between the genus rhododendron and another genus are not unknown either. 'Elizabeth' has been crossed with ledum and the resulting plant named 'Brilliant'. Rhododendron has also been crossed with kalmia. (Note: Ledum is now classified as belonging to the genus Rhododendron).

At the international conference on rhododendron classification held in Fife, Washington, it was interesting to observe the difference in approach to taxonomy between the European/North American and the Chinese. I was told that this was the first time the Chinese had participated in a forum like this. As they have a major portion of the genus within their own backyard, clearly their approach is going to be very influential. The Chinese were using the classical morphological methods, size, and shape of scales, leaves, ovary, corolla, etc. They also were very concerned with distribution. On the other hand, the European/North Americans were extremely interested in the biochemistry of the plants and were talking about leaf waxes, flavonoids and other esoteric substances. Perhaps the ultimate determinant will be DNA.

When the debate showed signs of becoming too contentious, I think it was Brit Smith as chairperson, who brought the subject back to earth when he said, "The subject is serious, but not that important". How true; but it's surprising how many people it keeps in a job.

Deadheading
October 1989

You need a dead head to deadhead. There is no doubt I can be totally dead in the head quite often on any given day on a wide variety of topics but after about five minutes of deadheading, I start to estimate how many more five minuteses will be needed to remove all of the pesky capsules. Even with our contemporary appreciation of astronomical numbers – those with strings of zeros on their tails – the task becomes incomprehensible. Paradoxically, I have an appreciation of the meaning of infinity.

Why do rhododendrons not have good fruit? If they had nice brightly coloured berries we would gladly leave them on the branch. If they were edible…oh, what a pleasant thought. I even try to convince myself that all this spent biomass that is being strewn at the base of the plants must be the best mulch in the world for rhododendrons. But that only makes the plants more luxuriant, which compounds the problem next year.

There is a school of thought that says, "Why deadhead? It only makes the critters bloom better next year". I recommend you weigh this advice carefully. It has merit.

I think that there should be an extra number used in rating rhododendrons – one for ease of deadheading. One of my most favourite rhododendrons is *R. auriculatum*. The plant is at least twenty years old and I enjoy it every day, twelve months of the year. It has never flowered. *Auriculatum* would get a 5 in my rating scheme – so would most of the *R. talienses* – they never flower either. For plants that do flower, I would rate things like 'Loder's White' quite highly. I'd give it a 4.5 (5 is reserved for plants that never flower and for plants where the darn things fall off by themselves). The

14

spent rachis on 'Loder's White' has the attribute of breaking off at the right point on the plant, assuming one is reasonably careful. Frequently on other varieties I end up with a whole whorl of leaves in my hand and more often than I like to admit, whole branches.

R. augustinii I would give a 1. By the time the flowers are faded, the new growth buds are elongated to just the right length to make them easier to knock off than the immature seed container. Actually, on some *augustiniis* the old flower pedicels are not attached all that well and a lateral blow will detach them quite easily. Try placing a curved index finger on the pad of the thumb and flicking quickly while taking careful aim at the object to be beheaded. With practice, you will soon knock them flying. My neighbour returning from his daily ten mile jog saw me executing this method. Reflexively, running on the spot, he half-raised his arm in greeting – paused – then hurried up the road shaking his head. I am now careful to use this method only when I am sure no one is watching.

Incidentally, I don't know why *augustinii* is classed as Triflora. I swear all of our plants have at least four flowers in the inflorescence.

All of the *lapponicums* get a Zero, a big fat goose egg. The fungus-like excrescences on impeditum just have to be ignored. There is no way they can be removed.

But the worst rating goes to *R. racemosum*. I would rate it right out there in negative numbers. I furtively pick a few of the cursed blobs and give up quickly. I always have a ready supply of seed of *racemosum*. When some ingénue asks, "Are all rhododendrons hard to grow from seed?" I put on a benign smirk and reply with feigned generosity, "Here, let me see if I can find you some seed of *racemosum*; it's a good one to start with". The seed capsules on *racemosum* are more persistent than the leaves. The deer occasionally browse on the leaves – never on the seed. Come to think of it, have you ever seen a weevil notch on a seed capsule?

In this deadheading business we also have to take account of the stickiness factor. I wonder if the manufacturers of "Crazy Glue" know about 'Ruby Bowman'? Maybe I'm

15

onto something and can make a million. I know now why Lem (or was it Elliot?) called 'Jingle Bells' 'Jingle Bells'. You deadhead the plant and you'll be hearing Jingle Bells on the radio every day before you get the gunk off your fingers.

It's no use using gloves. They do more damage than enough and the cloth fingers are soon irreparably forever fused. Scissors are needed to get the intended protection off.

Talking of scissors, they are quite an effective tool for deadheading the long sturdy pedicels of the *R. campylogynums* and *R. glaucophyllums.* I used to think that using scissors was an affectation, like using sugar tongs to pick up slugs, as the ladies in Oak Bay do. But it really is a good method for these particular species of rhododendrons and for this reason I would give them a 2.5. If you try to pull off three or four of the old flowers at one time on a *campylogynum* you risk pulling the plant out by the root. The stalks have remarkable tensile strength.

The deciduous azaleas have very high stickability indices. It's strange how the leaves fall off regularly as clockwork every year but the seeds seem to know another Ice Age is on the way. They are going to hang on until it's over.

I occasionally find a dead bee inside a wilted flower – stuck to its supposed feeding source. It is a good thing that we are quite a bit bigger than bees or every rhododendron grower would be trapped in early efforts to deadhead and all of this would be academic, which, on reflection, is what it is supposed to be.

There has been a huge increase in the number of hybridizers of late. I know why this is so. It is much easier to pull off the petals and the anthers before, or just as the flower opens, than it is to pull off the entire flower when it has wilted. The excuse they use is that the seed capsules may contain the next wonder of the world.

These are, however, superficial thoughts. Sooner or later, even if you are only a five minute spurter like I am, you have to ask yourself the fundamental questions, "What am I doing? What are the consequences of this act? When does the life of a rhododendron begin?" I hesitate to say it but perhaps we need a free vote on the subject.

Happy New Year and Some Chewy Thoughts
1989

The year's at the spring
And day's at the morn
Morning's at seven
The hillside's dew pearled
The lark's on the wing
The snail's on the thorn
God's in his heaven –
All's right with the world

That little piece by Robert Browning has a nice comfortable feel to it and is perhaps appropriate for starting the New Year and also wishing that we can make the last line more of a fact than a hope.

Still, that bit about the snail is a bit unsettling; why is the snail getting involved with everything being alright with the world? Weevils are bad; deer are a menace; but that first cousin of the snail, that slimy, elongated, terrestrial gastropod, the slug – is the worst of all.

There are armies of them at our place and the various regiments of the armies are subtly distinctive in their different uniforms. The heavy artillery are the banana slugs powering their way into every pot, devouring flower and foliage. They eat everything but are especially cruel to the young and old, seeming to prefer the newest tissue and the dying tissue.

The grey slugs are the armoured corps. They are the most vicious. I'm told they attack and bite bananas. Then there is the infantry – the one with the orange bottom. Its uniform is quite attractive, if you like that kind of thing. It's not quite as big as the Banana but can insinuate its way to the plants just as effectively and is equally voracious. The black ones are the commandos sneaking up surreptitiously and lethally.

Slug bait is ineffective and the cost prohibitive for a large area. Routine spraying with a twenty percent metaldehyde solution is also very expensive. Muscovy ducks were suggested as a control, but on checking with the Provincial people, they tell me they will not eat the big ones. Geese might drive the slugs away but they are also pretty effective at driving people away. 'Tis a thorny problem alright and the snail being on it only compounds it. Browning didn't grow rhododendrons.

Precipitation as Fertilizer
1989

I've heard on more than one occasion that snow brings with it more nitrogen than rain does. This piece of folk-lore serves to comfort gardeners in that when their shrubs and bulbs are covered with snow they are getting a good fertilizing making up for all the inconveniences that the white stuff brings with it.

Sorry about that, but snow has significantly less nitrogen in it than does rain. I don't know the figures for Victoria but for the plants (trees) of the eastern Rockies, over a third of their intake comes from precipitation and, as a large proportion of that is in the form of snow, Victoria's proportional intake should be higher.

Be doubly joyful when you sing "Raindrops Keep Falling on My Head".

Fall for Rhododendrons
1990

In the gardens of coastal British Columbia the best time to plant broad leaf shrubs and trees is the fall. In October and November the soil is still warm, the autumn rains have begun, and conditions are the best for the development of new roots. If you plant in the fall, plants will become

18

established before the burgeoning demands of spring signal the roots to send more nutrients for swelling blossoms and expanding leaves.

As long as the ground is not frozen the roots of the broad leaf evergreens are purposefully working. To the human eye there does not seem to be much going on above soil level but the plant is still photosynthesizing. Sugars and starches are being manufactured from the nutrients the searching roots are pumping up to the leaves.

When a plant is dug up and replanted, or taken from a container and put in the ground, the roots are always disturbed. To assist them to grow into soil in their new environment, the roots of a potted plant must be teased apart quite vigorously so that they can make intimate contact with the welcoming environment of their new, freshly prepared home. For rhododendrons this means an open, friable soil with a high content of organic matter, located in a well-drained site. Rhododendrons hate standing in water: they drown. Their roots need loose, airy, humusy soil around them.

One of the best and easiest ways to give them this open soil and the right acidity is to incorporate bark mulch. Up to 50% of the mix in the planting soil can be bark mulch – not too coarse and not dust either. Many people like to use peat moss, but much of the moss available today is so fine that if it ever dries out, it is very difficult to moisten it again. Furthermore, peat moss breaks down far more quickly than bark mulch. The number one cardinal rule for growing rhododendrons is that the roots must never go dry.

If your soil is a black humus-rich loam, you are fortunate indeed and no amendment may be necessary. You can plant the rhododendron as deeply as it was in the pot. But if the natural soil is a heavy clay, then 8 to 12 cm of coarse sand should be dug in to a depth of 30 cm before the addition of the bark mulch. Composted leaves, preferably oak, can be used instead of bark mulch. If the soil is heavy clay, you can plant very shallowly, bringing the amended soil higher than the soil level at which the plant was previously growing.

19

Mixing some fertilizer in the planting hole is beneficial but make sure it does not come in contact with the roots. Avoid using animal manures that are less than a year old. An excellent fertilizer you can make yourself is a mix of : 4 parts canola, 4 alfalfa, 4 blood, 1 bone, 1 kelp, 2 dolomite lime and 1 rock phosphate.

Most of the rhododendrons we grow are hybrids. Hybrids result when two or more of the plants found growing in the "wild" – the species – have been combined by cross-pollination. Most of the species that have been used to make these popular hybrids come from climates that have relatively dry winters and high summer rainfall. In the Victoria area, we have the reverse. One of the consequences of our persistent winter rainfall is that the nutrients that are at the surface of the soil get leached downwards quite quickly. Rhododendrons, which are very shallow-rooted can in fact be starved in our winter because all the goodness goes past them before they can catch their fair share. If the roots can't supply the nourishment, then the plant will draw from its stored reserves – its rainy day account – leaving less for production of flowers and foliage. The regime that I follow is to feed sparingly with a chemical fertilizer (10-8-6 with all the minor elements), five times a year. I start in November and feed every two months with the last feed on Canada Day. Rhododendrons are not gross feeders, but they do like three meals a day, light ones in the winter, heavier ones in the spring.

Choosing the right variety for the right spot is important. There are now more than 30,000 registered hybrids. This is a daunting number but, from its very size, you can be sure that the right plant for your particular location can be found. Some need almost no direct sun, some need full sun, some will grow to be trees and some will never be more than 5 cm high, some will bloom in December and some will bloom as late as August, some are deciduous, most are evergreen. Colours range through the entire spectrum except for the pure gentian blue. Even that is now a possibility with our increased understanding of genetics.

One of the convenient characteristics of rhododendrons is that because they're shallow-rooted they are very portable. For gardeners who would really like their plants to come with wheels so that they can move things around until their concept of horticultural artistic perfection is reached, rhododendrons come quite close to being ideal. They can be moved at any time of the year. The huge majority are planted in the spring and they do very well. The very best time, however, for gardeners in our area is the fall.

The Ten Best Dwarfs for the Rock Garden – An Update
April 1990

A few years ago, I wrote about my selection of the best dwarf rhododendrons for the rock garden (ARS Journal, Vol. 40, No 3, 1986). Perforce, the choice was made for plants which I had grown and which were more or less easily obtainable.

A little later, Felice Blake, our Australian colleague, wrote about her preferences (ARS Journal Vol. 41, No. 3, 1987) and, of course, they were so convincing that I could not but agree with them. Felice has also written about the dwarf form of *R. keiskei* and its hybrids and this article was published in our book, "Rhododendrons on a Western Shore". She has expanded and updated her review of *keiskei*'s progeny in an article in the latest Journal (Vol. 44, No 1, 1990).

The passage of time – age – makes a great difference to a rhododendron, and probably even more difference to its grower. Albert de Mezey once told me that to grow rhododendrons, all that was needed was a physical age of thirty and a longevity of three hundred. So at best, making choices is a subjective, temporal whimsey, but at least it's not like picking horses – there are no losers.

Another comforting thing about making a list of good plants is that the species/hybrid debate becomes a total affectation. I don't think the plant itself knows whether it's a

21

species or a hybrid and if it did, I don't think it would care much. I certainly don't, and so this revised list is a mix of both species and hybrids.

I would still rate *R. keiskei* among the top ten. 'Yaku Fairy' is the name given to the most dwarf, tight forms of this species. It is important to get this form, as some other expressions of *keiskei* are by comparison gangling roustabouts. Some dwarf forms are very prostrate, creeping across the ground like Cotoneaster 'Dammeri '. They are good garden-worthy plants but to me not as pleasing as the tiny, bun-shaped ones which have every piece of foliage covered by their pale yellow flowers in April.

As Felice Blake's latest article attests, *keiskei* has become one of the most popular parents. A couple of these hybrids are now generally available and certainly make the cut for the ten best. Both are Warren Berg hybrids.

These are 'Patty Bee' and 'Ginny Gee'. 'Patty Bee's other parent is *R. fletcherianum*. The result is a plant that is larger than *keiskei* but of good rounded form with abundant yellow flowers of a darker hue than that species. Some other *keiskei* hybrids that I now grow have truly deep daffodil yellow flowers. 'Golden Bee' (*keiskei* x *mekongense* var *melianthum*) is one. For me, the yellow is too brassy and the foliage is not as good as 'Patty Bee's', its sister seedling 'Golden Princess' is another. This is rated a 5/5 by Clint Smith of Benjamin's Nursery; I am prepared to be convinced of this but as I've only grown it for a couple of years, I'll leave it out of the top ten for now. Another *keiskei* hybrid, this time crossed with *hanceanum nanum* is certainly a contender, as is 'Princess Anne'. Out of flower, it has the same general effect as 'Patty Bee' but the flowers are paler and some of the foliage goes bronzy in the winter which, for some, is probably a detraction. There is another plant of this cross called 'Shamrock'; this has even paler yellow flowers. I like its pale green flower buds, attractive and unusual but not sufficiently to give it top rating.

Still with the yellows, Cox's 'Chikor' and 'Curlew' have to be included in our select few. The former (*chryseum* x *ludlowii*) gets the nod from me for being the more choice. The yellow is clear and the flowers match the size of the small leaves. There are two clones with this name. One was given an Award of Merit by the R.H.S. and the other received a First Class Certificate. I'm not sure which form we grow here in Victoria. By contrast 'Curlew' (*ludlowii* x *fletcherianum*) has huge flowers. It has received all the awards including the Cory Cup for the best hybrid of any genus. I find it a little difficult to please; it seems to do better in some shade and because of that, and because of its large flowers, it is only marginally a rock garden plant.

I'll just mention one other pale yellow hybrid that I saw in flower at our convention last year. This is the David Leach hybrid 'Tow Head' (*caroliniamun*, white form, x *ludlowii*). Coming from Leach, it is very hardy, to -26C, it is claimed. My early impression is that it is good enough to compete with the hybrids already named, but another couple of years will be needed to see if it makes the grade.

That was supposed to be all I was going to say about yellow hybrids, but two more come to mind. The first is 'Wren' (*ludlowii* x *keiskei*), another Cox 'Bird' hybrid. So far with us it seems awfully slow, but it is a good yellow and Felice Blake calls it "absolutely bewitching". The second is another 'Bird' hybrid – 'Chiffchaff' (*hanceanum nanum* x *fletcherianum*). Cox says it is not as good a doer as some of his other hybrids but it does well for us and its loose trusses of four to six lemon-yellow flowers are showily refined.

'Ginny Gee' must be one of the most floriferous rhododendron hybrids ever produced. It is *keiskei* crossed with *R. racemosum*. Its foliage stays dark all year and the pink/white flowers cover it completely in April.

I think *racemosum* is almost at the bottom of my list in the ratings of rhododendrons. It is leggy, suffers dieback, and has ugly seed capsules that need a Job's patience to remove. It sends up long sappy shoots (these do bear axially the flowers the next year which, blessedly, can be removed to make excellent cut sprays for flower arrangements). These are out of character with the rest of the plant. Its other virtue is that it passes only its good features on to its children.

'Ginny Gee' is a plant you should have in your garden. The Cox's, who have themselves bred not a few of the best dwarf rhododendrons, rate it as one of the best ever raised. The contrast between pink buds and white flowers is always effective and is especially so in this plant as it has so many to show. Watch out for the later Warren Berg hybrids 'Wee Bee' and 'Too Bee'. Both are *R. campylogynum*, *keiskei* crosses and seem very promising.

White flowers always seem to attract gardeners and often you will hear them talking about "the rare white form". It is, therefore, a pity that good white flowered rhododendrons are few and far between.

In the small-statured plants, Cox's 'Ptarmigan' is not bad, but it is a spikey, straggly grower. Kenneth Cox, when he talked at our convention last year, said it was improved when given a haircut. I haven't found it produces very many flowers; it can't be classed as a luxuriant plant. It reminds me of *Daphne blagyana*; its flowers are welcomed, but then forgotten.

In my opinion, the best white flowered dwarf is the species *R. anthopogonoides*. If you can get your mouth around the name you certainly deserve to grow it. Peter Cox says there is probably only one plant in cultivation. We have a plant and are now propagating it, especially after seeing a plant with the same name in Warren Berg's garden, thus authenticating it for me. All of the plants in the Anthopogon Series (now called Pogonanthum Section) are so distinctive with a whitish cast to the leaves and their flowers in small tight trusses. Most have very pleasantly aromatic foliage.

Anthopogonoides with us as a ten to twelve year old plant, is about 50 cm high and is nicely, if somewhat openly and twigily formed. The flowers are of good substance. It is a better doer for us than *anthopogon* itself. The form of this that we have is called 'Betty Graham' after Sheriff's wife. (Sheriff was half of the Ludlow and Sheriff plant hunting team). If you haven't read her account of their trip to Lhasa etc. in Fletcher's "A Quest for Flowers", it's worth searching for it.

'Eider' should probably be included in the top ten. My plant died before I could really appreciate it. It is certainly on the most wanted list.

Still in the Pogonathum Section, I have to include *R. trichostomum* for which I have a great affection. It is a classy doer and a great plant for bonsai. It has a twisted, spiral growth habit with light ginger-coloured exfoliating bark. The flowers are pink, small and tubular in a tight round truss. They have a good substance, lasting about a month or so. It is quite late blooming for a species – May. There are different forms, some of them named, but probably only available in Britain. It would be worth trying to get them.

I wish I could grow *R. campylogynum* better than I do. Euan Cox described it as "the rarest and most perky and self-satisfied of all dwarfs". With me it is not as self-satisfied as I would like it to be. Dora Kreiss grows a marvelous specimen. It is tight like a ball of bread dough ready to pop in the oven.

Most of the tiny rhododendrons take a bit more sun than their larger cousins, but I think *campylogynum* likes half-shade and is happiest in moist, but well drained situations. Generally these tiny plants come from high elevations – up to 16,000 feet, and while the light is intense at that altitude, there is not that much of it. Clouds and mist are typical and snow cover lasts many months. And remember, these species get most of their moisture from the monsoons during the summer growing months.

One can go crazy trying to distinguish the different forms of *campylogynum*. It is probably best not to bother overly much – just enjoy them. If it has a very long flower stalk (pedicel) and a nodding bell for a flower, cherish it and call it after your daughter or your dog. Flowers are pink, white, yellow, but typically plum coloured and have a unique bloom like a grape on the outside. There is one form, 'Bodnant Red', that is as close to a red as one gets in a lepidote rhododendron. Another plant worth growing is called 'Canada'. It also has nearly red flowers. It originated with the Greigs of Royston but was distributed by Jim Caperci of Washington State, who gave it its name. Yet another is called 'Kim'. I like it very much. Cox, however, thought it was muddy and tender and threw it out. *"Vive la difference."*

Colour preference is personal and I'm told, sociologically based. I have read that Western races do not like mauve/blue because when industrialization took hold, the working garb was of that colour. Still, we talk about blue bloods, blue stockings and blue chips. In any event, I like rhododendrons of this hue but as usual, some are much better than others. *R. pemakoense* is a blue-pink – a strange colour reminiscent of some Penstemons. I like this species, but for garden worthiness its hybrid 'Rose Elf' is better. It was on my original list and it will remain on this one. It's a pleb, easy to grow, easy to propagate, easy to find but such a happy doer and so undemanding that it gets overlooked. Give it rock garden room and it will reward you.

There are no true blue rhododendrons. The pure pigment of the gentian does not exist in the genus. Coming close, however, is *R. hippophaeoides*. It is a larger plant with grey foliage. I am skeptical of the named forms of this species. After being through three or four hands, it is easy to get the 'Tower Court' form mixed up with the 'Barto' form. The point of this remark is that the form that I grow has the tag 'Haba Shan'. I have seen other plants with this name but they don't have quite the same clarity as the light blue colour that ours does. Maybe the soil has something to do with it.

There are many good blue dwarf hybrids. The list is extensive but the differences are often small. So I will not enumerate them in the interest of space. At this time it would take another article to do them justice.

I am not sure whether there are fewer than ten or more than ten in this selection. It really does not matter – the whole thing is arbitrary. It is a great blessing that we do not agree on liking the same thing. What a boring world that would give us. As someone said, "We boil at different degrees".

My Favorite Rhododendron
December 1990

Make an array of $100 bills in front of me and ask me to pick my favorite one. If I use the bill to help pay for the groceries it doesn't much matter which one I pick. If I want the bill as part of a collection of currency the one without crinkles and folds is the most desirable. If I want to have a chance of getting more than a hundred dollars for it I have to look for one with some imperfection in the printing.

With so many nearly perfect rhododendrons to choose from the one that's slightly off the mark may sneak into top spot in one's affection.

Apropos imperfection recall that when one overhears *R. augustinii* being introduced one usually hears this apology: 'True, there are no true blues in rhododendrons – the pigment does not exist in the genus – but perhaps the one that comes closest is *augustinii* . . . ". Isn't that a bit like saying, "This egg is nearly fresh"?

Look at the ratings of rhododendrons. There are no 5/5s. Perfection has not been achieved so we have to look for 4/5s or 5/4s.

First, it's got a lot to do with the same kind of process that makes the Swiss like that singularly ugly flower, the edelweiss, and makes the Welsh rhapsodize about a leek. But if *augustinii* does not beget these emotive reactions in you let's try some more objective arguments.

It's a species. For me that gives it a slight edge. What nature has taken 70 million years to produce gives it some seniority over plants produced manipulatively in the last 25 years.

Then, coming from the drier sides of the steep monsoon washed slopes of the mountains of Tibet and western China, it tolerates more drought than many other rhododendrons and so it generally looks content in the garden.

However, since it is possessed of small scaly willow-like leaves it doesn't much matter whether it looks very content or not – it just blends into the landscape – except in cold, cold temperatures when these same leaves look like composting wood shavings.

I also like it because it is fast growing. It is easy to have a six or seven foot plant from a cutting in ten years, and it starts blooming when it is four or five years old. My regard for it is additionally enhanced because it seeds itself – the only rhododendron in our garden to do that. This gives an excuse not to deadhead.

But the best thing of all is the bloom. The flowers (not blue, remember) come in shades of deep magenta through all of the mauve and lilac tints to white. There are many named forms, some with poetic names like 'Azurense' and 'Blue Cloud'; but others have proprietary names like 'Barto Blue', 'Tower Court' and 'Fraser's Form'. One, which I like very much, I grew from seed and call with affected modesty 'Firwood Best'.

The cognoscenti have judged that those with contrasting lighter throats are the ones to covet but the ones with the dark throats like Marine sell best.

Some say the blue tones come through best after a mild winter but we noted stronger, purer colours after the Great Cold of February 1989. Hue may have more to do with who holds power in Ottawa than with temperature.

The colour does depend on the specific environment. Plants grown from cuttings of an outstanding form in one garden do not always reproduce that same form in another garden.

Lastly, I like its name. It is called after Augustine Henry who first described the plant. He was a medical doctor of Irish/Scottish ancestry who when he retired from doctoring in China had a fulfilling second career as a professor of forestry and who in his elderly years was described as being a fascinating bore. I say 'no wonder' and 'good for him'.

Last Year's Surprises
October 1991

It's therapeutic to stand back from all of the cataclysmic geopolitical events and reflect on some of the things that have been surprises in the last twelve months – things that happened on our own little bit of dirt right under our own little noses and caused us to stop and wonder.

The first noticeable thing about last year was the severity of the winter. Some plants that complainingly struggled though and survived the effects of February 1989 took the easy way out in January 1990 and called it quits. Still, a few that looked as if they had made the final decision had second thoughts and have pushed up new growth from the roots. The *R. edgeworthii* has done this and although not vigorous is proof of that strange power of survival. A *R. davidsonianum* which had never flowered but had reached a height of over 6 feet, which was given up for dead in '89 recovered to reach 8 feet and was mourned again this spring. August saw it pushing up new shoots. Twice a cryogenic phoenix!

The message here is not to give up on an apparently dead plant too quickly. Even a year after apparent death, the resurrection can take place. Conversely, things that appeared to have survived have recently turned up their toes. A mature 'Unknown Warrior' has succumbed; its only use now is to be cut up for Margaret Buffam's membership tags.

This was a case where a plant had its roots swamped in the heavy rains of early winter – there was standing water followed by a hard freeze. It croaked – no oxygen.

With roots deprived of oxygen for several weeks, other smaller plants have also passed away this summer. Some of these were *R. johnstoneanum;* some were forms of *R. arboreum* and some were the big leafed ones like *R. arizelum*.

Surprisingly, a good form of *R. falconerii* lost all its leaves but has come back and looks in excellent health. One 20-year-old *R. sidereum* is clearly brain dead but has put out one miniscule shoot from the old trunk. The Duchess of Montrose's rhododendron, *R. montroseanum* alias *mollyanum,* had its 16 inch leaves freeze to a tobacco brown which then fell off. It has now developed new, half-size leaves and with no more unpleasant surprises could be back to its usual voluptuous self next year. (It didn't make it.)

It is a really serious whammy to broad-leaved evergreens when they lose their leaves. These plants store their nutrients in their leaves – deciduous ones in their twigs and branches. If the roots can't supply the nutrients they draw them down from these folial reserves. Evergreen rhododendrons are actively growing all year as long as the ground is not frozen. Work at Oregon State University showed that winter feeding was beneficial so I now feed 5 times a year starting in November, then in January, March, April and the last one on Canada Day. It is true that the winter applications are wasteful as most of the fertilizer is leached or washed away. If you still have some of the 10-8-6 special formulation which is available from the club, perhaps you should give this regime a try starting in November. Small amounts are adequate for the three early feedings.

I get surprised every summer at how hot and dry things get. Every summer I realize just what a rotten place Victoria is for growing plants whose provenance has wet, wet monsoon summers. Victoria is a summer desert. Vancouver is a much better place to grow rhododendrons, but we get brainwashed here in Victoria by Vancouver forecasters who feel that they have to prove their worth by catering exclusively to cancer-seeking sunbathing Victoria apartment dwellers with their constant apologies for anything other than blistering sunshine.

Well, to some of the good surprises; 'Vulcan' was a knockout. This was a plant I had dismissed as plebian, unrefined, couthless and good only for $1.49 day. I have never propagated it and was almost proud I didn't stock it in the nursery. What prejudice! This year it took me three goes to deadhead it. On the last effort I counted the open trusses – 246. So this plant which is probably 16 years old and about 6 feet through, had more than 600 trusses. Each truss conservatively has 12 flowers. So there were over 7,000 flowers on it! That made for what Ed Sullivan used to call a "really big shew".

One of the other great shows of the garden was 'Cinnkeys'. I'm afraid that such a splendid profligacy will signal a terminal climax. It started blooming in April which is a month before it usually does and it still has some blossom – five months of flowering. It is one of the most trying plants to deadhead under normal circumstances – this year impossible. The *cinnabarinum*-type multipediceled inflorescenses have tiny seedpods that defy pulling and have to be pinched off, which usually results in pinching off the new growth. Excellent vision is needed to do a good job, but I have to do this with moderately impaired vision because if I wear my bifocals, the distance at this precise nipping range coincides with the line where neither the reading nor the long distance part of the lens is effective.

Maybe this was 'Cinnkey's' last hurrah, but I think not. Some of the new leaves are very small and some of the branches that held the 30 or more flowers are dead, but I think it will pull through. I have taken quite a few cuttings. Small plants need some coddling. I don't know which form of *keysii* was used in the cross with *R. cinnibarinum* to make 'Cinnkeys', but some forms of *R. keysii* are definitely very, very tender.

The other surprising thing (to some people) about 'Cinnkeys' is that it is a rhododendron and not a honeysuckle. It is one of the more interesting of the taller lepidote hybrids. Another interesting one that surprises me every year is one I brought back from Scotland from Cox's. I grow it as *flavidum* x 'Lady Roseberry' and I thought it was a cross that Peter Cox had made. But he attributes it to Lester Brandt so when I brought it in I was only returning it to North America. Cox was intrigued by this cross as 'Lady Roseberry' is a tetraploid hybrid and was consequently thought to be a difficult parent. Brandt evidently called this cross 'Flip' but it had not been registered. It is a narrow upright grower. It is surprising in the

31

flowers not being tubular shaped as one would expect from its parentage. The colour is a curious mixture of pink and yellow which seems to me to be crying out for tenancy in the traditional English country garden.

I have a small plant of a hybrid called 'Burnaby Sunset' which is the same cross. This has not flowered for me yet but evidently caused quite a stir when its peachy-cream flowers were shown in Seattle some years ago. Surprise happens every day; a garden is never static – the weeds most certainly are not. Currently I'm surprised that the plants are getting by with so little water, but don't be surprised if you hear me complaining about fertilizer that's been washed away due to too much rain, or about unseasonable temperatures. One of the easiest things for me to do is give the specifications for an ideal climate – not a surprising thing at all for a gardener.

The Price Of Snobbery
February 1993

You might think this piece is a bit snobby, and it is. If you come 'round my garden', I will point out some plants using a very revering tone of voice. I will need to point some of them out because you would most likely overlook them otherwise. Most of them do not make any real contribution to the landscape; most never flower and yet they are among my most prized possessions.

I have a couple of *R. proteoides* – both are grafted. One is the Greig form. It has about six leaves on top of a six-inch stick. Most people would pull it out mistaking it for a misshapen piece of *mahonia*. Perhaps Dave Dougan is right when he says growing spinach is more rewarding.

Next to it is *R. pronum* – a pricey plant if there ever was one. But you would never know from looking at it. It grows at an undetectable rate and will never bloom in my lifetime. Even worse is its neighbour, *R. recurvum*. Clint Smith gave me this and I thank him every time I see it or him.

It is so rare that I didn't know I lusted for it – still, it is easily overlooked.

At the Western Regional Conference last October were 2-inch specimens of a cross made by Cecile Smith – *proteoides* x 'Bambi'. They had been propagated by the Bowhans. Because they were so insignificant and puny I just had to have one. If you didn't know it was there you would never notice it. It has way less garden impact than a poorly grown dandelion.

I have three forms of *R. recurvoides*. They all have peculiar indumentums on the undersides of their leaves, but no one ever looks there and if one did one would be tempted to spray. None of them has ever bloomed.

We have a 28-year old auriculatum – way taller than I am. It has never bloomed and gives no sign of ever trying to.

Another plant I will point out to you is *R. taliense* – titular head of a tribe notorious for being shy bloomers. This one does bloom but I wish it didn't. The flower is a miserable apology of a thing that cannot excuse itself for its lack of grace. Thank goodness there are no flower buds for 1993. The bush is about as useful in the landscape as a broom – maybe not quite.

I keep telling my wife that when I croak she must treat the *talienses* as her inheritance. We have two or three but they too have never bloomed and they grow with painful slowness. Dora Kreiss has a marvelous specimen and I told her it should be specially mentioned in her will.

I don't think I will forgive Jack Lofthouse for selling me a seedling of a cross he made of *R. macabeanum* and 'Promise of Spring'. That was 20 years ago. The plant is 10 feet high but nary a flower. I keep growing it because it has a pretty nice shape to it and it reminds me of how my two dollars has grown.

One of the most miserable plants in the garden is a Joseph Rock introduction of *R. forrestii* var *repens*. This was a layer in Albert de Mezey's garden which he kindly gave to me. The plant now spans about two feet. It has bloomed but a slug ate the flower before I had a chance to see it. Probably the flower only lasts one day anyway.

However, all is not gloom and doom. *Macabeanum*, *R. grande*, and *R. wightii* all have set flower buds for the first time. Now that I have written that, probably a deer will have them off before spring.

I have never seen deer look so fat and well clothed, and disdainfully unconcerned about the damage they are doing. Homo sapiens may be on the edge of extinction but not *Odocoileus hemionus* ssp. *columbianus*.

Water on the Brain
May 1993

Keats said (I looked it up): "I am in that temper that if I were under water, I would scarcely kick to come to the top". I'm not in quite such a desperate frame of mind as Keats evidently was, but reflecting on our times it would not be a bad way to go.

Here we are in this great city of gardens and we are faced with water restrictions. It is not that this really affects me directly as we rely on well water and consequently I face a restricted water supply every summer anyway. Each year I despair of losing some of my treasures, but the fact is, most survive. It does take quite a bit of effort.

"Never let the roots of your rhodos dry out". I suppose this is the single, most important bit of cultural advice needed for growing rhododendrons.

Nearly all of the rhododendrons we grow in our gardens come, or their parents come from areas of the world where most of the annual precipitation is in the summer months. Many get that from the summer monsoon blowing over the Indian Ocean from the southwest.

In our environs, particularly on the southern tip of Vancouver Island, there is very little rainfall from mid-May until mid-October. Supplementary water in these months is essential to keep our plants growing "normally".

It is true that well-established older plants can remain alive through a typical Victorian summer without irrigation, especially if there is some rain when the new growth is being formed. However, they will be heavily stressed and will not go into the winter in very good shape.

The smaller plants – the impeditum-like things, because of their liking for sunnier, more open places in the garden and because of their smaller, shallower roots, will not survive without their transpirational needs being met artificially.

Some plants, like some irises and our native arbutus have evolved to survive arid summers. Rhododendrons have developed a physiology particularly good at getting rid of excess moisture in the warmer months and conserving it in the colder months. Some, for example, have developed scales covering their stomata and some curl up their leaves when the roots can't supply enough water in drought, or when frozen.

On very hot days, I see plants that even with moisture at the roots just can't get the phloem and xylem working hard enough to keep the plant in good health. This is the reason why so many plants we grow in the Pacific North-West will not survive a summer in Osaka.

One good thing that should be stressed is that rhododendrons do not need as much water as a lawn. The Water Board is telling us that one of the most significant things we can do to conserve water is not to give our lawns more than an inch of water a week, and that we should support our fisheries by buying lots of canned salmon so we can take the empty cans and spot them all over our still verdant swards and when we water, fill the cans to a depth of 25.4 millimeters, precisely. This same amount of water – 25.4 mm per week more or less precisely – will keep our rhododendrons sudatory and satiated, ensuring their being thrifty and our being happy.

For an individual plant of about 3 feet or 914 millimeters, using a half-inch (13mm) hose at full bore for two minutes will provide an inch of water over the area of the roots.

If you have 30 rhodos, each 3 feet high or wide, you will need to spend an hour a week at the end of a hose. That is not really overwhelming.

What may, however, be overwhelming is discovering the financial consequences of our current water shortage. There is an immutable law of contemporary public administration that holds that the surest way to secure increased revenues for a utility or public service (and hence increase the status of those in charge of providing the service) is to create a crisis – preferably one that can be blamed on previous management. It will always be claimed that the crisis can only be solved by spending a lot of money hence justifying any increase in rates. These increased costs are irreversible and even if a one-time expenditure could overcome the crisis, the operational costs of the utility always rise to meet the increased revenues.

While on this tack, there is another immutable law that applies in situations like our water shortage. This is known as the Law of Upward Comparability to the Highest Common Denominator. This states that, for example, if water costs x times more in London, Ontario or San Diego, California, then the cost in Victoria is unreal, non-egalitarian and discriminatory and that costs should rise to that of the least efficient, most expensive example that can be found and that we citizens should feel blessed to be so well served.

There have been so many articles recently on how to "xeriscape" (horrible word and horrible concept) our gardens that I don't need to mention the use of mulches, watering when the sun is low, not using overhead sprinklers but using micro-heads and soaker hoses, saving the potato water and my own secret – but not recommended for smaller gardens – acting naturally when the bilges need pumping when outdoors.

The second last piece of advice I can give is to recommend that everyone go to at least three places of religious worship next weekend.

The last piece of advice is to encourage you to write to every radio and TV station and complain about the way

36

weather forecasts are given. "Good" weather to them is always sunbather's weather. We know that too much sun can give us skin cancer. The plain fact is that in these parts "good" weather is rainy weather. Even a bit of acid rain is alright. Rhodos love it.

For the Cat Who has Everything
December 1993

Did you notice the word 'who' in the title? If you do not think of cats as persons, this article will not interest you. It will interest you if you are in that most frustrating of situations when you just can't think of the ultimate present for that most significant cat in your life – to be given on that very, very special cat day. I have the answer and it may surprise you. It is *R. roxieanum* var. *oreonastes.*

Don't turn off right now because you think *roxieanum* var. *oreonastes* will be too difficult a name for your cat to appreciate – just hang in and read a bit more.

You see, cats don't know many things by their names. And it is pretty well useless trying to get a cat to understand abstract things, (e.g., things like 'the Natural Law Party' or 'relativity'). Cats recognize most things by smell. That is how they recognize pretty well all tangible things; smart cats can even sense a few abstract things using this sense.

Anyway, *roxieanum* var. *oreonastes* sends cats into paroxysms of ecstasy. We all know that paroxysms do not always occur as pleasant events but when you see that closed-eyed Cheshire look on your cat's face and feel the vibes from its tremulous twitching little nose, you will know this purring paroxysm is a good one. You could also object to using a fairly abstract word like 'paroxysm' for your cat's intemperately orgasmic raptures, but even if your cat does not know that precise word, you can be sure it has a complete fix on the idea.

37

R. roxieanum var. *oreonastes* is a classic rhododendron fit for the garden of the most fastidious connoisseur. It kind of looks like a land-based green sea urchin. (That is *Strongylocentrotus droebachiensis*, just in case your cat is of the more than normally curious type, still alive and might like to know that).

R. roxieanum var. *oreonastes* belongs to the Taliense affiliation and, at least from a nurseryperson's point of view, possesses all of the bad qualities of that tribe, i.e., it is almost impossible to propagate from cuttings, is not easy to graft, and as it takes eons to bloom, it is hard to get seed and when you do, it might not be viable. When it does bloom, however, it is a real joy to behold and if you find yourself in the position of beholder, you could be excused for having one of these paroxysms all to yourself.

Being such a coveted plant, it makes sense for those who do own this rare and expensive rhododendron to be discreet and selective in letting the fact of your ownership be widely known because most of the specimens of *roxieanum* var. *oreonastes* in captivity are of a very portable size and the visitor could have a paroxysm of envy and greed which could end up in thievery.

You might think, then, that it would be logical, if you value your status as a collector of rare plants more than the love of your cat, not to tell your cat you have one in your garden.

However, I would advise against not telling your cat because it is a sure bet that your cat will sense the precise minute *roxieanum* var. *oreonastes* crosses your lot line. And anyway, you, having read this far, must be darn nearly desperate to let your cat experience one of those incontinent paroxysms.

If you know your Latin (I don't, so I'm just waiting for someone to tell me this paragraph is all nonsense) you will quickly intuit what the name itself – *oreonastes* – gives away about this interesting reactionary feline phenomenon. The *roxieanum* part of the moniker is something of a letdown because it's one of these commemorative names, eternally memorializing a Mrs. Roxie Hanna of Tali-fu, China, who was a friend of the plant's discoverer, or at least describer, George Forrest. Too bad we don't know more about Mrs. Roxie Hanna – perhaps – who knows – she may have had a weakness for aromatically induced paroxysms.

It's the *oreonastes* bit that is the mother lode. The 'oreo' portion really means 'mountain' in Latin, but cats are not too well versed in dead languages and, get this, they recognize the modern meaning of 'oreo' (i.e., 'cookie')!

Ah ha! So then we move on to the '*nastes*' bit. You may not believe this, but this is the exception that proves the rule; cats have almost instant recognition of what 'nastes' means in Latin. They do not make the correspondence to the modern English meaning of 'nastes' (i.e., 'unpleasant'), but go right to the Latin word 'nasitortium' which means 'distortion of the nose'. You look at your cat in its oreonastical paroxysm and you will see what 'nasitortium' means. The Romans knew what it meant and so does your cat. Nasturtiums evidently gave Romans nasal paroxysms and that's why they called them *nasturtiums*.

Romans almost certainly never said or smelled *roxieanum* var. *oreonastes*. It's almost impossible to be absolutely sure what kind of paroxysms they would have had had they done so. Most likely, they would have given it a very wide berth after Pompey's 67 B.C. army's unfortunate run-in, which quickly developed into a run-out, with the poisonous honey from the Pontic azalea (*R. luteum*). In that instance, Pompey's army surely had a debilitating and paralyzing collective paroxysm that cost most of the soldiers in the army their lives at the hand of Mirthridates, King of Pontus.

Perhaps this does bring up a cautionary point. Watch out that there are no predators around when your cat is having its paroxysm because they are sitting ducks (??) in that state and to compound it, you yourself, might end up having a paroxysm of grief when looking at the moribund remains of your pet.

At this point I'm sure you want to know how I came by all this dope on God's ultimate gift to mousers. Well, the first *roxieanum* var. *oreonastes* I had I kept in a pot. At that time, I did not know how addictive it was to cats, but anyway it must not have been cat-accessible. Probably I kept it in the greenhouse, and it got to be about fourteen or fifteen inches tall and in age produced a flower bud. I must say my mind ran to thinking about installing special security devices to protect from human predation but I was guilelessly unaware that there were four – count them – "Tristan', 'Smudge', 'Timmy' and 'Kate' – incipient paroxysmatic pussies right in my very own home.

I wondered why all of those exquisite narrow, lanceolate, indumented botanical marvels of advanced photosynthetic evolution were lying around the base of the plant. Then the flower bud disappeared and I had to look more closely.

We all know what rhododendron hairs are but the hairs I found were 2.1 to 4.6 cm. long, glandular, glabrous, white, sometimes black and white, orange flushed brown or black. These weren't rhododendron hairs. They were cats' hairs.

Next piece of evidence. At last year's club picnic I won the door prize – a *roxieanum* var. *oreonastes*. It was a beautiful plant in a four-gallon pot. It had been expertly grown by Clint Smith. I went home thinking that the '93 picnic was the best we had ever had.

It sat on the deck where it could be admired from the kitchen window – by people. But it was admired much more closely by the purring pussycats that lodge (dare I admit to thinking 'temporarily') at 5631 Batu Road. They had an orgy of paroxysms and one of the main branches was amputated – covered with cat hairs.

Some of you may see this as presenting a dilemma. Which or who comes first, cats or rhododendrons? I suspect most of you will plunk for the former and you will want to ingratiate yourself to your fat feline friend – by getting him,

40

her or it, that transcendentally perfect gift, *roxieanum* var. *oreonastes*.

Don't be tempted by the claims of shysters touting catnip. This is like comparing slug's eggs to caviar. Go for the best; but be prepared for difficulties because *roxieanum* var. *oroenastes* is not easy to find. You will have to be committed and resolute in being your cats' benefactor responsible for providing the greatest hallucinogenic rapturous paroxysms by acquiring – preferably by theft – *roxieanum* var *oreonastes*.

Cats truly pass this way but once. Dismiss that view that a cat has more than one life or that a cat's life is a vale of tears; make it a Garden of Eden. You have the answer.

For more information on paroxysms caused by ingesting rhododendrons or rhododendron products, see David Leach's article "The Two Thousand Year Curse of the Rhododendron" in Rhododendron Information, A.R.S. 1967. Also "Puzzles in Rhododendron Poison" by the author in 'Rhododendrons on a western Shore' Ed., A. McCarter, VRS 1989.

Fertilizers for Rhododendrons
October 1994

The size of my stomach bears testimony to how well fertilized I am so if you put any faith in the ancient herbal Doctrine of Signs (or Signatures) then you may decide that this messenger is good (i.e., well-fertilized) or bad (i.e., over-fertilized).

Photosynthesis is the process whereby plants capture the sun's energy. This energy can be stored or transported around the plant to make it grow and thrive. Very simply, photosynthesis is the chemical reaction whereby carbon dioxide in the air reacts with water to produce sugars and starches (carbohydrates) and oxygen.

All plants are made up of these three elements – carbon, oxygen and hydrogen plus thirteen other essential

41

mineral elements. Some plants need other elements but all have this list of thirteen. They are the six MACRO NUTRIENTS: Nitrogen, Phosphorus, Potassium, Calcium, Magnesium, Sulphur – the first three are called the Primary Nutrient Elements – then the seven MICRO NUTRIENTS: Iron, Chlorine, Copper, Manganese, Zinc, Molybdenum and Boron. In nature these are provided by decaying living material and by the weathering of rocks.

In their natural environment rhododendrons have evolved to obtain all of their requirements, obviously, right in the spot on which they grow. Plants, unlike animals, don't move around much in search of food. If any of the thirteen minerals is not on the dinner plate the plant will not survive. Some plants have evolved to have a need for additional minerals; salt marsh plants need sodium, for example; however, rhododendrons have not yet been shown to have any other essential element in their diet.

If we make a broad generalization about the provenance of rhododendrons, we can say they occur where there is (1) ample rainfall in longer daylight months for those from more northerly climes and evenly distributed rainfall for those nearer the equator, (2) acidic soils because of the fairly slow rate of biomass decomposition, (3) a more or less shady location, and (4) humus accumulation because temperatures are moderate.

A simple mnemonic for the culture of rhododendrons is that they are easy to grow if one remembers to **WASH**, (i.e., (**W**)ater, (**A**)cid, (**S**)hade & (**H**)umus).

The biological productivity or the busyness of plants depends on light and ambient temperature. That special group of plants called broad-leafed evergreens is active all year long. Even when the soil around the roots is frozen and there is no liquid water to suck in with the dissolved mineral ions the leaves can still be transpiring, and some react to this by curling up their leaves to reduce this transpiration. Rhododendrons want to grow the year round; to do this they need water at the roots. In our mnemonic if we take away the

(W)ater we are left with (A S H) and this has happened to my plants too often, especially this summer.

This biological productivity has been measured and it doubles for every ten degrees Celsius increase in temperature. At 10 °C the busyness of the plants is twice what it is at 0 °C. At 20 °C it is about four times. Imagine how busy a rhododendron wants to be when grown in a container in the full sun with soil temperature of 40 °C or more. Internal constraints like size of the plumbing just can't cope and again we end up with (A S H).

Another thing which is important about understanding the care rhododendrons need is appreciating where they store their nutrients. I found particularly interesting and important the advice coming from Oregon State University as reported at a couple of the ARS conventions. It seems broad-leaved evergreen plants store most of their nutrients in their leaves. A healthy plant has quite a bit socked away in these botanical RRSPs and when the roots can't meet all the plant's needs it draws down on these stored starches and sugars. We humans don't want to use our RRSPs – if we have them at all – unless and until we have to on a rainy day. The difference with the plants is that they usually save them for a dry day not a rainy day! However, here in the Pacific North West, as far as rhodos go, it can often be the rainy day after all when the reserves are called on. We get so much rain in the winter that the soil nutrients are leached away and escape the ion-pumps of the shallow rooted rhododendrons. In a large proportion of the natural rhododendron habitat winter rainfall is small or the plant is covered with snow and there is not too much being leached away. Here, our plants will benefit by having their essential nutrients supplemented with a feed of fertilizer. Of course our chemical supplements will be leached away too but the scheme is to give the roots a chance of catching them on the way past.

The regime I now follow is to give them quarter strength feeds in November, January and March (soil temperatures are low and productivity slow) and full strength feeds in May and late June or early July.

The mix I use is one developed by Tom Brown of the Vancouver Chapter. He spoke about this at the Regional Conference at Whistler a few years ago. A test of his formulation followed and it was found to give good results.

Its analysis is: Nitrogen 10% (half of this is sulphur-coated urea), Phosphoric acid 8%, Soluble Potash 6%, Sulphur 8%, Magnesium 5%, Iron 1.8%, Zinc 0.04%, Boron 0.02%, Manganese 0.04%, Copper 0.02%. This formulation (10-8-6) differs from other commonly sold fertilizers for rhododendrons, typically (4-12-8), in that the proportion of nitrogen is much higher.

There is a myth the rhodos don't need a high proportion of nitrogen. Analysis of rhododendron plant tissue confirms a high percentage of nitrogen. My own experience is that when a plant shows chlorosis – a paleness of the green colour between the veins in a leaf – it can usually be cured by a shot of nitrogen – provided the pH is in the right range. Ammonium sulphate (21-0-0) is a soluble source of nitrogen instantly available to the plant. Caution is needed in using ammonium sulphate as too much can burn the plant. Calcium nitrate is sometimes used, I'm told, to give a quick greening up to foliage. To the ammonium sulphate I usually add some magnesium sulphate (Epsom Salts) (1 gram for 3 liters) and some fritted trace elements (FTE) because all the books talk about iron chlorosis and magnesium deficiency. I haven't observed these FTEs doing much good, but because a magnesium atom is the central one in the chlorophyll molecule it is essential. For a quick pick-me-up 20-20-20, Fish (5-2-2) or 30-10-10 are also very good. I get Tom Brown's mix specially made and buy it in quantity. Members can get this from me at cost.

Of course some growers have ideal natural conditions for rhododendrons with bushels of well-composted oak leaves and fir duff inches deep. They don't need any supplemental feed. My own soil is thin glacial till with very little humus. There are no rich alluvial accumulations. The ice scouring can still be seen. It only left about 11,000 years ago and the Douglas Firs didn't start growing until about 7,000 years ago so there haven't been many generations of big plants to build up a decent duff. My rhodos need all the help they can get, which means bark mulch, oak leaves, a lot of sawdust or any other natural kind of dressing so the supplementary chemical feeding becomes doubly necessary.

Still Slugging
December 1994

"Let us accept slugs for what they are – slimy ugly voracious creatures. Not unlike people, to whom we owe money."

I remember writing a piece for the newsletter some time ago about the various regiments of the rapacious army of slugs that inhabit our place. At the time I didn't think too many people had felt compelled to write about slugs, so recently I sensed a swelling in my chest and an unusual slippery buoyancy when I read a letter to the editor in the Globe and Mail by Margaret Atwood.

Now when Margaret Atwood, (an author who knows this world well and one who is recognized even by the literary elite of France as worthy of a decoration), says something about slugs ... that really hits home.

In a previous edition of the Globe and Mail, Andrea Schluter of Vancouver had written an article defending the wilderness and its creatures and had quoted from an Atwood poem which Schluter used – so Atwood claims – to make her sound like a nature hatin' coyote-bashing meanie. Atwood goes on to say that slugs and coyotes are ... quite different things. I have to quote the last two paragraphs of her letter. They are so good that even if you have already read the letter it's worth a second read.

"For Ms. Schluter, however, they (coyotes and slugs) are both symbols of wilderness. I would be happy to pack up my own slugs and express them to Ms. Schluter, who is by definition bound to foster them. They'll turn the inside of her house into a natural paradise, at least until they run out of food.

And that's the problem right there: food. And what eats what, be it Pomeranians, my lettuces, or Ms. Schluter. Liver flukes and plague-carrying fleas and cholera bacteria are part of the natural world, too. I guess it's just a matter of where you put that fence, eh?"

You will understand that I'm in a high state of gastropodal excitement reading all this and my head is nodding emphatically in support of Margaret Atwood. It probably won't stop until I buy her latest book. And it doesn't stop there. Someone who knows my sluggy feelings give me "The Little Greenish Brown Book on Slugs" by Eve Corbel. The quotation at the top of the article is from it. On its cover it says, "They come out at night and devour everything that grows." You quickly appreciate its editorial bias. Another good quotation from it is, "A slug will also eat a living animal (Ms. Schluter?) if the creature will stay still long enough." How about, "the word gastropod means belly foot, and refers to the way slugs, like Napoleon's army, walk or march on their stomachs".

For those of you who are really into all of the current rights issues this little book (3 x 4.25 in.) is reassuring. It says, "Just last year a spokesperson for the United Nations told me that slugs are not protected by international treaty." I think I appreciate some of the basic precepts of biodiversity and the need to conserve complete ecosystems but slugs – which I learn are not a group of closely related animals but merely have a similar body type – have their highest population density in Coastal British Columbia – as many as three per square foot (Harrowsmith).

I also think they are the world's best recyclers. Slug casts are probably every bit as good stuff as worm casts for enriching soils but when these casts are made from the rarest indumented species of rhododendron, I would rather keep a Saskatchewan potash miner and an Albertan oil driller in a job and use a little nice clean chemical fertilizer. Slugs are not an endangered species. Listen: a slug's heart is myogenic, i.e., it will continue beating when removed from the body; slugs can withstand total immersion in water at 10 ° C for over five hours; slugs have both sexes in the same animal and if push comes to shove they need only one to survive. My little book says, "Both partners are fertilized during copulation", giving rise to the question: who did what to whom?

It is clear it's our lifestyle not theirs that is threatened.

I had intended to write about the unrelenting fight we are having this year with rabbits. Our neighbour started with two nice black ones. She had them in the house, but thought they would be happier outside. She fed them. They were happier and multiplied – you know that rabbits are sex machines. So you can thank Margaret Atwood for sparing that ongoing tear-some tale. Slugs, sebaceous and omnivorous, are back on my hit list as number one enemy, along with rabbits. In an effort to be somewhat fair to slugs, I'll close with one more quotation from the little book,

"Human beings have courtship habits far stranger than those of the slug".

Reference

The Little Greenish—Brown Book on Slugs; Eve Corbel. Arsenal Pulp Press, 1062 Homer Street #100 Vancouver BC V6V 2W9. 1993. ISBN 0-88978-267-9.

Great Moments In History
March 1995

"Dr. Livingston, I presume?"; "Et tu, Brute!"; "The Eagle has landed".

Some phrases take on an historical and symbolic significance that sinks deep into our cultural psyche and provokes long trains of thought in our dream wanderings, many of which would no doubt surprise even their original utterers. But here comes one phrase well considered by its utterer and made some time in advance of its actual happening, – that is assured of being on the lips of the *cognoscente* from here on into eternity "The *auriculatum* will bloom."

I have been making this promise, prediction or threat now for fifteen or more years but this thirty-year old plant has at last come out of the closet and declared itself to be a sexual creature. Finally, it has flower buds. So, let the phrase "The *auriculatum* will bloom" resound through your halls and echo from the boles of your forests.

This is being written just before Christmas and I sense a similarity about the magic that Christmas holds for children – and even some adults – where its anticipation holds more of its essence than it does its realization. Maybe it's the same thing with "The *auriculatum* will bloom." Certainly there is a downside to the blooming of *auriculatum*. As with kids at Christmas, the guessing is gone when the wrappers are off. Waiting for a cherished plant to bloom is one of the most effective and inexpensive life insurance policies one can acquire. Will I now be able to transfer the *auriculatum* policy to *proteoides* or *basilicum?* Last year I had a customer who was buying one of the big-leafed species. I said to him, "You know this will not bloom for twenty years". "That's OK", he replied, "I'm seventy-three. That gives me twenty years to watch it grow and ten years to enjoy the bloom." Does that mean I have ten years at most to go?

The next problem is that I will have to start deadheading *auriculatum*. That won't be easy as the thing is fifteen feet tall, clearly a very hazardous undertaking. Also as *auriculatum* blooms in late July or early August, there is a danger of encountering a really hot spell. The floral display, reputedly so fragrant and luxuriant, could be of short duration. I will not only be worrying more about getting enough water to the plant but about its being short-changed for its debuted presentation.

I bought this plant from Bill Lammle, who with his wife had started Rhodoland on the Pat Bay Highway. This was a specimen garden plant and had not been for sale though Bill knew I coveted it. When the decision had been made to sell Rhodoland I got my chance and Bill and I came to an understanding on the transfer of its ownership. I would very much like to get the word – the phrase – "the *auriculatum* will bloom" – to Bill Lammle. He would appreciate its significance right away. Maybe he will sense it anyway.

The late Peggy Abkhazi told of the big *auriculatum* in her – now Chris and Pam Balls' – garden. She said it was about twenty years old when she acquired it and it took another forty years to bloom. So Bill Lammle's plant is quite precocious by the Abkhazi standards. I tell this Abkhazi story to visitors to our garden. It is part of the standard repertoire. I suppose I can still keep the bits about her plant almost the same but I will have to change the whole spiel about our thirty-something youngster. It sure changes the whole point of the story. But still "The *auriculatum* will bloom" will be on everyone's lips by then and I will probably give the best impression if I am just smugly reticent about the whole thing. Some have greatness thrust upon them and all that stuff.

So now you know. The Americans have "Remember the Alamo"; we have "The *auriculatum* will bloom."

Going for the Alphabetically Challenged
November 1995

One word that jumps out at me from the printed page and makes me all twitterpated is 'oxymoron'. A few years ago this word was a complete stranger to me. Now I see it used in literal overdoses, in newspaper and magazine articles by writers who should know better. Last night I cringed at Peter Newman's use of it in MacLean's. William Safire, that prophylactic proctor of American-English usage in a recent article used the phrase 'oxymoronic rhetorical trick'. My understanding is that 'oxymoron' means something like 'acute falsity' or ' a blatant contradiction'. 'Rhetorical' has the sense of artificial persuasion, and 'trick' means fraud.

What the semantic sum of Safire's phrase equals is not very clear to me – but that's not my point.

The significance here is the use of the words containing the letter 'X'. Letters at the end of the alphabet have been getting short shrift for a long time and now they are out for revenge. This is the advent of Glottal Charter of Rights. Zealous watchers will also have noticed increased use of words with an intermediate, not terminal, 'Y', as in 'oxymoron' and the present zestful fervour for the use of words with 'Z' in them.

As an example, one word that's getting the tops and bottoms of its letters abraded by overuse is 'xerophytic'. One cannot read a gardening magazine or attend a horticultural meeting without being deluged (a super word in this context) by 'xerophytic', 'xeriscaping' and 'xeromorphic'. The popularity of these words, no doubt, reflects the perceived need by their users of probity, prudence and political correctness in broaching sensitive subjects like global warming and raising the Sooke dam. But to me their overuse makes the message more xerotic and less germane. Do you not agree with me that there is something oxymoronic about a xerophytic garden?

Recently a customer called wanting *Rhododendron xanthostephanum*. I was impressed. I had never had anyone ask for this plant before. The prospective grower said he wanted it because he didn't have a rhododendron in his garden that started with an 'X'. He also said that he wanted it to add to his collection of rhododendrons but you will immediately see how 'au fait' he is in attempting to meet his quota for the alphabetically deprived.

This got me thinking. If my theory on the resurgence of the alphabets nether extremities is not all wet, (i.e., xerophobic, and holds water), then the best selling rhododendron species are going to be *xanthostephanum, xanthocodon,* and *zaleucum. Xanthocodon* has been having its lumps recently, having been demoted to a sub-species of *cinnabarinum* by Cullen and Chamberlain. (Good old Davidian, the gardener's taxonomist, still gives it specific rank and says it differs markedly from *cinnabarinum*.) I will keep giving it its majority not only because of its distinctive appearance but mainly because of the noise the word makes. To ensure it makes the top ten all we need is to have Ian McTaggart-Cowan say it to as many people as possible. One usually hears it as zan-tho-co-don, the way a six-year old who is still being taught to read phonetically would pronounce it. Ian must have learned the 'whole language' way and it rolls off his tongue with a dynamism that brings back youthful memories of hearing the famous locomotive – 'The Flying Scotsman' – roaring through the border country.

Anyway, after my customer's request, I immediately struck some cuttings of *xanthostephanum*. I have to admit that I had forgotten all about having a plant of *xanthostephanum* in the garden but quickly rediscovered it. I also put some *zaleucum* but couldn't find a *xanthocodon* (Go on, say it) and so had to make do with *concatenans*.

I will now make another prediction which if I were truly selfish I would keep to myself. There will be a huge splurge in the popularity of that cousin of the rhododendron – the Sourwood or Sorrel Tree – *oxydendrum*. My goodness, does this have a lot going for it! Not only does it suit many suburban gardens with its modest nature – August blooming, lily-of-the-valley flowers and great fall colour, but its name carries a double merchandizing whammy. We've got the hot ticket 'oxy' at the start and then the tympanic shocking beat of the 'drum' at the end. It's almost too good to be true.

The 'drum' part is especially good because many people like to call our favourite plants 'rhododendrums'. It is, arguably, easier to say it that way but it is probably too late to change. No matter, '*oxydendrum*' has a virile vibrancy to it and gardeners are going to be visually and aurally satisfied by growing it. (I have not been able to trace why the 'drum' ending became accepted. It seems to come from the same 'tree-dendros' Greek root.) In any event Bailey (New Encyclopedia of American Gardening) called it *oxydendrum* over a century ago. Another plant in the same band is *clerodendrum*.

Concurrent with the craze to grow plants without water is one to grow only 'native' plants. The Newfies call people not born on the island "Come from Aways". Newfoundlanders are such friendly people that it is surely not a xenophobic appellation. For some neo-gardeners there is, however, a real phobia about growing "Come from Aways". I have a challenge for them. One of the most majestic of our BC natives is Bear Grass. I remember being so impressed by it the first time I saw it growing among widely spaced Ponderosa pines. *Xerophyllum tenax* – what a name! It meets all the specifications of our politically sensitive contemporary gardener. It has two 'X's', it is 'native', and it wants a dry environment. Unfortunately, it needs other conditions not easy for us in Victoria to provide but that should just add some cultural zest for the anti-exotic enthusiasts.

I am sure readers can think of many more examples of 'new wave' plants. Share around. One I caution about is Zygadenus. It has locution, it is native, but the overall flavour is not good. The Death Camus was carefully culled out from the beds of nourishing Camus by our native people. We should do the same no matter what the trendy political mores are. And remember, don't be an oxymoron, whatever that means.

The Season's Starters
January 1996

It's a bleak, fireside-tugging day. The last leaves are still on the mountain ashes and the dogwoods are giving some colour, but there is not much blooming. The pond which usually does not overflow until December started sending its surplus down to Elk Lake a couple of days ago. Many people are saying we are going to have a hard winter.

Still, in about six weeks the first of the rhodos will be in bloom and a whole new season gets into swing. The first to put on its petaled cloak is usually *R. dauricum* or at least the two plants I have of what I call the Abkhazi form of *dauricum*. Some years this will open its first flower on

Christmas Day, but I think it really wants to be in a Scottish person's garden and wait for Hogmanay to put its purple first foot into the New Year. It's a welcome 'first foot' and is a fitting leader of the levee as its New Year's dress is the best it has and, after its blossoms are gone, it dons the hodden grey attire for the next eleven months and is easily overlooked.

Of great stature and close behind in timing is *R. ririe*. Our plant is in a very shady spot and I suspect it's trying to tell me that if only I gave it a bit more prominence it would feel justified in showing off more. It does end up with some mushy brown flowers most Januarys when the temperature drops to minus two or three, but the unopened buds will bide their time until the temperature warms up so they have a chance to make some seeds. It is, however, a very easy plant to grow and, provided it can be given the space it needs, and its owner can wait for a few years to let it get to flowering maturity, its somewhat somber but distinctive pink colour with its dark nectaries makes it a favoured New Year friend.

When we are introduced to newcomers it is often difficult to get their names right the first time. Once we know these new friends by their given names we are likely to keep calling them that even if they were improperly introduced in the first place. And if a plant has a catchy, easy name we recall it more easily than if it has one you have to say over two or three times to get it into your registry. 'Christmas Cheer' is such an easy alliteration that I suspect that many plants being called this are happy enough (as are their owners) with the appellation. But I think there are many, many 'Christmas Cheers'. The plants we grow in our garden with that name don't open a flower until the end of March and would be better called 'Easter Cheer'. The plant we call 'Rosamundi' starts its show in October some years and goes on blooming until April. The flowers are smaller than those of its later blooming cousin but more welcome for their earliness. Some critics decry the weak colour and the smallness of bloom on 'Christmas Cheer' and 'Rosamundi' but I think it is a bit of a cheap shot and a horticultural injustice to say that plants like 'Christmas Cheer' and

53

'Rosamundi' would be thrown on the bonfire if it were not for their early show.

The above two are given in the literature as being *caucasicum* hybrids. Both have been around for a very long time – well over 100 years. Of equal or even older vintage are some hybrids listed as being *caucasicum* x *arboreum*. These are not well known in the Victoria area but I think they are probably better plants. 'Nobleanum coccineum' and 'Nobleanum venustrum' are two that are available from time to time. Could it be that their names have limited their popularity? My favourite of this clan is 'Lee's Scarlet'. It will bloom before Christmas and continue for two or more months – never a great mass of colour but with enough of the dark rosy pink flowers with a deeper blotch to warm up a short January day. If you have the room put 'Heatherside Beauty' beside it. This plant – same cross and habit – has pale, almost white pink flowers possessing an elegant refinement.

For early whites, however, my vote for the plant with the classiest, most pristine flowers would go to 'Tessa Bianca'. There is just that touch of warmth in the white that makes you want to stand closer. I haven't tried this but I think it would look superb growing with pink or purple *Helleborus orientalis*.

I will just mention three more hybrids that make the best choice list in the catalogue in my mental, very floppy disc. These are 'Crystal Pink', 'Airy Fairy' and 'Clipinense'. The first two both have *R. lutescens* as a parent and there is no blue at all in the flower. 'Crystal Pink' comes in more than one clone. One is known as 'Bodega's Crystal Pink'. Place it where you can see it from the kitchen window or where you can see it while eating breakfast. It will make the coffee taste better. 'Airy Fairy' has a touch of whimsy in it. Maybe it's just the name, but even though it has the same willowy habit as lutescens, it seems as if it will never grow up. It is a perpetual teenager, all limbs and hormones. 'Clipinense' is probably the best known of the small, early rhododendrons. The watercolour blending of pink and white on a spreading mound of shiny, hairy leaves makes it a prime candidate for front of the border. It is one of Lord Aberconway's creations. And saying that compels me to mention one more that you shouldn't be without – 'Seta'. Aberconway was really inspired when he made this cross – *spinuliferum* x *moupinense.* The flowers are pink with deeper pink stripes on the outside and face upwards like young nestlings with their craws open looking for a feed.

I could go on. If you have space, the early giants like *R. calophytum* are truly impressive as are the big leafed things – the *R. macabeanums* and *R. montroseanums*.

There are many choice dwarfs like *leucaspis* and *pemakoense*, but these are for another story for another time. Enough for now, the new season is almost here.

Ernie Lythgoe   (1902-1996)
February 1996

Ernie Lythgoe's long, full and rewarding life came to an end on the 8th of January. He was a member of this Society from its beginning and was an Honorary member. He and Elsie created a garden of note which was visited and enjoyed by many, many people.

No one enjoyed that garden more than Ernie and Elsie. We all hope that Elsie will continue to do so for a long time to come. Ernie's enjoyment of their garden was not a simplistic thing, just as Ernie was not a simple person. Most of the plants in the garden were chosen because they were individuals who knew their place in the big scheme of things and fitted in the smaller scheme of the garden. Ernie treasured the Hairy Manzanita and the Lewisia Tweedyi which grew above the pool, because they were native and were survivors that flourished and were beautiful despite some pretty hard times, and were now in a friendly location.

Ernie was a teacher and a musician. To be right, things must be composed and conserved, and be as comely and congruous as possible. He loved the wild plants – the species – and was suspicious of man-made hybrids.

I can think of two examples where Ernie's philosophies were given expression in our garden. When *R. yakushimanum* was first introduced, Ernie got some seed of this treasure. One of the plants that resulted was clearly a hybrid. He gave it to me as I liked it. It is tough, reliable, showy in a refined, unostentatious way, but very floriferous and getting better each season. Over the years, Ernie would admire it, having forgotten its origins. I would tell him I was calling it 'Lythgoe's Legacy' and ask if he would like a plant as I had been propagating it for some time. However, it was still a hybrid.

The other chuckle I would have with Ernie every year would be with 'Top Banana'. Ernie would spy this yellow blossom. "That is a good yellow", he would say. "'Wardii'?" When I told him what it was, his face would fall in disgust. "Bah, I'll wait for the bottom banana."

Ernie was a teacher, both a professional and an amateur one. I have known Ernie for only the last twenty odd years. He had retired from the classroom when we became friends. But he spoke of many of his students as friends and of his many colleagues in the same way. He loved having gardening students in his garden. He loved sensing his knowledge being absorbed. I'm sure he enjoyed saying to me, "We'll make a gardener of you yet," as much as I appreciated hearing it.

One day I needed a new handle on an axe. I watched in fascination as a craftsman did a job that included details I had never imagined. The resulting fit was perfection. He was always ready to help – pulling stumps, identifying a plant, making labels for the plants at the University or working in the rock garden at Beacon Hill Park.

Elsie was his life's partner and his complement. She is in our thoughts. When many of us gathered at the Lythgoe house on Saturday the 13th of January to pay our respects to our late friend, Elsie was as gracious and appreciative and welcoming as she always has been. She too will be supported by her memories of Ernie – she has her Lythgoe legacy.

A Tale of Thailand
March 1996

One late spring day in 1996, I had an unexpected
visitation by a busload of travelers from Thailand. I was not
too enthusiastic in my welcome, as I had only 20 minutes
notice of their coming and I had not in the past made any
special connection between Thailand and rhododendrons.
Their leader, on alighting from the bus, was immediately
identified as such by his headgear – a baseball cap on which
was artistically emblazoned "The Dogfather." After the initial
hand-shake, he drew attention to its prominence. Keeping
pace with his purposeful stride was the one woman in the
group. When I asked her name and was told, my attempt to
repeat it was so far off the mark that the lady said, "Just think
of Rhododendron *makinoi.* " I did not know it then but all
Thais have nicknames and this lady's nick-name was "Noi." I
did know then that I was dealing with serious plant people.

The group visiting our nursery was one half of the
senior staff of the Mai Fah Luang Foundation of Thailand.
The other half was visiting our British Columbia museum and
investigating the local craft outlets. The "Dogfather" was M.
R. Diskul Disnadda (Khun Chai, more informally), Secretary
General of the Foundation and Noi was his wife. The group
had a short tour of the nursery and garden. This was followed
by very courteous thank-yous and with promises to keep in
touch. My thought at that time was that here was potential for
establishing a chapter of the ARS in Thailand.

Later that year, there was a phone call from Bangkok
from Dr. Charlie Mehl. Dr. Mehl looks after the international
interests of the Foundation. He invited my wife and me to
visit Thailand. "Just get to Bangkok and we will look after
you from there on." At that point all we knew about the Mai
Fah Luang Foundation was gleaned from the couple of
pamphlets that Khun Chai (The Dogfather) had given me on
his visit. The Foundation had been established by the late
Princess Mother of Thailand who was appalled at the
devastation that was happening to both people and land up in

the northeast corner of Thailand. This is where Thailand borders with Myanmar (Burma) and Laos. This is the area notoriously known world-wide as The Golden Triangle.

The Hill tribes in this region had, since the sixties, become commercial growers of the opium poppy (*Papaver somniferum*). The hill people had been growing the poppy for hundreds of years, probably since it was introduced to the area during the spice trading days of the 14th century. They used opium medicinally and it had become an inherent part of their culture. Now, there is a total proscription on its growth. The opium poppy is a plant that does well on poor soils. I don't recall where it came from but it grows quite well in our garden. In recent years poppies have given better economic returns to the Asian growers than other crops. The hill tribes became dependent on selling to the drug lords. They also became enmeshed in the sex trade, trading their teenagers to prostitution.

The authorities recognize six main tribes, most of which practice "swidden" farming. It is also called slash and burn, shifting, or rotational agriculture. With the exponential increase in the demand for opium, the tribes responded by burning more of the forests to get more acreage into production. Some of the tribes had originated in Burma; some originally came from China and some from Laos. None identified in a civic sense with the current political boundaries and all had their own language, although about half had their ancestral roots in the territory of Thailand.

Apart from the squeeze for land to grow opium, the larger causes of deforestation in Thailand were the conversion of forested areas to agricultural crop production by lowlanders and by logging. I learned a new meaning for "clear-cut." In fact I despaired of seeing teak trees, but eventually did see lots of reforested young ones. Later we saw elephants working with teak logs. Teak grows in a narrow altitudinal range. To be rich in Thailand is to own teak trees. One reference cites a statistic that explains the urgency for new government policies. One hundred years ago 75 percent of Northern Thailand was forested. In 1989 only 30 percent of the forests above 800 meters elevation remained. In that year the Thai government banned logging of any kind, although some observers note that illegal logging accounted for at least three times the legal quota and that it still continues.

It is hard to believe that the lush luxuriance that we experienced at Doi Tung was a clear-cut just ten years before. Plants grow quickly in this region of tropical fecundity. Eighty-five percent of the Foundation's lands are now in forest – some deciduous and some evergreen. We experienced no rain during our visit and the temperatures were salubrious, in contrast to the steamy heat of Bangkok. December and January are the driest months in the north. This is when the deciduous trees drop their leaves. Doi Tung has, on average, 1400 mm of rain falling on 145 days of the year – a relatively dry micro-climate in this part of the world. Other parts of Thailand experience two annual monsoons. We were told that during the June to September period it is very damp indeed. With daytime temperatures in the twenties and the coldest recorded temperature being 5°C, I would have thought that they would be able to grow many other horticulturally desirable genera like proteas, but proteas evidently cannot tolerate the prolonged dampness of the monsoon.

In 1987, the Princess Mother assembled 150 square kilometers of this devastated mountainous land to form the Foundation. She built a residence – a palace – at Doi Tung. Doi Tung means mountain of the flag. She also set up an ambitious social/economic program to give the hill people alternatives to growing poppies: introducing better varieties of rice, making paper from mulberry trees, growing coffee (as good as Kona coffee), making textiles, and growing cut flowers and house plants.

There are 26 villages within the boundaries of Doi Tung. During our visit we saw only one of the villages. That was the occasion of one of our happiest memories. We stood watching as a couple of dozen 3 and 4 year-olds in the village school boisterously acted out the words of the songs they were singing in such an engaging fashion that we found ourselves trying to follow their motions and getting quite caught up in their enthusiasm.

However, we had been invited to Doi Tung for the purpose of discussing rhododendrons. Khun Chai, in his plan for the development of the estate, has set aside 50 hectares for growing

59

rhododendrons. *Rhododendron* is not a common plant in the wild, and apart from those at Doi Tung about the only others we saw were beautiful bright potted evergreen azaleas at the Sunday Market in Bangkok. Thais love bright colours, especially red.

At Doi Tung, there are already immaculately landscaped gardens with sweeping lawns: great swaths of colour from roses and geraniums, salvia and petunias, punctuated by towering spikes of Italian cypress in a panorama that rivals Butchart Gardens in Victoria, British Columbia. The road that climbs steeply and twistingly from the plains up to the 1500 meter elevation of Doi Tung is lined with tall poinsettias with colors so intense that we were awed by their brilliance even when, on the night we arrived, we could only see them by the headlights of the vehicle and by the light of the stars. In the greenhouses were orchids (many are native to this area) and anthurians and begonias and thousands and thousands of African violets. Many were being grown by tissue culture, as were pineapple and rice and a special vetiver grass that is being used to stabilize the steep slopes of the deforested areas. This grasses' roots go down 3 meters but the disease resistant clone they use does not reliably set seed, hence the need for micro-propagation. The propagules are grown-on in square Johnny Walker whisky bottles, which are set out on the ground under shade cloth. One nursery grows plants solely for the royal residence. The residence where we were accommodated was certainly "royal" by any standard. The floral display in the main living room would have stocked Victoria's largest florist quite easily. On Christmas Eve the decor changed to one we were familiar with. The "tree" was a *Pinus kesiya,* one of the species used for reforestation.

Khun Chai is a man in a hurry. He has set aside 50 hectares for a rhododendron garden. His first priority was to get the hard landscaping completed. The paths and the stairs, built of local sedimentary rock set in mortar, are aesthetically sumptuous. The gazebos and pavilions are architecturally inviting. Right on the edge of the ridge, where the border with Myanmar (Burma) runs, is a semi-circular lookout. There, the view over the hills goes forever and the sunsets are of tropical subtlety. We could see some areas on fire but whether these were natural occurrences or not we could not determine. Close to this grand viewpoint were two Rhododendron *smithii* (now R. *argipeplum*, subsection Barbata) that had been relocated from China. They were estimated to be 100 years old. They were anchored in with tie-downs, but they were in bloom on Christmas Eve when Princess Mahachakri Sirindhorn was in residence at the Foundation. We were fortunate to be introduced to Her Royal Highness. Some of the slopes on the site had been planted with an evergreen azalea native to Thailand *(R. simsii)* and these were doing well. Also doing well were Yunnan plants of *R. decorum, R. fortunei* and *R. delavayi* (now *R. arboreum* ssp. *delavayi).*

Other areas were planted with *R. maddeniis* – mostly *R. taronense* (now *R. dendricola*) – also brought in from Yunnan. These were mature plants, 3 to 4 meters in height, but they were thin and twiggy with small root balls and had been defoliated badly although many showed new shoots coming from the base and along the trunks. Just a meter or so from the Burmese border were specimens of *R. lyi* and *R. ludwigianum,* both native. Unfortunately the sun had set when we saw these plants, and as I had not brought flash equipment up to the ridge I was unable to photograph them. If one were a bird watcher and keeping a lifetime "sightings" list, then having seen these species "in the wild" would be a major event, but there was so little light when I saw them that I could not make note of any distinguishing characteristics.

The scale of the rhododendron "garden" at Doi Tung is so immense that it calls out for large plants. However, great gardens do not quite happen overnight. But clearly the climate and the site are so benign for rhododendrons that it should be possible to grow all but the alpine species. With a frost free environment all of the vireyas should flourish as should all the species in subsections *Falconera* and *Grandia.* Recalling how quickly the plants had grown at Pukeiti in New Zealand, it is not difficult to imagine the little plants that are now being grown from the 1998 ARS Seed Exchange, luxuriantly clothing the steep slopes at Doi Tung. My mind had difficulty with the idea of growing hybrids on this natural setting but clearly many of the most exotic will flourish. I really tried to take a plant of David Leach's 'Bangkok' with me but I couldn't find one locally. It would probably not thrive in that soft environment, I rationalized.

Perhaps we rhododendron growers will soon give an altered connotation to the one we usually have of the Golden Triangle. My wife and I will always think of Thailand in golden terms.

Let's Have a Little Respect
November 1996

'Cynthia' has been on my mind and in musing about her, I decided she has been done dirty by me – and by others too.

I recently got an order of rhododendrons and among the exotic and rare species were ten plants of 'Cynthia'. "Cynthia," I cried, "Who's going to buy 'Cynthia'?" Well, I don't know who's going to buy 'Cynthia' but I bet if I get her to blooming size she will sell herself. 'Cynthia' doesn't get the respect she deserves.

On our bus tour after attending the Rhododendron Convention in Oban, Scotland, we visited Blackhills, which is world famous, among other things, for being the home to one of the finest specimens of that choice and rare rhododendron, *R. lacteum*. We were being guided around its 25 acres by John Christie – its present owner. John is the third generation Christie to have the pleasure and the responsibility for its well-being. Blackhills is in Morayshire in the northeast of Scotland. The climate there is not moderated as it is on the west coast by the Gulf Stream, and the general lay of the estate is northerly. Rainfall is modest too – not too different in total amount from Victoria's, but distributed much more evenly. About 30 miles away in Inverness, temperatures in the winter of 95/96 got down to -20 ° C, yet at Blackhills only a few degrees of freezing was experienced, a Scottish example of an Oak Bay microclimate.

The first generation Christie had been a "planter" in Asia and, when he laid out Blackhills early in this century, his intention was to replicate Himalayan rhododendron country. I suppose Blackhills comes as close to being in the Himalayas as I will ever get. Led by John Christie (who along with the Coxes of Glendoick) had won most of the trophies at the Convention show) we were trekking up one side of the valley and I spied this blaze of colour on the other side. Excitedly I exclaimed, "What is that?" With obvious lack of enthusiasm and somewhat dryly, John replied, "Cynthia". I admit that among all the *R. hodgsoniis* and *R. rudes* and *R. fictolacteums* 'Cynthia' could be considered not quite "pur laine". I accepted the wordless emanations from the owner that signaled that if it weren't such a big and thriving plant, 'Cynthia' would be removed.

In our own garden I don't worry much about how plants are placed. Species and hybrids are mixed indiscriminately. Some attention is given to height and colour, but not much. Dave Dougan's thesis that a rhododendron doesn't know if it's a species or a hybrid, so choosing the plant for its looks and not for its long name or rarity is pretty well accepted – except that I do give a little bit of preference to the rare and unusual. After all, if they are never going to bloom as with a lot of species, why worry about colour clashes. So as I reflected on the Blackhills 'Cynthia' episode and on my initial reaction to acquiring some for sale, I started to feel sorry for the poor old girl. She should get a little respect.

I recalled how, like Paul on the road to Damascus, I had completely changed my opinion on the merit of 'Vulcan'. 'Vulcan' was one of our first purchases and for years I snobbishly gave it no respect. After all, you could get 'Vulcan' in any garden centre. I think I reported in a previous newsletter years ago that 'Vulcan' had gone up in my rating when I had to deadhead over 200 trusses. This year I counted again and got to 444 when something interrupted the process (it was never finished). So now I have a great deal of respect for 'Vulcan' and I recommend whole-heartedly growing it where you want a medium-sized, June blooming, totally reliable red.

Lionel de Rothschild, the grandson of the other Lionel who founded Exbury, makes an interesting reference to 'Cynthia' in his article 'Hybrids in the British Isles: the 19th Century'. This is one of the chapters in 'The Rhododendron Story' published this year by the Royal Horticultural Society. There he suggests that the parentage of *catawbiense* x *griffithianum* given by most authorities for 'Cynthia' is suspect as the plant was first mentioned in the catalogues of Standish and of Noble in 1860. They issued separate catalogues after they split in 1856. Noble's name for 'Cynthia' became 'Lord Palmerston'. Rothschild says that since *griffithianum* had bloomed for the first time in 1858, its contribution to 'Cynthia' can be discounted. He offers no suggestion for what was mated with *catawbiense*.

There weren't too many other parents available in 1850, so it should not be too hard to determine. *Griffithianum* was first introduced by J. D. Hooker in 1850. The fact that it bloomed only eight years after introduction gives me hope that I may yet see a bloom on my plants. The two larger ones I have kept in pots as I am not sure how hardy they are, but as *griffithianum* has been measured at 50 feet in its natural setting this is obviously not a long term solution. In their garden, Evelyn and Nick Weesjes have a fine specimen, the scion for which came from the Fortescue garden in England.

Parenthetically, the Noble nursery became known as Sunningdale Nursery, which was the topic for Alleyne Cook, our speaker for the October meeting, making this discussion of 'Cynthia' somewhat timely. As an aside, Rothschild notes that on the dissolution from Noble, Standish said that 'two suns could not stand in the same horizon'.

But back to 'Cynthia', she went on to make a further outstanding contribution to the rhododendron world as she had a part in producing 'Pink Pearl' which held title to being the 'most popular' rhododendron for a very long time. 'Pink Pearl' is another plant that does not get the respect that she is due.

Both 'Cynthia' and 'Pink Pearl' have what we now class as average foliage. On the rating scale it rates a 3. That may be part of the reason for their dropping in popularity listings. Also, they are fairly big plants and I have to admit that if a big plant is required, 'Lem's Monarch', 'Point Defiance' and the 'Wallopers' are somewhat more dramatic in flower, but if the garden result that is wanted is a huge mass of pink, then the oldies will do the job just as well.

So do not dismiss 'Cynthia' as an old crone; true she is about 150 years old, more than any of us will see. Remember to show a little respect for your seniors.

The Scales of Injustice
January 1997

"This article is not intended to be about taxonomy; it is really about discrimination."

Scaly-leafed rhododendrons are not so popular as the non-scaly ones. I suppose the two main reasons for this are the smaller flower truss, or the absence of a truss, and the smaller sized leaves. Most of us are initially attracted to rhododendrons by their big showy burst of many flowers all stuck together in a multi-based mammiform, and the aim of most hybridizers (not only those working with rhododendrons) has been to produce bigger, more obvious blossoms. Bold and dramatic foliage are also desirable attributes.

The word 'lepidote' means having scales. These are found on the leaves, mostly on the underside, and often on the twigs and flowers. The word Leprosy (Roman) has the same root. The elepidotes (not having scales) include all the big-leaved species like *R. macabeanum* and *R. falconeri* and *R. fortunei* and many with the most interesting foliage. The indumented species are nearly all elepidotes, for example *R. yakushimanum, R. pachysanthum, R. fulvum* and *R. arboreum*. Go to any garden centre and you will find only a few lepidotes. You can probably find 'PJM', 'Curlew', 'Blue Diamond' and perhaps *R. impeditum* but the vast majority being offered for sale will be non-scaly ones. Azaleas are elepidotes too.

Most breeding effort with elepidotes has gone into the low, dwarf varieties. The Birds and the Bees are renowned worldwide. Cox's Birds include 'Curlew', 'Ptarmigan', 'Wren', 'Egret', 'Phalarope', and 'Razorbill'. Warren Berg's Bees started with 'Patty Bee' and went on to include 'Too Bee' and 'Not Too Bee' (now called 'WeeBee') but Warren went on to muddy the waters, for purposes of this article anyway, by giving his 'Bee' moniker to elepidotes when he registered 'King Bee' and 'Wanna Bee'. This roiling of the waters is just typical of the classification, the taxonomy of rhododendrons, and Warren Berg may even have a justifiable claim to consistency.

By and large elepidote rhododendrons will not cross with lepidote rhododendrons. The evolutionary lines of the two groups diverged long ago. Most elepidotes have the basic number of chromosomes ($2n = 26$) (i.e., they are diploids). Most lepidotes are polyploids, with the greatest number of species having $2n = 78$ and the next most frequently occurring about half as often as the former with $2n = 52$. Some go as high as 156. This is one of the reasons why there are not as many lepidote hybrids, as it helps to be a mother if your intended mate has the same number of chromosomes as you do. W. J. Bean, the late great English plantsman put it this way: "Lepidotes are less indulgent to the hybridizer and seemingly unpredictable."

But there are other significant differences between the two main groups of rhododendrons. The flowers are curled up one way in the bud in scaly rhodos and the opposite way in the non-scaly ones. The seeds have different shapes too. The natural world is a bit too complicated to fit into neat boxes that would make the lives of those of us who are row-and-column accountants cosy and predictable. We just have to accept the fact that there is a lot of chaos out there and that there are a lot of exceptions to the rules that we so cleverly devise.

According to the Senior Registrar for the genus Rhododendron there are over 30,000 hybrids on his list. (He is still struggling to get them onto a computerized database.)

I would guess that only a small percentage are of the scaly persuasion. Just because the elepidotes are so numerous and so many are so similar (man-made chaos) the lepidotes stand out by their individuality. Our club logo is a lepidote, 'Transit Gold'. Its profile of hanging bells at least narrows one's guess at the plant's identification to something manageable. (What more could one say of an outline of 'Trude Webster' than that it was a rhododendron?)

The most damaging and insulting misconception about the lepidotes is that they are often confused with azaleas. I suppose it is asking too much to have gardeners carry around a small magnifying glass in just the same way as they carry pruners, but a sneak peek would quickly show the difference. Azaleas don't have scales, but they have long hairs lying on the tops of their leaves pointing towards the tip just as a cat's hairs point towards its tail. This is easy to see with a 10-power glass. Many azaleas have five stamens while most other rhododendrons have ten or more and that is often, but not always, diagnostic.

As I remarked at the beginning, this article is not intended to be about taxonomy; it is really about discrimination. I can understand the small ones being confusing but to call a *R. augustinii* an azalea is very demoralizing to that noble plant. *Augustinii* belongs to a pretty distinctive group called the Triflorum Series, or if you prefer the latest revision, the Triflora sub-section, a group that is among the most garden-worthy in the whole genus. The colour range is from white through yellow, pink, near blue, purple and almost red. The smallest form of *R. keiskei* is tiny, but most are in the 2 to 3 metre range.

February brings *R. lutescens* in a good clear yellow that rivals *R. forsythia*; then comes the white elegance of *R. rigidum*; the pink of *R. davidsonianum*; white and coral of *R. yunnanense*; the sheets of blue *augustinii*; more yellow of *R. ambiguum* and ending the season in June with the smokey purple of *R. tricanthum*. Most of these are never seen in garden centres. Their leaves are willow-like, as is the growth habit, but the foliage is not without interest year round. *Lutescens'* new foliage is red while *R. oreotrephes'* and *R. rigidum's* are quite blue.

Broad generalizations always need retractions. The claim that the lepidotes are distinctive falls down when it comes to the 'blue' hybrids. *Augustinii* will cross with every rhododendron in the Lapponicum Series. *R. impeditum*, *R. russatum*, *R. fastigiatum*, *R. intricatum* et al. love to get together not only among themselves but with *augustinii*. And so, perhaps in an effort by hybridizers to show that they know lepidotes exist, they have gone to town with this group. Blue hybrid confusion reigns, absolute man-made chaos. 'Blue Diamond', 'Blue Tit', 'Bob's Blue', 'Songbird', 'Blue Chip', 'St. Breward', 'St. Tudy' 'Oceanlake', and on and on. It's almost as bad with the elepidotes where, to give one example, I counted 32 registered hybrids of 'Mars' x *yakushimanum*. The best blue hybrids in my opinion are 'Crater Lake', 'Blaney's Blue', and 'Ilam Violet'. If you have a mind for the more evocative try 'Passionate Purple' or 'Vibrant Violet', maybe even put them in the same bed.

All of the Vireyas, the tropical species, that we don't see too many of here in Victoria, as they can't take frost, are lepidotes.

Some of them rival orchids in their exotic flamboyance and where they can be grown outdoors, in Australia or California for example, breeding of Vireya hybrids is an exciting business.

There are physiological problems in crossing the hardy lepidotes we can grow with the tropical show-offs, but where similar problems exist in other genera, (e.g. lilies), ingenious ways of making them compatible have been found. Also, we are on the threshold of gene splicing and all that genetic engineering that we are reading about, so my guess is that it will not be long before we see very different and luxuriant lepidotes. Furthermore Vireyas can bloom at almost anytime of the year, presenting another great opening to the rhododendron hybridizer.

In the meantime if you have a space of say, ten square metres, try a planting of one *augustinii*, one *davidsonianum*, one *yunnanense*, one *ambiguum* and one *R. concinnum*. Draw lots for which goes where; put them where you can see them from the kitchen table and drag in all your neighbours for ego-gratification and a cup of coffee.

Blizzard 1996
February 1997

This is a subject I really do not want to write about. I think I am fairly philosophical about things that fate throws my way, and in terms of most tragedies where life and limb are involved, what happened here on the 29th and 30th of December 1996 is of no great consequence – but it hurt.

As I write this, nearly three weeks after the storm, there is still a lot of snow on the ground, and the full extent of the damage is still to be determined, but enough can be seen to assess that damage as major. Examples: we had a group of *R. augustinii*, about eight of them. They were more than 20 years old and were ten maybe twelve feet tall. These have all been broken off at the main trunk about two feet above the ground. I am pretty sure they will regenerate – probably quite vigorously – but that great sheet of blue that graced our Aprils will take years to re-establish. *Styrax japonica*, the 'snowdrop tree', has had the branches ripped off on one side leaving long torn gashes to a depth of half the trunk. *Magnolia* 'Susan', whom we had watched grow from a young lively four year old to a mature and graceful lady, is a polypelagic. *Acer griseum*, was not only barking up the wrong tree, but has hardly any of her cinnamon bark left at all. *R. taliense*, not a common plant in any garden, which grows in Yunnan at 12,000 feet where one would expect that the living is not all that easy, does not appear to have one branch left on the trunk. Two of our native dogwoods, at least twenty feet tall, were flattened and smashed. As I was sawing them up I was fully aware that I needed a permit from Saanich to make this butchering legal. I was also probably breaking a Provincial statute, but my teeth, and not just the ones in my mouth, were ready for any challenge from officialdom.

I think my favourite tree is the *arbutus*. Not just because it is a first cousin of the rhododendron and one of the biggest of the heather family, but because it is such an individualist. It grows every which way, twisting and contrary and straining for light. The main trunk is often skewed far from the vertical. It paid for its idiosyncrasy. That snow that fell on the 29th was so cohesive, the flakes stuck to each other like herring roe at spawning time and piled up on the branches of the firs and cedars and all things with branches – straight up it went on some *arbutus* – with a perpendicular angle of repose – great blades of white potency ready to fall like the Bastille guillotine.

Nanaimo recorded a greater amount of snowfall but got nowhere near the damage we got. A friend was describing his experiences and got quite spiritual and lyrical when he told of the divine wind that blew every quarter of an hour or so to dislodge the dreaded build-up. On Bear Hill, ten-inch *arbutus* were torn to the ground and fell with impunity. And a strange observation is that the dead limbs which *arbutus* are prone to have, stood up to the onslaught better than the live branches.

We had a big sprawling unkempt *Pyracantha* in a stone planter. I knew something should be done with it. In a moment of fantasy I thought it should be clipped and trained to be a square-rigged three mast ship. Then I was inspired by Bill Reid's masterpiece, "The Spirit of Haida-Gwaii" in the Canadian embassy in Washington and in the new terminal at Vancouver airport. Impressive. Well, the *pyracantha*'s been dismantled and decapitated, and I can devote more dreaming time to tonsures with topiary with a much less cumbersome subject.

Of course the second greenhouse has collapsed. There were some treasures in there and most may be recoverable but the insurance company now says – after all the estimates are in and the paper work done – that it was not covered by our policy. I can understand their reluctance to pay for rebuilding this structure once more as they paid to do so six years ago when a tree demolished it, but they are now saying that it wasn't even covered then – they made an error – and they won't make another one. While we debate I don't want to touch it and the fate of the trapped plants worsens.

How so much damage was done to plants in containers is a mystery. The mechanics of the breakage are not obvious. Side limbs and leaders seem to have suffered equally. Compact mound shaped plants fared just about as badly. *R. yakushimanum* has evolved to its bun shape form because of constant buffeting from the elements. But these millions of years of conditioning and selection were no defence against Blizzard '96. I don't own a chipper, but I could give the whole place a significant mulch of rhododendron chippings if I did. The surprises were those that came through relatively unscathed. The best flowering cherry we have is one called 'Pandora'. She looks as if she had just come from the hairdressers – not a hair out of place. *R. arboreum* – twenty-something years old – lost only one or two small branches and *R. auriculatum*, that hoary veteran that took 26 years to produce a flower, found its protection under the smothering cover of a cedar tree that had I been less indolent would have been trimmed last summer. I was worried about the recently grafted plants but the unions seem intact. Colin Millar was not so lucky. His prized *R. roxieanum oreonastes* was snapped off right at the graft.

So many plants have long, sheared splits where branches fork. One can splint and tape up these wounds and I am doing this in some cases, but it is generally not good practice. The bark/cambium may join, as in a graft, but if the branch has any caliper the strength of the inner fibers is gone and the fork will split again with even more modest loading. If the branch is much more than one centimeter in diameter it is best to grit your teeth and amputate. You can take some anesthetic afterwards.

71

I think I have become a melancholist – one who counts losses. In a year or so maybe that will change. But I still appreciate sympathy and the best I got was from my 18-month-old granddaughter. As I was carrying her through the deep snow when they were leaving to go back to Vancouver after the holiday she said, "Damn snow. Grumpy. Damn snow". I wonder where she heard that.

"Show and Tell"
April 1997

At this time of year I get bored by all the exhortations from the garden clubs I belong to. "Pot up something now, today, to enter in the spring show". "Every member should have at least five entries"; "the club depends on the show to raise some revenue so we can keep our dues at a reasonable level". And on and on and on.

It's the same thing every year and I think most of us get a bit fed up hearing the same tired old litany. Still, I compete in the annual show perennially and even though most of our rhododendron branches with flower buds were torn off in the blizzard this winter, I am sure I will find enough to make the cut this time too. It's a lot of effort and it's always done in a human blizzard of frenzied shears and overturned unstable beer bottles. The plant names become mixed-up and individual flowers fall off the best trusses. An attempt – far too hurried – to trim the top leaf to remove the evidence of what a weevil has already removed results in a shape that would win a prize in origami. Squeezing all the bottles into a cardboard box that is far too small results in more mutilation to the best spray from the *R. augustinii*. It's a hassle all the way and time just evaporates like water from a birdbath in August.

You bolt down a sandwich while filling in entry cards and it sits in your stomach like the plug of sand at the bottom of the bottle that you should have put in the bottom of the bottle in the first place, to keep the darned thing upright.

72

When you get to the hall – and this year we have the added hazard of watching out for photo-radar – you wonder why you bothered because there are so few entries from the other members and the hall looks sterile and bare and the poor lighting brings out all the blue tones in your 'Jean Marie de Montague'. It's the same colour as the blood blister you have on your left index finger that you gave yourself when you missed with the hammer trying to smash the stem of *R. haematodes*. It's no consolation that *haematodes* is well named.

Then you have to find which class your blue 'Jean Marie' should be in. You will be helped by one or more members – saying different things. They don't exhibit. ("Not a thing in the whole garden – that's the way the cookie crumbles. Ha, ha, ha."). They get their jollies from seeing the few exhibitors' unsteady hands trying to top up narrow-necked bottles with wide-mouthed spouts.

The hall floor is awash and a skating rink. You are in danger of doing a triple axel. The show stewards have set up tables to conform to some impressionistic idea of colour harmony which has no numerical logic. Class 41 is next to Class 17. The organizer obviously had had difficulty at school counting after the number of fingers had been exceeded but has remembered saving all the red Smarties to the last.

When you do find the right place for your entry with the now sodden black paper skirt stuck to the half-empty bottle you find that some selfish show-off has nabbed the best place on the bench. Innocently, you move it to the side and put yours in its place. This assuages the tension in your stomach a little. But when you come back with another truss on the now routine quarter mile trek to find the right class, you find that not only has yours been moved right off to the far side but turned around to show the hole in the truss where you knocked the flower off with your sore finger and you remember your language matched the colour of your blue 'Jean Marie'.

Your stomach is now worse than ever. Then into the hall comes this cool cat that in successive leisurely trips brings in box after box of huge, multi-hued 45-flower trusses. The only consolation you have is that this latest competitor hasn't a clue which classes his blousey barmaid trusses should go in either. You leave that to the two non-competing helpers to decide. Still it doesn't help your stomach much. But at least the hall is beginning to look a lot better. The non-competitive entries arrive and the hall starts to look resplendent. But there are still a lot of empty spaces. The judges are going to have an easy time this year, you think.

Once again you think that the rules should be changed to allow people to bring in entries on the Saturday morning. Then I have a flashback to my childhood. I recall my grandfather planning to put an entry of gooseberries in the local 'Cattle Show'. He had sacrificed all the fruit on the bush but five. They were as big as plums. On the night before the show someone stole all five. I don't remember the language but I think I remember the blue smoke rising in great clouds from his well tamped pipe. Maybe it is better to have all the entries in on the Friday night: anyway the judges will have little enough time to make the wrong decisions.

So you go home on the Friday night vowing that you will have better entries next year and that you will try to encourage others – with tiresome exhortations no doubt – to compete. And then you find you got a blue ribbon and a couple of Honourable Mentions and you decide you had a good time and the old stomach wasn't so bad after all.

Country Life
September 1997

It seemed somewhat soothing and a bit of an anodyne to the current provincial dyspepsia from a diet of forests and fish when I came across this:

"How blessed he, who leads a country life,
Unvex'd with anxious care, and void of strife!
Who studying peace, and shunning civil rage,
Enjoyed his youth, and now enjoys his age."
                                    Dryden

Despite my lumbar aches and my scaly skin, I thought Dryden had sent me a personal message as I reflected on my country life.

It looks pretty good right now (mid-summer) and an awful lot better than it did in January. I recall being admonished, after complaining at length about the disaster that the blizzard had wrought, that after a couple of years one would not know that anything untoward had happened.

At the time I thought the person somewhat insensitive but I now look around and see healing and regeneration.

I was taking cuttings from an *R. augustinii* recently. Eight feet up in the air a one-inch diameter branch was still caked in mud where it had been driven into the ground by the weight of snow. All along that trunk were new shoots that had sprung from dormant buds.

The twelve-foot *R. davidsonianum,* which had been reduced to a two-foot stump with nary a leaf, has several sprouts that look as if they don't want to wait another twenty years to get to twelve feet.

My polyplegic magnolia 'Susan', which I had written off as being no more than an excuse to start my victim's recitation on the trauma of the blizzard is now really quite presentable and while giving the appearance of youth is, in fact, enjoying her old age. *Magnolia grandiflora* is another matter.

But on to other things: the Propagation Group, by the very nature of its purpose, is a forward-looking bunch. As most of you know it meets on the third Monday of the month, usually at Ken Webb's house. One of the ideas that germinated at a spring meeting was to try to create a new hybrid that would be suitable for giving to attendees to the 2005 convention which our club will be hosting. For my effort, I used a plant in a pot as the mother plant and brought it into our bedroom where it could be pollinated and kept safe from the bees without all that mutilation that has to be done outside.

After the flowers had faded and the pollen was happily united with its intended, the plant was moved back to the open elements close to the back door where one could watch the capsules swelling and anticipate the sowing of the seed. But best laid plans – a passing neatnick saw an undeadheaded rhododendron.

* * *

I have always cherished rhododendron 'Faggetter's Favourite'. In fact we brought the plant with us when we moved here twenty years ago. I have, however, not had much success in propagating it. Faggetter was the head gardener at Slocock's nursery in England. One Saturday morning a lady called to ask if we had 'Faggetter's Favourite'. Could she come to see the plant? The lady was Mr. Faggetter's grand-daughter – all the way from Australia. We didn't have any little plants but we immediately put down a couple of layers which will be transportable next year.

* * *

A few days later I had a call from our bank saying that one of my checks had bounced. Having been guilty of such a sin in the past I am very sensitive on the matter and full of self-righteous umbrage I immediately tried to call the bank whose cheque I had used.

Have you tried to telephone a bank recently? You get a machine. "If you want this, Press 1 ; If you need this, Press 2?". If you just want to talk to someone you are out of luck.

Frustration at trying to prove my innocence was eruptive. In the midst of all this phone activity was an incoming call.

"How the heck do we get to your place?" "And who the heck are you?" I barked back, thinking it might be the World Bank or the Securities and Exchange Commission. "I'm the bus driver with your load of visitors."

"I don't know about any visitors and it's polite to be invited before landing on someone's doorstep." "We'll be there in twenty minutes."

"Where are you from?" "Thailand".

And sure enough, twenty minutes later a busload of Thais spilled out over the landscape led by one with 'THE DOG FATHER" blazoned on his baseball cap. Still smarting from the indignities inflicted by the modern banking system, I proffered a limpish handshake.

Very quickly, however, I learned that these strangers were knowledgeable. The second-in-command was a lady and when I asked her name and I stumbled over its pronunciation she said, "Just think of rhododendron *R. makinoi*."

I knew I was talking to plantspeople.

They were from the Mae Fah Luang Foundation, an organization working on improving the living conditions of Thais in the northern part of the country. One of the projects was the creation of an arboretum. I have since been in contact with Mr. Diskul, the Secretary-General (the wearer of the dog father cap) and have mentioned the possibility of forming a chapter of the ARS in Thailand. That would be an interesting and possibly mutually beneficial development.

The reach that the genus rhododendron has is truly universal. I wouldn't be surprised if NASA finds rhododendron pollen on Mars.

* * *

But thinking of age again, koi are known for their longevity. A few years ago we put some in the pond to keep the regular goldfish company. The big blue heron got all but one. When I chased the heron off the pond he was so full he could barely gain enough altitude to reach the lowest branch on the nearest Douglas Fir. Only one lonely koi remained but

77

he seemed content enough with the remaining runts of goldfish and I liked him as did our granddaughter. He was 'the big fish'. He would swim around followed by his underlings. Maybe he imagined he was wearing a cap with Koi Father written on it.

During March, and still now, every time we go near the pond there is a huge splash caused not by fish but by bull frogs which presumably trekked up Batu Road from Elk Lake. A neighbour who lives nearer the lake told me he had shot five of these eastern intruders, with five pellets from his air pistol after having found half eaten goldfish in his pond. A sixth despite a fusillade of lead is still on its predatory bonanza.

* * *

A last paragraph and a happy report about my prize *R. sinogrande*. It is grown from seed and I think it is now eight years old. I first noticed it when it displayed a mauvish metallic sheen on the new foliage. Each year the leaves (beloved by slugs) get bigger and bigger. This year they measure over 24 inches in length. The plant is not much more than that in height.

Peter Cox records its leaves reaching 30 inches in its native habitat and in some British gardens but that occurs in very moist monsoony conditions. Perhaps the wet spring has suited it as well as it has the bullfrogs. When *sinogrande* first bloomed at the Royal Botanic Garden in Edinburgh in 1933 they cut the truss and marched it down Princess Street accompanied by the skirl of the bagpipes. I think it had taken about forty years to get its first bloom and it took another forty years to bloom again. Well I don't think this old man will stage a similar procession on the Causeway no matter how great the benefits of living in the country.

The Garden Visit
February 1998

Beverly Nichols advised that when faced with a garden visit and when that inevitable time barrier hits you head on, trim the edges of the lawn and leave the grass uncut. I don't have any lawn so his advice doesn't help me at all.

I have never – not once – been able to get our place in shape for visitors. I always tell myself that people like coming here because they go home feeling their own garden is Eden compared to ours.

As a consequence of the perpetual unmaintained look I try to sound superior about it and call it a 'natural West Coast garden'. It doesn't really fool anyone but it eases my own sensibilities a little.

I am sure you know this line well, but despite its triteness, I find it still works quite effectively. Actually there are two lines "You should have been here last week", and "In two weeks time this will be a blaze of colour" and I always have a few horror stories ready. Visitors then think how lucky they are and they then don't ask so many embarrassing questions. I usually start by informing them that I carry extra insurance because the place is so dangerous. Then I point out *R. aureum* which Dr. Koelpin used to try to cure arthritis, which it did a bit, but killed his patients in the process. I also point out the poisonous berries on the *Daphne laureola* and the remains of our Heritage Tree – a native dogwood which needed some dead limbs removed. The butchers who came to do the job misunderstood the arborist's instructions. They thought they were to "remove the dogwood" when the order was to "remove dead wood". That gets some sympathy as I lead them past a particularly noxious patch of brambles.

I find it helps to just keep talking – don't give opportunities for questions or comments. Nothing will spoil your day more than when some insouciant visitor tells of his specimen of such-and-such that is twice as big as yours and blooms the whole year. The late Maggie Whitney had a tactic that was pretty drastic but worked well. When someone would say, "It must be beautiful when everything is in bloom," she would reply. "If you don't think it's beautiful now you are not a gardener so OUT", and she would point the way. But don't use that method right after the "You should have been here last week" line.

It helps a bit if you have some juice or pop or coffee available and some chairs. A lot of visitors will just stay near the refreshments and forget all about going round the garden. Normally I serve the coffee from the greenhouse but last year I had one group – all nice blue-rinse ladies – who came when I wasn't ready for them. My wife was out of town so it wasn't just the garden that needed maintenance – regardless, I just gave them the run of the house. They found the ugliest spoons and mugs for the coffee and used paper towels instead of napkins. They were in every drawer and cupboard looking for utensils. While I was called away for some other commitment they fended for themselves just fine.

One thing I have observed is that a surprising number of visitors arrive with full bladders – the coffee station has some consequences to it too, which should be borne in mind. So this year we are going to build a toilet that is accessible without going through the whole house. I say ours is a private garden and by that I mean that some of us can remedy the bladder problem *en plain air*. But that is not satisfactory for all guests, so one has to be prepared to offer other arrangements.

If you really want to put on the dog think about charging admission. This will bring you a lot of respect I have noticed. People will talk in hushed tones when going around. You can say the admission is for a charity if you want the voices to be even more hushed. However, paying people will stay longer to get their money's worth and more will come with bigger pockets to take home samples. This spring I took pride in four little plants of *R. recurvoides*. After one noisy visitation I had three and after the next there were two. A lot of garden visitors know their onions.

Some garden owners ask visitors to sign the guest book. We don't have one. We are waiting to get an autograph that is really worth something before investing in a fancy album. But it has the advantage of giving you a record of who might have made off with the prize *R. proteoides.*

I think it is important to wear grubby clothes when taking people round the garden. It shows you are a worker and closer to Lady Chatterley than most of the observers. I always look at peoples' hands. If they are not as dirt engrained as mine I write them off as being theoretical gardeners only.

From experience I now know that it will be impossible to get the place in shape for the Royal Visit so I don't worry about it anymore. You will no doubt be asked to show off your garden this year as members of our club just love coming to criticize all your hard work. Remember that you can be the visitor in many more gardens than you can be the host so just check that you have something to drink and a convenient toilet and if you have a lawn do the edges first.

Have a Nice Day, Give a Plant a Smile
January 1999

Several weeks ago, a couple of newspaper articles got me thinking about smiling. One article was about the way checkout clerks in a large grocery business were being instructed on how to treat customers. They were being cautioned by their employer that failure to look customers in the eye and smile would result in disciplinary measures being taken. The second was in the same vein and applied to cabin personnel in airplanes. Evidently the captains of industry figure a smile is worth a million dollars whether sincere or not.

Our culture is full of songs and poetry about smiles being sunshine and sweet and all that. I'm not one of these people that do not show their teeth when they smile. I like to smile. But my sensibilities get riled when a human behaves like a robot. Why not just have a computer give you a smile –

and it could give you a pat on the butt at the same time –
without the risk of being hauled up for sexual harassment.

I really quite like supermarkets too. They are among
my favourite stores. Some days, however, when I know I
have only $50 in my wallet and am scared that the contents of
the cart are going to total more than that I feel like
abandoning the buggy and fleeing the store when I see that
gingival excess bounded by perfect ivories and hear this
recording which emits from them, "And how is the world
treating you today?" I have the same reaction when tied in a
too small airplane seat and think I can smell smoke coming
from the cockpit and the steward says, "Enjoy". And isn't it
strange that gasoline companies are so keen for a buck that
they all price their product to the tenth of a penny, yet still
order us to "Have a good day" when they hand back our
credit card.

What I'm trying to get around to is important. It's
about smiling at your plants. There have been many
speculations and indeed some serious claims that plants
respond to conversation, music, good feelings and maybe
even to "Have a good day", or "Take care". I admit I may be
biased but I think rhododendrons are among the most
sensitive of plants and do respond to this kind of treatment.
And among rhododendrons there is one that I certainly go out
of my way to be nice to. This is *R. rirei* – the smiling
rhododendron. It is called after the Reverend Ririe who
worked for the Chinese Inland Missions and was a friend of
Chinese Wilson. I don't know if he spoke French as well as
Mandarin but likely his ancestors came from France and they
were always happy and that is how they got the name *rirei*.
Rire means "to smile".

What better to make you smile in our January gardens
than the large luxuriant flowers of *rirei*. They are a kind of
pinky-mauve (the same colour as the dentated gums of our
favourite check-out clerk) and really quite showy so early in
the year. A feature of the flowers that to me is remarkable, is
that they have huge dark violet nectar pouches which are just
replete with flowing goodness. I have never seen insects on

82

the flowers and it could be that with us all this sweetness gets wasted but maybe there are insects buzzing around in its native land of Sichuan at that time of the year. Maybe I'm so busy smiling that my vision gets impaired and I can't see properly but I don't see them being pollinated. The nectar must have some utility other than to sweeten the flower's smile – and mine.

Rirei keeps its smile, without any orders from corporate headquarters, until we get a frost. Then the opened flowers brown and I have to admit, despite my great admiration for the good Reverend Ririe's rhododendron, that this browning happens with less intensity of freezing than some of the other early bloomers. 'Rosamundi' and 'Lee's Scarlet' and certainly 'Snow Lady' will take minus two degrees centigrade of frost without browning.

Rirei lives up to its name also because it smiles wherever you put it in the garden. It is happy to please and it is easy to please. Ours is in quite deep shade but still grins away. It lost some of that grin in the great Christmas blizzard of 1996 when several of its limbs were amputated. It showed that that disaster had not caused it to lose its good nature for long as it bloomed last January (1998) more profusely than ever. I'm sure I could make it even happier by giving it a bit more sunshine but it's too big to move now. It's a big plant and can get to ten meters eventually.

The Thais are a smiling people. They always smile no matter the subject. It is said that Thais have ten different smiles, all recognizable. Just like our rhodos are graded 5/5 or 2/4, so the Thais grade smiles from 1 to 10. If a Thai says to you, "What a lousy hair-do you got this time", you can tell by a No.1 smile that the remark is sincere. Here's a culture where how sincere the "Have a good day" is can be detected immediately by grading the grin.

But when we get a gratuitous No.10 smile every time we spend money at the grocery store then we have lost one of our means of being spontaneously pleased and pleasured. I would rather pass up the imposed smile than have to smart at myself as I say, "And you too" for the umpteenth time. When

I pass *rirei* it always gets at least an impromptu, sincere No. 5
– at least.

A Rhododendron Who's Who
February 1999

That the culture of rhododendrons reflects the
mainstream of humanity – local, national and international –
is a proposition to be easily understood by our Society's
members. To illustrate this truism, that noted commentator on
both public and horticultural affairs, Norman Todd, has
offered several examples of this vital connection. Some of
these are listed herein; others will be included in future
editions of the newsletter.

Martha Stewart
Rhododendron 'Unique'
A perfectly manicured hybrid with too perfect pink
and cream flowers regurgitatively evocative of icing on a six-
year-old's birthday cake. Trusses can be used to decorate
wedding vehicles or floated in the dog's water dish. Foliage is
thick and stiff and makes a good besom. Does not get mildew
in Martha's garden.

Bill Clinton
Rhododendron *nudiflorum*
It comes from Eastern U.S. It is very hardy and easily
layered in cultivation. One authority says it is stoloniferous,
another says it is not. Indicating the presence or absence of
this characteristic seems to depend on the affiliation of the
observer. It is not easy to propagate vegetatively although the
capsules ripen early and split open easily. The stigma are very
long being three times the length of the corolla. It does best in
full exposure, in fact languishes if not in full light. Some
hybrids of *nudiflorum* and *alababamense* (geographically
close to Arkansas) have a yellow streak.

Glen Clark
Rhododendron 'Solidarity'
     A fairly recent plant of super hardy parents. It thrives in ! /--:-. abusive conditions but resents competition from other plants, especially *magnolia cambellii* but will accept grass root encroachment from red fescue. The flowers are red at first but fade with age especially if stressed. It loves aged horse manure.

Kim Campbell
Rhododendron 'Canadian Sunset'
     This is a B.C. hybrid which is reportedly doing well in California. It was so named because the flowers have a different colour every day. Greer describes it as being 'quite different'. It was once thought to be the best yak hybrid ever but has now been largely replaced by those with more liberal flowering habits.
     Readers are encouraged to submit brilliant rhodomorphisms of their own. More next month.

A Rhododendron's Who's Who (cont'd)
March 1999

     As everyone knows, anthropomorphism means the attribution of human characteristics to any form of animal life (my daughter holds to this belief, preventing me from dispatching slugs in her presence). Phytomorphism is the belief in the humanity, with all of its noble and nasty elements, of plant life. Accepting these concepts is not difficult, so VRS members will find it easy to become practicing Rhodomorphists. More evidence in support of this movement is supplied by our house philosopher, Norman Todd:

Judy Tyabji
Rhododendron 'Airy Fairy'

This is an early bloomer. It looks delicate but is really quite resistant to the vicissitudes of garden culture. It is showy when in flower but can be overlooked when not. Half of its lineage – *lutescens* – was a Wilson introduction. It tends to be leggy.

Bill Gates
Rhododendron *ponticum*

Now a very widespread and domineering plant. It will support almost any kind of elepidote graft but will grasp any window of opportunity to overcome its 'parasite'. This species was the basis of the recent huge expansion in the popularity of the genus rhododendron. Now considered a threat to other plants, especially apples, in some gardens. Some forms are protected by patent.

Monica Lewinsky
Rhododendron 'Sappho'

Monica is not related to 'Mrs. T .H. Lowinsky' which is a fine plant but has suddenly fallen out of favour. The name 'Sappho' evokes different images with different people. For some it is poetic – for others it has a more salacious connotation. It has a beautiful flower but a terrible growth habit and if grown should be placed at the back of the border. I now prefer the more compact 'Peeping Tom'.

Rhodomorphs We Have Known
April 1999

By now we are all convinced of these marvellous incarnations. Norman Todd has added yet another three identities to the array.

Margaret Thatcher
Rhododendron 'Point Defiance'

This is a plant of "major" stature and very strong habit, renowned for making its point defiantly. It has tough leathery foliage not readily attacked by pests. It is quite compatible with 'Independence Day' but not with 'Party Pink'. One observer says it is surviving in the Falkland Islands. Reports of it being carnivorous are probably incorrect although I certainly have noted many dead bees in its flowers.

Lucien Bouchard
Rhododendron *schizopeplum*

A rare plant in gardens, preferring its native conditions. The name means 'with a split covering'. It has recently been demoted and is now classified as a variety. It has had a number of name changes. Hybrids are rare and seeds usually come true although it has bred with one form of *californicum*. The genes of *schizopeplum*, however, are dominant. It prefers significant separation from other plants but has been known to accept occasional hybrids of foreign origin especially those with *soulei, delavayi, fargesii,* or *davidii* in their parentage.

Pavel Bure
Rhododendron *caucasicum*

This species comes from a tough environment but is inclined to be difficult in our climate. Reports are that it really likes a harsher winter and thrives in soils low in organic matter. Keep it if you are a fussy grower but if looking for flower power in the garden perhaps you should trade it for a newer hybrid.

Now you are all earnestly exhorted to submit your candidates for this horticultural pantheon.

Black Beauties
May 1999

Two final entries in the Rhododendron Hall of Fame have been received:

Conrad Black

Rhododendron 'Black Magic'

A vigorous, aggressive grower, demanding full sun. Of all rhodos, this one is known for a strong flowery statement but its colour is rather dark and gloomy, best seen back-lit near sundown. Noted for its tough fibre, suitable for paper production. Flourishes in Canada and the UK, but languishes, rather, in Australia. Certainly a plant with an opinion on its own worth.

David Black

Rhododendron 'White Gold', aka 'Nisga'a Nemesis'

The polarity of the names of plant and person is not without significance. The paper-white flowers are fully recurved to reveal a golden flair. Though a genuine North American hybrid highly adaptable to most urban environments, its constitution may be challenged unless grafted to aboriginal roots in the interior. Widely accepted throughout B.C. but its relative lack of cold-hardiness is a serious handicap. 'Black Magic' will limit its spread to eastern gardens.

The World Would Be a Better Place...
October 1999

We read and hear a lot these days about genetic engineering. We are promised an end to hunger with an abundance of food. We are tempted to hope for longer life by reading that the world's best minds have created the technology to grow replacement organs from embryonic stem cells. The ethical problems raised by these scientific advances are far beyond my understanding but the promise of a longer life, I admit, has some attractions. When I first became interested in rhododendrons one of my mentors was Albert de Mezey. As we strolled through his famous garden on Foul Bay Road he advised me in his richly resonant Hungarian

baritone that to grow rhododendrons you needed two things –
a physical age of thirty and longevity of three hundred.

I am musing on these matters as I am sticking cuttings
in my propagator. Today I put in five cuttings of *R. diaprepes*
'Gargantua'. I know that should I be lucky enough to get
these cuttings to develop roots, and I am then lucky enough to
get the roots to support some top growth and make a new
plant, it will probably be 2020 at the earliest before there is a
hope of that plant bearing a blossom. I also know that even as
I am absorbed in this stone age style of attempting to create
another living entity, the new bio-technologies will not be
available soon enough for me to see that flower on this
particular *diaprepes.* Quite quickly, I reason with an amazing
appeasement of my initial unease, that the world will most
probably be a better place with one more *diaprepes* in it, and
certainly not any the worse for me not being in it, and I
should quit making any connection between the life of that
cutting and my own.

I think, therefore, the world would probably be a
better place if we all got at least one cutting to root and made
a new plant and to heck with a three hundred year life span
for humans. Just be glad that rhododendrons have it. And so
with this primitive process that I use, I become a creator and I
can look forward to the hugely fulfilling feeling I will have
when I gently tamp those rooted cuttings into a six inch pot
and tie a brand new label on each fledgling plant.

In the past I have had groups of people come to my
not very sanitary greenhouse and the group sits on a plank on
one side of the propagating bench while I do a demonstration
of how to make a new plant. I have a supply of Styrofoam
coffee cups and a pail containing a mix of moistened peat and
perlite, a small container of rooting hormone and some clear
plastic bags. These groups are often what I call the 'blue
rinse' set – middle-aged ladies who have immaculate gardens
as well as immaculate hair-dos. (Middle age in these
genetically enhanced times goes from 55 to 85). Then they all
prepare their own cuttings: removing all but three or four
leaves and cutting those leaves in half; wounding the base of

the cutting just through to the cambium under the bark; dipping the cutting in the rooting compound, then dibbling a hole in the 'dirt' filled coffee cup and popping in the cutting. After labelling and making a little greenhouse with the plastic bag sealed by a rubber band they take off for home, trooping out of the greenhouse in single file with smugly satisfied smirks on their faces and the precious plastic bag held delicately between thumb and forefinger, each of them looking as if she was reliving the taking home from kindergarten of that first finger painting to show to an admiring parent. For me, the most satisfying part comes when these people come back and say, "Do you remember when we took those cuttings of that azalea? Well, I put it on the kitchen windowsill, and now it has grown three inches. Should I plant it outside?"

If you would like to know some more about making new rhododendrons and have not attended a session of the 'Propagators', contact Ken Webb for more details. The group usually meets in the middle of the month. It is a very informal group and meeting times and locations vary.

If you do participate, you will quickly become aware that certain varieties – 'Lem's Cameo', for example – are notoriously difficult to root. You will also be amazed at the success you will have with your first efforts. Neophytes have a high success rate. I attribute this to beginners' cleanliness and the extra care taken but there is no doubt beginners have chlorophyll in their fingertips. When I first took cuttings of 'Lem's Cameo' twenty years ago, I put in ten cuttings and I got ten plants. Every year since then I have put in ten cuttings of 'Lem's Cameo' and just occasionally get one with roots. The latest 'must have' species is *R. pachysanthum*. It is very hard to root. I have never been able to do it. Some of the 'Propagators' find *pachysanthum* easy. It's the same with *R. tsariense*. However, just to make sure that you are not the exception to this 'novice-no-problem', or 'tyro's triumph' phenomenon, take a few cuttings of an evergreen azalea or 'Elizabeth'. Now there are those who would say that the world would not necessarily be a better place with another

'Elizabeth'. However, she is a turn-on, as she is so easily propagated. That initial success is crucial to your continued career as a plant creator.

New plants can also be created from seed. Seed may be obtained from our local society and also from the Seed Exchange of the American Rhododendron Society. You can also be really creative and do some hands-on genetic engineering and make your own hybrid, taking the pollen from the anthers of one flower and putting it on the pistil of another. There is a faction, to which I belong, that thinks that there are too many registered hybrids, and that the world would be a better and certainly simpler place if more restraint were exercised in registering new names. That does not imply that there should be fewer new plants but only that those enshrined in the Rhododendron Registry be distinctive enough in habit or blossom or hardiness or some other characteristic, to merit inclusion. I once counted 32 registered plants with *R. yakushimanum* and 'Mars' as parents. No one grows or knows them all but it is doubtful that more than a few are worth having a special moniker. That having been said, I sure would like to have one named for my granddaughter – and there is another grandchild on the way – so you can see that when we do our little bit of rhododendron procreation and want the world to know about it, we should take some pains to make sure we are, in fact, making our world a better place.

Compared to plants like soybean, cotton or wheat, the level of effort going into genetically engineering new varieties of rhododendrons is minute. Some of the latest offerings from some of the big nurseries are genetically engineered. They have had the number of chromosomes in their cells augmented. It is claimed that these plants are tougher, with thicker foliage, longer lasting flowers and are good 'doers'. This induced polyploidy can now be achieved by the amateur by using a colchicine-like chemical on seedlings. Such increase in chromosomal numbers is very low-tech compared to adding new material to genes – which is the cause of so much concern and debate with GM foodstuffs. Still, isn't it tempting to think of adding genes from a plant that blooms all the time – *impatiens* for example – to our rhododendrons so that we get a longer period of bloom? And I think it would be nice to put in a gene or two to make rhododendrons unwelcoming to powdery mildew. However, it is at this point that our cautionary alarms should go off. If there are no root weevils are there subsequently no strawberries?

Once afflicted by the compulsion to create new rhododendrons, the pressure can lure you into questionable practices. I am told that when a truss of 'Point Defiance' was first displayed at a show, a pollen thief swiped every grain. There was an outcry. I also recall being with a group on a garden tour and among the group was a well-known hybridizer. Going round the garden, I was astonished to see this hybridizer, in a manner that certainly looked subversive, snap a truss from a bush of 'Phyllis Korn'. I was embarrassed for him when our eyes met. He really did look guilty as sin, but obviously he wanted that pollen. Later, when the subject of polyploidy was being discussed, 'Phyllis Korn' was singled out as being a naturally occurring polyploid, having come from open pollinated 'Gomer Waterer' seed. The discusser bemoaned the fact that 'Phyllis Korn' was totally sterile. The famous hybridizer's face fell to the floor. He has, however, produced so many good plants that I am sure in the final reckoning he has made the world a better place and his lapse in etiquette has been forgiven. Had he asked politely for a cutting, he would not have been refused.

We are told that biochemistry and cell biology will be the technologies of the 21st century. Meanwhile in the last months of the 20th century, we can, with very little effort or expertise, improve the ambiance of our habitat by making a new plant which has the potential, without having any modified genes, to live into the 23rd century. It's an act of faith, of course, but there are rhododendrons in our city that are now well into their second century. I think you'll agree they do add just a little to making our world a better place.

Touched by the Magic
November 1999

We saw the brushed cream and pink and mauve dawn behind the slender boat masts; we saw the mile long shards of mirrored glass that sealed the surface of Kennedy Lake; we saw the surreal shapes of ancient cedar stumps – huge and silent on Clayoquot Island; we saw a dome of rhododendrons as a'maze'ing as Hampton Court; and from that dome we could see forever across the sound, over the low treed islands to the still snowed sides of far-off mountains. And for three days we saw our island at its Beautiful B.C. best and not a drop of rain – but the dew on the plants in the morning would make our Water Board postpone raising the Sooke dam for yet another ten years.

Our contingent (the Propagators) numbered twenty-two. Our hosts, Ken and Dot Gibson, did the work of an equivalent number. A welcoming vase of flowers graced our motel rooms and a dram warmed that welcome, up at the house. The conversation flowed. One lives with history in Ken's presence. In Tofino one is conscious of ice ages and explorers and settlers – and some unsettlers – when contemporary issues are discussed. Rhododendron growers, past and present, get equal time with logging, fish farming and fiberglass molds for patio slabs. Grafting techniques are explained and powdery mildew bemoaned. At other times the hikers can exercise their legs on the sand smoothed beaches, leaving the praters to continue exercising their tongues on good and bad doers.

Magic it was, and probably a record too, to sit outside eating brunch in Ucluelet on Saturday morning, the sixteenth of October. The table umbrellas had to be unfurled so the menus could be read, the plates were the size of old growth stumps and the toast the thickness of a barn shake. George Fraser's maples were in full fall colour.

Back at the dock in Tofino, Captain and Master Gardener Chris was waiting with his launch to ferry us over to the Island and our numbers were such that he had to do it twice. Waiting on the Island was Master Gardener Sharon and her tribe of visitor-starved raccoons who no doubt are now suffering from distended stomachs, the consequence of the bag of buns Alison Hawkins took for them so she could have them eating out of her hand. The plants we remembered had grown and were more at home than ever and there were lots of new plantings to see. If Sharon especially liked a plant it was a "she", and if it was just so-so it was a "he". She had the blue and the pink wisterias interplanted so it seemed her segregation proclivities could be eased if aesthetic priorities prevailed. She was so energetically poetic in her descriptions of her creative endeavors that we also were breathless and unable to utter our approvals. She described the initial coolness of a couple of English B.B.C. photographers making a documentary on the flora and fauna of the land and water, and how that coolness changed to bubbling reverence once they were 'touched by the magic' of the island. A thing of magic was the Mushroom gazebo. Built from driftwood, fitted together like the great hammerhead roofs of mediaeval cathedrals; sheathed with shakes split from curving logs to give the mushroom profile; its seat a slice of a great donut of a cedar with grain so fine it could have made a violin; it was of classic beauty and a work of art. Their tomatoes were quality too as were all their vegetables. Sharon claims curative properties for her soap. One of the few items not totally homemade was Chris's rum, which, I'm told, also had curative properties. Dot's apple spice cake complemented the magically curative ambiance.

Dinner that evening was good. For those who haven't tasted it, the Schooner's clam chowder is, of itself, worth the trip to Tofino. We sat at a table next to a couple who had almost finished their meal. We tried to encourage them to leave so our group could be together. It turned out, however, that they were from the Vancouver Chapter so we had to chat a while. Rhodo people were everywhere. Next day at Coombs, with the goats on the thatched roof, we bumped into the president of the Mount Arrowsmith Chapter.

Sunday morning the cutting raid began. Ken Gibson behaved like a frustrated IWA. logger, disappearing into the massed greenery and throwing out great limbs of rhododendron. The group descended on these with hungry clippers just as the goats at Coombs savaged the maple branches being thrown up to them. Plastic bags were stuffed with precious cuttings and many times one heard the plaintive cry "What was the name of that one?" This orgy was followed by more Gibson hospitality on the deck with the sun still blessing us. Most of us then set out for the glorious drive home. Some of us set out twice, as when we got to the junction for Sutton Pass my wife recalled leaving her jacket in the motel. Others enjoyed the beaches and Karen Morrison found magic in the seaweed of Chesterman Beach. Evidently she looked like a mobile kelp stack.

We all felt we had been touched by the magic and want to thank our hosts for that.

The Numbers Game
December 1999

Some numbers are hard and some are soft and some range in between. The date is a hard number. There is nothing you can do to change it, even if you are in debate about when the millennium starts. The unemployment rate is a soft number. We read its value every day but most of us don't know how to measure it and many of us think that those who do measure it don't know either. Some would say that recent B.C. government budgets contained some very soft numbers. The amount you owe on your Visa is both hard and soft. It's hard because you have to pay it sooner or later, and then some, but you can postpone some of the hardness by paying only the soft part on the current bill. Rhododendron ratings are soft/soft numbers.

Most of us refer to commercial catalogues and reference books to get descriptions of rhododendrons and we note their ratings. We read 4/4/4 alongside a name and this

95

tells us that it has an above average flower, an above average leaf and an above average habit. This is useful information but we have to remember they are soft numbers. I was surprised to read in one of the issues of the Scottish Chapter's newsletter that many of the plants we cherish so much here are disasters over there. John Hammond reports that 'Noyo Brave' and 'Haida Gold' , for example, are not good plants in Britain. In Victoria, we love the big leafed *R. rex* (3/4/3-4). It is almost certainly the best big leaf rhododendron for these parts. However, I am told that there is only one lone sole specimen of *rex* – a super-hardy clone – growing on the entire east coast of the American continent and that is in the spray-swept garden of Walter Ostrum at St. Margaret's Bay, Nova Scotia. For east-coasters this plant is a ?/5/5 but here it might only rate a ?/3/3. We grow the east coast specimens and they have never bloomed, but it stops them in their tracks when they see it.

The British, particularly the English, ruled our horticultural world, here in B.C., for a century – from the mid 1800's to the mid 1900's. Then, local breeders on the Pacific west coast started to do their own thing with gardens and with plant breeding. The Washington/Oregon/British Columbia region jumped ahead, not only with the creation of better rhododendron hybrids but also with interest in the entire genus. Rhododendrons became important garden plants. My observation is that only in Britain and in our neck of the woods is the rhododendron the most revered plant for the landscape. I would guess that in New Zealand we saw at least five camellias for every rhododendron. Hans Hackmann of Germany has done monumental wonders in creating a market in continental Europe for rhododendrons where they are now becoming more and more popular. In 1996 he was a worthy winner of the ARS Gold Medal which was awarded to him at the Oban, Scotland convention. His 'Fantastica' is deservedly given a high rating (4/5/4); it should be in every garden, even though Mr. Hackmann's acceptance speech took nearly as much time to deliver as it took him to make the plant. The Dutch have been exporting the latest horticultural wonders for an eternity and fifty years ago were still the main source of rhododendron hybrids in B.C. In those days rhododendrons were rated like Michelin does hotels and restaurants – with stars. The 'Loderis' were given ***** and 'Bow Bells' **. That was a composite rating for all characteristics of the plant. I am not quite sure of the process by which these ratings were determined, just as I am not sure how the current three number ARS rating is derived.

Isn't it strange that we have endless debate on some matters, like Free Trade or clear cut logging, often without conclusion and yet on something as important as rating rhododendrons, the number just appears – bingo – no debates, no campaigns, no protests, no pepper spray. And there doesn't seem to be anything we can do about it. Perhaps, we rhododendron growers are quite civilized after all.

However, one fact that makes me feel fairly comfortable with the current ratings is that with over 30,000 registered hybrids there are no 5/5/5's. One does wonder if the rating may, from time to time, be influenced by how easy the plant is to propagate or how many plants the grower has on inventory or if that grower is a committee of one. These are spurious codes and one must always remember that the plant that is a garden treasure in San Francisco will probably not do very well in Helsinki. The ratings are soft, soft numbers.

Conversely, there are quite a few plants among my favourites that have rotten ratings. I know I should have the courage of my convictions and not be all that concerned about what others think but that's a bit like admitting to liking Kraft Dinner; you need to be made of pretty stern stuff to sing its merits. For example, take my adoration of 'Airy Fairy': my spring would be barren without it ; it's as welcome as the first humming bird. Some references give it a 3/2/2. For me it's a 10. When did you last see 'Nobleanum coccineum' in a nursery or even in a catalogue? It's rated 2/2/3. It's better than 'Christmas Cheer', in my opinion, and 'Christmas Cheer' gets a 3/4/4. Here is a case of a plant getting a bad name because it has a bad name – no one can say it, or if they can, don't want to, especially if they have dentures. The 'Nobleanums' have been around since the 1830s, as has 'Christmas Cheer' and probably have the same or close to the same parentage but are definitely the black sheep in that family.

People who don't associate 'Cowslip' with a primrose and take the name literally, cringe at that name. I've heard people say they would not grow a plant with such an inappropriate name. I tell Clint Smith that he has no one to blame but himself for a 3-4/3-4/3-4 rating on his 'Woody's Friggin Riggin'. It's a super plant but often goes without a label, either because of the unpoetic, prudish sensibilities of the gardener or because there is never a large enough label. Clint, of course, would like to be the Robert Service of the rhododendron world. Jack Lofthouse, who has made some superior hybrids, had a spell of giving them names that I would rate as 1/1/1's – things like 'Pink Petticoats' and 'Hot Pants'. 'Taurus' is a good name for a good plant and it is rated appropriately. There is no question the name influences the rating. People in the entertainment industry often adopt new names for commercial reasons. Think of Cher and Madonna. With rhodos that can't be done. Once named, no amount of deed polling can change it.

Most good stories contain a moral and if there is one here, perhaps it is that reducing the worthiness of a rhododendron to a number is simplistic and subject to the same political scruples that beauty pageants now suffer from. The contestants are under lascivious scrutiny for only a short time and that is in a glitzy, show-biz setting. The true character of the entrants is marginalized and the superficial aspects are emphasized. Another moral may be that... "What's in a name?" That which we call a rose "by any other name would smell as sweet" may be true if your name is Romeo or Juliet; it isn't always so if you are a rhododendron and are about to be rated. Names and numbers are soft commodities. Samuel Johnson said it 250 years ago: "Round numbers are always false."

'A' is for Arboreum
February 2000

One of the difficulties in writing about rhododendrons is that the facts that allow one to make useful encompassing generalizations need about a century of observation. One can be a writer on Canadian federal elections or U.S. presidential elections and make some interesting, even predictive, comments by knowing what happened in the last ten or fifteen of them. Writing about contemporary art requires only the study of a static object or two and a stack of metaphors. Commenting on women's fashions involves no risk at all because the creations being analyzed will never be worn by anyone reading the article. Pontificating about life forms with a longevity greater than our own may be risked only because at the end of the day those reading this will not be around to criticize for significantly longer than the writer will.

These thoughts are prompted by a predilection to claim that one of the best species for a large garden in these parts is *R. arboreum*. Also, I think *arboreum* is currently underused in hybridizing. This hunch or bias is based on observation of a very small number of plants over a mere thirty years.

I have read about and even have slides of arbutus-sized *arboreum*s in Nepal – sentinel columns of blazing red. I am aware of a grand one in Dunbartonshire, Scotland which measures over forty by forty-five feet. I am also aware of avenues of fifty footers in Ireland and of many other Methuselahs in Southern England which reputedly came from seed collected by Dr. Wallich, Superintendent of the Calcutta Botanic Garden. He was not the first to collect seed of *arboreum*, this distinction going to a Dr. Buchanan Hamilton. (What would we do without medical people?) It seems, however, that it was Wallich's seed that arrived at the Liverpool Botanic Garden in 1815 and at the Royal Botanic Garden, Edinburgh in 1821. *Arboreum* had been 'discovered' by a Captain Hardwicke in 1796 on the Sewalic Mountains of India. This species and *R. thomsonii* were the first large red rhododendrons to be seen by covetous, grasping Western horticulturists. Readers are referred to Davidian, 'Rhododendron Species', Vol. 11 for a fuller account of *arboreum's* introduction.

Arboreum, with its several sub-species, has a very extensive, patchy (disjunct is, I think, the proper word) distribution throughout India, the Himalayas and neighbouring China. There are remarkable isolated populations in southern India and in Sri Lanka. Some of these forms, usually with red flowers, are not hardy here and are only suitable for semi-tropical locales. On the South Island of New Zealand we saw specimens that were centenarians. It has also become naturalized in Jamaica.

Local gardens have some notable, but still relatively young, examples of the species; the *arboreum* ssp. *cinnamomeum* in Dora Kreiss's garden comes prominently to mind. There are some good plants of perhaps the most famous of all *arboreum* hybrids – 'Sir Charles Lemon' – at the Finnerty Gardens. My premise that more use could be made of *arboreum* rests mainly on the few plants I know well – those in my own garden. In the deepest, darkest days of winter when only the odd hellebore and camellia and viburnum are in flower, 'Rosamundi' and 'Lee's scarlet' and 'Nobleanum' are glowing photon-emitters of warmth. Half of their genes come from *arboreum*. Many gardeners are disappointed when the 'Christmas Cheer' they have cherished and coddled for a few years, blooms in late March. It was baptized as 'Christmas Cheer' in the 1820s when those who could afford to buy rhododendrons had large conservatories and this plant could be forced to bloom for Yuletide decoration. My point is that we need more of these dark day dazzling denizens. There is a strong demand for bloom in the winter months.

This early season blooming can be obtained from *arboreum,* and this characteristic along with colour selections that are clean and clear; indumented foliage, that is crisp and precise and resistant to weevils and mildew; and good plant

100

habit make *arboreum* an attractive parent. The Social Services Agency for Horticulture will approve.

The subspecies of *arboreum* – *nilagiricum*, I have never seen. It may not be hardy here but its hybrid, 'Noyo Chief', and that plant crossed with *R. yakushimanum*, to give 'Noyo Brave', are contemporary garden-sized plants with outstanding foliage and good flowers. Even better is the New Zealand hybrid 'Rubicon' which is 'Noyo Chief' x 'Kilimanjaro'. This has only 25% arboreum in its lineage but (proving the importance of grandparents) this is evident in the foliage. 'Rubicon' may well be the best compact red rhododendron yet developed for gardens in our area. It is an April bloomer. *Arboreum* ssp. *nilagiricum* has been reintroduced within the last ten years. Keen growers and hybridizers should be on the lookout for this plant. Some of the newer introductions could be hardier.

The red-flowered plant of *arboreum* that I have is now about 12 or 14 feet tall and 30 years old. The leaves are not as large as the two-toned pink form (yet unbloomed for me) and have silvery indumentum. The really outstanding feature is the reliability of blooming and the duration of the bloom. Last year it was in flower for a full two months. My second flowering plant is pink and it had a somewhat later but almost as prolonged bloom. The plant had its first flowers two years ago and these were miserable, small, recycled looking things. After such a dramatic improvement with the second blooming, I have hopes that the show may be even better this coming March. I had bloom on ssp. *delayvayi* for the first time last year and this was a clear primary red. The habit of the plant is tidily symmetrical and the foliage a notable dark matte green. This sub-species has had no winter damage during the last ten years, although it is recorded as being a tender plant. I have also bloomed a white form of *arboreum* ssp. *arboreum*.

Already referred to was 'Sir Charles Lemon'. This, Cox opines, is *arboreum* with *campanulatum*. It is famous for its cinnamon indumentum. It is a plant to look up at. Another hybrid of this parentage from the 1800s which I have recently

101

acquired also has good foliage and judging from photographs, probably better white flowers than 'Sir Charles', is 'George Cunningham'. This commemorates, I believe, the Cunningham who ran Comely Bank Nursery in Edinburgh. He is more notorious for 'Cunningham's White' which could well hold the record for the most propagated rhododendron ever and is likely to remain so, as it is still the best rootstock for grafted plants and used all over the world for that purpose. Still yet another hoary old hybrid from the mid 1800s which is seldom seen and seems worth a place in a large garden, is 'Boddaertianum'. This one originated in Ghent, Belgium at Van Houtte Nursery and commemorates their foreman. Other foremen have been commemorated such as Faggetter and Wiseman. The Finnerty Garden curator has a form of *R. williamsianum* named for him. Would it be a good idea to have a Curators' and Foremans' bed at U Vic? I will mention one more early blooming hybrid that I think is overlooked and that is 'Bibiani'. This is a Rothschild plant that has blood red flowers in late February. There is a good specimen in the University Gardens.

I am not a hybridizer, so the following suggestions may have been tried without success or be otherwise unworkable, but in the attempt to get early blooming varieties with bigger pastel coloured flowers, how about using February blooming 'Heatherside Beauty', (the records show this as *caucasicum* crossed with an unknown but that unknown looks like *arboreum* to me), with the new hotshots like 'Lem's Cameo', 'Naselle' and 'Horizon Monarch'? Or put pollen from an early blooming white *arboreum* on these mothers. For bigger early reds, would a trial of the biggest flowered red *arboreum* with 'Markeeta's Prize' or 'Very Berry' not be worth a shot? Examination of the ARS Seed Exchange may show there are lots of growers who have had the same idea in which case I encourage someone in our Chapter to get the seed and get some plants going.

The results may not get you to chair the Breeders' Round Table which is held at every ARS Convention, or get you royalties to match those of the Sultan of Brunei but it will be good for the ego. Even a rejection, if it gets enough publicity by a famous grower can boost the ego. I think of the case of the February blooming 'Praecox' and that famous plants man A. K. Bulley, (George Forrest's sponsor). Bulley refused to have 'Praecox' in his garden because of its mauve colour. 'Praecox' had received a commendation from the RHS in 1861 and went on to be crowned with the A.G.M. in 1926 and an F.C.C. in 1978. Even the Cox family damn it with faint praise. They write... 'Rather a harsh unfashionable colour...but flowering too early in the season for the *ponticum* prejudice to be very influential.'

'A' stands for *arboreum* but it could also stand for Achievement.

STOP PRESS. The first flower on 'Nobleanum Coccineum' was fully out on the 28th of October. For the greater good of the cause, this was picked and John Hawkins is storing the pollen for application on worthy mothers later in the season.

Conventionitis
March 2000

In five year's time our chapter will be hosting the Spring Convention of the ARS. We did this once before in 1989 and it turned out to be a great success. We were blessed with salubrious sunshine, a renovated Empress Hotel, a brand new Conference Centre and a great *esprit de corps*. All of our members – about 100 all told – banded together and worked with a common purpose. It was hard work. We set a record for the number of delegates attending any ARS conference – with close to 1,100. At the time I remember thinking as I walked – or ran – from auditorium to the Crystal Ballroom for the thirty-fifth time that day, that I was living a satanic nightmare – the simple but unforeseen consequence of wanting to grow a few miserable rhododendrons in my own backyard.

In 2005 our club will be celebrating its silver jubilee. We will be in a celebratory mood and will want to share that bonhomie with ARS members from all over the world. Our club has to start soon to get down to the nitty gritty and do some work but before we do I thought it might be amusing, certainly nostalgic, maybe even provocative to record some of the memories of that harried, stimulating, debilitating last week of April 1989.

I don't recall who first broached the preposterous idea that the Victoria Chapter should host a major convention. For years local politicians had talked about the need for a convention center in Victoria. In the mid 80s these plans started to gel and a site was chosen and plans drawn up. The Centre would abut the Empress Hotel which simultaneously announced it was undertaking a multi-million dollar renovation. Completion of the Centre was projected for late 1988 or early 1989. Our group believed it would happen. Expo 86 had been a success. I personally was involved with building the Institute of Ocean Sciences and that was coming in pretty well on time and close to budget. So I, at least, was full of what was, in retrospect, flimsy faith. It was a good thing we didn't have the Multiplex or the fast ferries to jinx us. As it turned out Opening Day was too close for comfort... And as I recall we did not have a good contingency plan for using alternative accommodations if the opening date was delayed. We did talk about the possibilities of the University and the Newcomb Auditorium and even the Coliseum but only in a very superficial way – we just believed it would all work out – no earthquake or labour dispute would put the kybosh on the Victoria Rhododendron Society. Our convention was the first major one held in the new complex. It still smelled of wet paint and freshly laid carpet when we christened it with the aromas of rhododendrons and the b.o. of our members.

There were lots of problems. No one knew how the audio-visual systems worked. Getting photocopying done meant scurrying off to Monks on Fort Street. Having a phone installed involved major engineering. Portable phones or pagers were only dreams back then. Even getting tack boards took hours to arrange. The heating and ventilation were still somewhat experimental. The Empress kitchen had yet to meet the challenge of preparing a meal for 900 people.

Our planning committee met pretty well every week for two years. As I recall the first major task was to establish a program and get the speakers lined up. We adopted a theme of "The Old and the New". The convention at Eugene, Oregon, two years before had set a standard we thought would be difficult to match and one of the first things we did was to contact Harold Greer who was a prime mover of that event and was the incumbent President of the ARS. Asking him for suggestions on speakers (he was the first we asked to give a talk) he said we should try to get Edmund de Rothschild. Hamish Robertson was in charge of Program and it now seems, although I am sure it was not that easy, we aimed high. Among those the Newfies call "Come from Aways" we lined up Edmund de Rothschild, Kenneth Cox, Warren Berg, and Brian Morris from New Zealand. And our "Old and New" keynote speaker was Gwen Bell. Locals included Ian McTaggart Cowan, Ted Irving and Richard Hebda, Jennifer Lort and Fred Hook, Bill Dale, Sue Mowat and Hamish Robertson. Diane McLaren accepted the huge responsibility of Treasurer. For drawing up a good itemized budget, with all the fixed and variable costs, Diane enlisted the help of Robin Reddicop of the Art Gallery. The breakeven attendance number was set at 600. We did a very competent job of identifying income and expenditures but a lousy one of projecting cash flow. The club had scant funds. I don't remember how much we had but I think we had less than $2000, and we soon realized that we had printing costs of twice or three times that amount and we had the cost of booking the yet to be completed meeting space, plus a myriad of other small items. We thought we needed a software program for registrations. I remember approaching one source and the up-front cost was going to be over $2000. It is hard to recall just how computer illiterate most of us were a dozen or so years ago. I also recall Dave Dougan, with me as seconder, saying we would co-sign loans to get us over the hump. In the event, we went to the fall regional conference at Everett, WA, and much to the embarrassment of some of our members, asked (pleaded) with the attendees there to fork out their registrations six months ahead of the convention. The response there and the response of our own members was overwhelming and we had enough cash to pay our bills.

One of our strategies that worked out well was of approaching four hotels we had chosen and blocking off a number of rooms. In return for assuring these bookings, the hotels agreed to give us enough free rooms so we could accommodate our speakers. These hotels varied in price so delegates had a choice. I think recent conventions have had low attendances in part because the hotel costs have been so high. This arrangement was not without the odd problem. I recall one speaker being upset at not being in the Empress and when the "slight" was compounded by sending him to the wrong hotel, our diplomatic skills were tested to the limit.

The renovations to the Empress had not been quite completed, especially at the reception area and there were a few mix-ups with registrants' accommodation. For example, the Dougans were given a key/card to a room already occupied by a very amorous couple. But the Old Lady looked resplendent. Mrs. de Rothschild was overheard admiring the new carpets and saying they made the carpets at Exbury look like dishrags. Jim Smith was Convention Manager at the Empress and if ever a person gave 110% to a job it was he. We almost cost him his job. The stained glass dome in the Palm Court had been uncovered and restored and the entire décor of the Palm Court and the Crystal Ballroom was of renewed elegance and refinement. In our agreement with the Empress we had secured the Crystal Ballroom for, of all things, the plant sale. The pile on the new carpet in the Ballroom was an inch thick and in we came with 6,000 plants. We came in carrying each plant by hand after completing a tortuous commando course from the loading dock at the new Convention Centre. One detail the architects had overlooked was how to move 6,000 plants into the Crystal Ballroom. The route from the loading dock involved a descent in an elevator into the bowels of the hotel, along a narrow doglegged passage several hundreds yards long and eventually up into the splendour of the Ballroom. No wonder some pots slipped from the exhausted grasps of the army of helpers, spilling their contents onto the luxuriant pile of the yet virgin carpet. Mr. Barber, the hotel manager, arrived on the scene. On seeing this devastation he almost went through the stained glass of the dome and his outburst easily drowned out the pealing of the clarion across the street. Jim Smith was really "on the carpet". Operations ceased until several rolls of 6 mil polly were purchased and spread from wall to wall. Another memory I have is of Clint Smith arriving with his truck stacked to the roof with plants, and realizing the enormity of the task of getting them to the place of sale, venting his anger. I can still hear him asking which idiot had dreamt up such an impractical arrangement – I still smart at its acerbity and accuracy. Among the many who heard his tirade was an unknown passerby – a fairly elegant lady who immediately downed her handbag, climbed into his truck and spent the next few hours unloading. Her identity has never been discovered – the "in extremis" blonde angel.

I think the plant sale was our weakest endeavour. At an early stage we realized we were being stretched to the limit and we did want to involve the other B.C. chapters so we asked the Vancouver Chapter to assist us with the sale and we would split whatever profits resulted. In terms of quality, the plants offered for sale were of Chelsea Show standards. Back then, for example, *R. yakushimanum* was still a rare plant and there were lots – at $25 for a yearling named variety. Les Clay had done a marvelous job but we sorely underestimated the number of people that were needed to set it up, sell the plants (acquiring a Visa account took days of negotiation), and tear it down. An associated headache, one probably remembered by many as the nadir of the Victoria Convention, was the issuing of Phytosanitary certificates to those returning to the U.S. This problem had been foreseen; we had discussed it with Agriculture Canada; we had trained twenty-four of our members on filling in the forms; all the plants had been inspected beforehand. But every plant had to be recorded on the forms and Doug Kyle, the chief inspector was very helpful – God Bless him – and he is still filling the same top job. I think he guessed what would have happened had he asked one of his staff to do the job. He had to sign every one himself. The Palm Court looked like a combination of Ellis Island at the time of the Irish potato famine and a U Vic examination hall with two dozen graduate students writing finals, as rhodo buffs clutched long sought for treasures and waited for over three hours. I remember Diana Whitehead, particularly, using all her school teaching experience to try to bring order to this feverish, frustrating fiasco. The Shearmans worked so hard that I am sure Doug Kyle wanted to offer them jobs at Ag. Canada.

We had our triumphs too. With a setting sun radiant on a green sward that stretched bucolically down to the lake, over 400 sat down to a salmon barbeque at Peter and Pat Stones' magnificent garden at Duncan. Organized by the North Island chapter, led by Joanne Foster, the delegates had a truly West Coast meal whose digestion was aided by the stirring skirl of bagpipes – a thoughtful extra provided by the Stones. One of the secrets of a good convention, I think, is making each day varied and leaving just a little time to relax and be able to talk to your neighbours. I don't think we had a delegate from Africa but we did have one from South America and thirty-three from New Zealand, several from Australia; there were delegates who were Dutch, Danish, Norwegian, French and even some from Scotland. There were lots of interesting people to talk to. We are fortunate in Victoria, as the gardens being visited are fairly proximate and lengthy traveling times are not involved. Thus half-day tours are practicable. Each day divided itself into talks in the morning, tours in the afternoon and some social function in the evening. This is still a heavy schedule and I was always amazed to see thirty or more people assembled on the causeway before breakfast, eager to participate in our Early Bird Walks.

Moving several hundred people on to buses which are sequentially going to the same locations but at prescribed intervals and which leave at a set time and return at a set time is an exercise that requires planning at a level of sophistication only seen in operations like D Day. Bill Dale was the tour manager. I've forgotten how many buses we used – it was something like sixteen. The weather cooperated and things went like clockwork. Weather was, however, always uppermost in our minds. February of that year will long be remembered by gardeners. When I first came to Victoria I was always being regaled by the old time gardeners talking of the winter of '55. That did terrible havoc, exterminating nearly all the Monterey Cypresses among other tragic things. The winter of 86/87 had been soft and mild – until early February. Then the temperature dropped to sub zero and the Arctic wind blew from the North East at forty knots for four long days. This was a climatic, climactic, and climacteric event that will rival the December '96 snowstorm in the minds of most members. I know I lost quite a few plants but strangely I do not now recall many of the gardens being damaged to the point where the enjoyment of visiting them was seriously affected.

So many "little" details go in to making a convention memorable. Margaret Buffam cut 1100 pieces of rhododendron wood and painted a rhodo and printed a name, varnished and put a pin on every one of them to make souvenir name tags, in addition to the donating of one of her best ever paintings for sale – one of *Rhododendron macrophyllum*. Leslie Drew used her writing and editorial skills to produce the insert for the ARS Journal. She and Alec McCarter produced a book – "Rhododendrons on a Western Shore" to commemorate the occasion. Lurana Dougan and Pat Stone collected 1100 baby food jars and filled them with their homemade jelly to put in every Goody Bag. Joyce Parker tapped Nestles to stuff that bag with candy and nuts. And if the convention gave you a headache or a tummy ache Margaret Buffam had sweet talked McGill and Orme into providing everyone with a packet of Aspirin and a bottle of Mallox. Island Seeds gave everyone a package of seeds. I recall asking Butchart Gardens to give us a postcard or some small thing and getting no response. Eventually I managed to get through to the manager, Roger Wheelock, and he said, "Bring everyone to the gardens as our guests." To my shame, I do not remember the name of the winery, but two cases of wine were donated – and consumed. Sybil McCulloch took on the responsibility for registration which she insisted on doing manually. She was later backed up by Diana Whitehead and Carmen Varcoe on computers. From the beginning I had a nightmarish fear of "someone being stomped on by an elephant" and we tried to practice Russian Engineering – 100% redundancy in all systems and a back-up for every person. I don't think we achieved that but we tried. We had a "rhododendron" quilt made by a famous quilter from Montreal and it was a moneymaker as a raffle prize. We had an official travel agent and an official airline who gave us a bonus of a trip for two to Hawaii. We had door prizes and more door prizes. We gave our speakers Cowichan toques, and Mayor Brewin, who opened the conference – half an hour late – a copy of "Rhododendrons on a Western Shore". I wonder if she read it. Ian McTaggart Cowan, who was to be our speaker at the Friday night dinner, occasioned great distress to himself, his family, and all assembled when he had to be rushed to hospital. Warren Berg decided to collapse when doing his talk. We rushed to the phone for an ambulance and it was surprising how many medics were in the audience. Fortunately, Warren's hiccup was nothing serious. A memorable sight – I wish we had a movie of it – was the entry of the Empress waiters at the banquet – in procession with laden trays, held on high. No one should have worried about the catering arrangements – except Judy Gordon. All one needed to know was that Judy was in charge. I remember only one complaint and that was from a habit-bound gent from the Deep South; for him coffee had to be served first. It was surprising how many personal items delegates left behind.

I know I have omitted to mention many people who performed heroics and have forgotten events that should be recorded. I hope this will prompt members to correct these omissions. We made a sizeable profit. I recall Dave Dougan saying, "That's going to be our big problem now", and in many ways he was prophetic. Not all our members thought we had the capability to be successful. One even wrote to the President of the ARS and suggested he put a stop to our efforts. But most of us thought it was worthwhile. We must have – to solicit doing it again in Victoria in 2005. It can be a very rewarding experience. Any volunteers?

Cross Words
May 2000

This is true. Every week I tackle the New York Times crossword puzzle printed in the Times Colonist. Most weeks I can't get it finished. But the other week – "Eureka" – all the boxes were filled in. The great mystery was that all the main clues – the theme of the puzzle – were incomprehensible to me. So it was a red-letter day in terms of the result but one that was attained with a deficient knowledge and a smidgen of intuition.

I think a lot of gardening is like that too. If we win a plant in the raffle we usually find a place to put it, not on the basis of some great master plan but on the very practical matter of where there is a small, unused snippet of soil. Occasionally, this does have some upsetting consequences – but not too often. However, one recent event that was somewhat unpleasant comes to mind. I was trying to satisfy a difficult-to-please customer. She did not have a paint colour chip with her although I have had her ilk in the past who insist the chip is necessary to get that perfect match. Even though the sellers of paint have a marvellous command of English, the words themselves do not do much to give the precision my difficult customer demanded. In struggling to remember the names given to paints, my attempts at poetic tincturesque vocabulary were clearly inadequate. In semi-desperation I admitted that I did not give great attention to what went next to what in my garden. At which point she hit me with a verbal KO – and it still smarts – "Yes," she said, "but you are not an artist."

We settled on a R. *yakushimanum*, which has to be the safest rhododendron to put in any garden. It is an easy doer, always looks neat and as my customer agreed, the flowers could be removed when they overstepped the limit set by those blest with taste. Such super-sensitivity to art versus nature reached its vituperative nadir, in my reading experience, with Germaine Greer in her 'Revolting Garden' column in a British publication. She spits her revulsion for rhododendrons with "...(they have) bloated heads of rubbery blooms of knicker-pink, dildo-cream and gingivitis-red." Obviously the paint companies are missing a trick by not having Ms. Greer do their colour descriptions. As counter argument to the rectitude of those who know what is pleasing, Brent Elliott remarks in "Rhododendrons in British Gardens: a Short History", "...as usual, it is unwise to assume that the taste of the general public corresponds closely to the recommendations of critics and designers in the horticultural press." Amen.

Having therefore demonstrated my lack of aesthetic credentials, there are a couple of plant groupings that give me a lift. They may be in the pop art category and do not possess much subtlety but they make me stop, look and admire. (Andy Warhol made the big time too.) Currently blooming at the end of March are the rich double purple blossoms of 'April Rose' – little dark Gardenias of perfection. This has 'Snow Lady' as a white foil and 'King Alfred' daffodils as a yellow one. It is so eye-catching a statement (of what is up to you) that it would cause the most unobservant to pause. A bonus of this grouping is that the colours do not change or fade (for once the paint chips work). It's a set piece for a month. Perhaps the Society would like to give a prize for the most Germaine (not Harold – although no stranger to hyperbole) Greerish description of that grouping.

Another grouping that pleases me is a mass of ten or twelve Williamsianum varieties. This needs more space than most of our developed gardens now have and only looks 100% when all the plants are old enough to fill the space. Then for an early start to the season choose 'Maureen' (pink), followed by 'Moonstone' (cream), next to 'Point Fosdick' (a shocking colour – fuschia plum, the catalogues say. One that the sensitive will shun.) The effect of a bigger leaf can be obtained with 'Rothenburg' (light yellow) or 'Gartendirektor Rieger' of the same hue. The white 'Olympic Lady' could complete the planting. Spring bulbs and Asiatic lilies can be used to fill the spaces in early and mid season. Begonias, fuchsias and annuals can add the bright tones of summer. This won't win an award at the Seattle show but people like me who want texture and colour in their garden will find it pleasing. Many alternatives to the rhododendrons mentioned can be found and the use of a colour wheel is not necessary.

For a third planting – again, coincidentally, without a Gingivitis Red – try using plants of the Triflora tribe. The season could be started in March with the bright yellow of *lutescens*. As good a harbinger, I claim, of the busy Technicolor inter-equinox times as is Forsythia – a plant not to be despised at all with its arching shafts of Diaper Ochre. There would be some overlap of this flaxen bloom with the Knicker Pink of *R. davidsonianum*. Then the Vestal (how am I doing, paint companies?) White of *R. rigidum*, the Denim Blue of *R. augustinii*, and last, in late May, the Bumbleberry Purple of *R. tricanthum*.

I didn't get very far with the latest New York Times crossword puzzle and it could be that there is a message in that. I would like to be known as a sensible person of taste but one must recognize one's limitations, and you know what George Bernard Shaw said about those sorts: "(He was)...a man of great common sense and good taste, – meaning thereby a man without originality or moral courage" and probably not very good at crosswords either.

Survivor
October 2003

For those readers who do not watch television or who have discriminating taste, the following is a précis of the 'plot' of 'Survivor'. This program attracted the second most numerous TV audience ever. Coverage in newspapers was extensive and required more time from a diligent reader than did the one hour per week for the TV show. Sixteen candidates were selected and taken to a small "uninhabited" island in the China Sea. The participants, at two day intervals, held a vote to reduce their number by one. When only two remained, the winner, who was awarded $1,000,000 US, was chosen by the seven last voted off the island. The only food provided was a small ration of rice. Water was available from a spring – a twenty minutes walk from the beach.

Let us now assume that the uninhabited island is Vancouver Island and the participants are rhododendrons and the necessities for the preservation of life, (i.e. food and water), are limited but sufficient to keep the strongest as survivors. Following the model of the TV show our contestants are divided into two tribes. I have chosen species and hybrids. Members of the species tribe are: – *R. augustinii, R. impeditum, R. macabeanum, R. macrophyllum, R. ponticum, R. proteoides, R. williamsianum* and *R. yakushimanum*. The hybrid tribe is composed of 'Cunningham's White', 'Fantastica', 'Ginny Gee', Lem's Cameo', 'Loderi, King George', 'P.J.M', 'Point Defiance' and 'Virginia Richards'.

It is interesting to note that "Castaways 2000", a British TV program of the same 'reality' genre, currently being aired, is reportedly plagued with contention. A group was sent to a windswept treeless island in the Outer Hebrides, in an attempt to establish a new community over a year's time. Many of the entrants almost lost their lives to influenza and other maladies – much more debilitating than the sand lice and rats of the tropical island. The candidates, for this show, were subjected to vigorous selection tests, and were chosen mainly, according to one article I read, not on the basis of resourcefulness and stamina, but on potential interpersonal incompatibility. Conflicts give higher TV ratings.

Our rhododendron selection is not chosen on a potential conflict basis, but at the end of the day there can be only one survivor, despite the fact that rhododendrons are sociable plants. Nearly all can be classified as 'good doers' in our current, here and now, 'sheltered' garden environment and so each has a reasonable chance to be the winner. Inasmuch as the competitors are not physically able to vote, I am exercising that prerogative for them.

The first to be booted out was 'Virginia Richards'. Despite being very beautiful and photogenic, she is not a good doer as she is extremely prone to powdery mildew – the AIDS of rhododendrons. The others wanted her in hell and gone fast. They were scared of infection. There were 15 votes against her.

The next to go was *macabeanum*. I feel devastated at this result, but it is logical. Here is a big plant that needs lots of water and nutriment. It is a happy plant in its own environment of Manipur – but a miff as an immigrant if it doesn't get cosseted and kept warm. Furthermore, it has little sex appeal to the others in the tribes as it is old-aged by their standards before it becomes fecund.

There are now fourteen. Some of the remaining group realize that to win, the most threatening competitors must be removed – and the sooner the better. And so the next to get the chop is 'Cunningham's White'. This is a plant I don't have in my garden but many gas stations do. It is a proven survivor. It's a tough, 150 year old hybrid, whose propagatability is legend. Hackmann, of Germany, uses it as understock for all of his nursery material. It is a dour Scot, of no great beauty. It is the rhododendron equivalent of George Forrest – persistently productive. If our game were taking place on the Outer Hebrides and not Vancouver Island, it would probably win.

The next two to be jettisoned are 'Lem's Cameo' and 'Loderi'. Both have the allure of great beauty and seductiveness – the Marlene Dietrichs of rhododendrons – but are hard to root and only contented if pampered. The latter's fragrance intoxicates the most jaded nose but counts for nought with our tough rhododendron tribes. "Neither of you can take the sun or the wind and you wimp if you are not fed", the others say. "You're out".

The competition is getting tough. Those remaining rhododendrons are scheming and pushing their roots out for all available food and water. 'Point Defiance' has a great menacing name and is genetically endowed to be a survivor. It is boldly brash. Its muscular physique makes the others feel inadequate. It wins prizes. It is too much of a threat and it has to go. The vote, however, is close.

Escaping notice so far because of its unassuming size and lack of pushiness is 'Ginny Gee'. She is really quite a show off and despite her diminutive stature gives an aggressive display every year. But she is a lepidote. She has scales. She is different. Racism rears its ugly head. No doubt the scaly rhododendrons are the oldest breed and have a lineage to boast about, and most are polyploids, but the audience likes the big bosomed belles – their elepidote cousins – better.

Williamsianum, despite its elepidoteness, is not one of the blousy barmaids. It is a good neighbour and a good parent. Its minuteness and slow growth are severe drawbacks. Furthermore, small round leaves do not show up well on TV. Willy is the next casualty.

Augustine Henry was a remarkable man – long-lived and industrious. The rhododendron, named to honour his first name, is virtually an aristocrat – almost a blue blood. Augustine Henry served in China as a medical doctor. His time with the Chinese customs would constitute a normal career for most of us. In retirement, he, however, became Professor of Forestry at Dublin. *R. augustinii* does survive pretty well on southern Vancouver Island as it comes from the drier sides of the deep chasms cutting south from Tibet and so is more suited to our monsoonless summers. *Augustinii's* fault, however, is that it is not blue blooded enough. Rhododendrons are bigots and not without an

116

internal hierarchy whose elite prefer pure primary colours. The true gentian blue is absent in the genus and blue pretenders like *augustinii* are of lesser caste and have to go.

This prejudice against the blue tinge is now aimed at 'P.J.M.'. Despite being a toughie – it even survives in Winnipeg – it has that racist strike against it, and it is scaly. It is a lepidote. It is voted out.

Hiding all this time, but quietly voting, is poor little *impeditum*. Being bluish and scaly, it can see that it is only a matter of time before its name is called. A true dwarf, a heather of the Himalayas, it has been inconspicuous so far, but it is not comfortable. Being an alpine plant, it will not survive global warming and so its future survivability on lower Vancouver Island seems limited. It belongs in colder, harsher climes.

Where do we stand now? Still in competition are *macrophyllum*, *ponticum*, *yakushimanum*, *proteoides*, and 'Fantastica'. Clearly, the species tribe are going to outvote any hybrid. After all the species have been around for 60 million years. The hybrid upstarts have to go. 'Fantastica', despite its beauty and strong Teutonic upbringing, can't compete with the four remaining old-timers. There are four votes for dismissal.

Proteoides is probably the most coveted of all rhododendrons. Dave Dougan is the one exception to this generalization. He says he would rather grow spinach. In its favour, however, is an unsubstantiated report that Bill Gates paid $1500 US for a three year old plant. Native to Tibet, it loves a long winter and a cool, moist summer. The climate on Vancouver Island is incompatible. It is loved by weevils so that it cannot survive without human intervention. Toast.

It is no coincidence that the last three are closely related. All are members of the Pontica, that group that spreads itself all over the Northern Hemisphere. *Yakushimanum* is the beauty and gardeners and the TV audience are clearly rooting for it to win. As a survivor, however, it is at a disadvantage. It is naturally an islander but there, on Yaku-Shima, at the southern end of the Japanese archipelago, it rains every day. It is a hog for water. On this basis it is dismissed.

It is now obvious that the winner must be *macrophyllum*. It is on its native soil and having survived the last Ice Age has good credentials for persistence. In some parts of the world its rival – *ponticum* – has proved to be a successful colonizer, in fact a weed, so it too has the characteristics of a good survivor. The deciding factor, drawn from the long memories of the judges is that *ponticum's* pollen is known to be toxic to humans. (It is now known that *ponticum's* pollen is not poisonous) Honey from *ponticum* makes people sick. Whether *macrophyllum* has a similar toxicity has not been proven but the local gets the benefit of the doubt. We have a winner.

Now all the armchair analysts and coffee break pontificators can have the stage and can write pages on the vicissitudes of a rhododendron's life. It's amazing the amount of trash that fills newspapers – and newsletters.

The Botanical Mr. Banks
December 2000

The name of Joseph Banks cropped up recently in the Newsletter in connection with *peonia suffruticosa*. Sir Joseph has a monumental connection to a huge number of the plants we grow in our gardens. At a recent meeting we were shown some of the floral treasures of Newfoundland – unjust though it is – a place not often thought of in connection with horticulture. Be it remembered though, that it was Joseph Banks, who is much better known as the founder of Kew Gardens – botanist to Captain James Cook on his first voyage; champion of Merino sheep; father of Australia; friend of George III; Vice President of the Society for the Improvement of naval Architecture; President of the Royal Society from 20 November 1778 until his death on 20 June 1820, and who introduced *R. canadense* to cultivation in

1767. He took it back to England on completion of his expedition to Newfoundland.

Canadense had been described by Linnaeus as Rhodora Canadensis in 1762, following receipt of herbarium material from the Swedish naturalist Peter Kalm who had traveled in Pennsylvania, New Jersey and southern Canada during the period 1748 to 1751. Peter Collinson of Pennsylvania had been sending seed of eastern North American plants to England for 25 years (1735-1760) but it does not appear that *canadense* was successfully introduced from his shipments.

Banks was a great arranger and organizer. He organized his own instruction in botany at Oxford and even if he did not formally graduate he seems to have learned a lot. He came of age in 1764. His father had died in 1761. Personable and curious, he inveigled an invitation for himself and Constantine Phipps to be passengers on H.M.S. *Niger* when she was dispatched on a fisheries patrol mission to keep an eye on the behavior of the French fishermen on the Grand Banks – a name which was no doubt viewed with approbation by the young Joseph. The *Niger*'s mission also included surveying the Northern Peninsula of Newfoundland and parts of Labrador and an instruction to improve relations with the Indians and Eskimo.

Banks made good use of his time. The first plant catalogue of his collections from Newfoundland and Labrador listed over 150 species although he undoubtedly collected more than that. (Banks was extremely modest in his need for public recognition of his exploits and he published no record of his journeys.) Averil Lysaght's monumental volume, "Joseph Banks in Newfoundland and Labrador, 1776", details the disposition and fate of his botanical collections and compiles descriptions of the extensive zoological material. From the very limited perspective of our Society's interest, we should note that Banks also described *Ledum groenlandicum* and *R. lapponicum*.

A second connection between Joseph Banks and contemporary rhododendron interest is in the use of

119

colchicum autumnale – the autumn crocus. Some new commercial rhododendrons have been "genetically engineered" by the use of cholchinine, an alkaloid drug obtained from meadow saffron or autumn crocus. This affects tissue metabolism and cell division (mitosis) and can be used to increase the number of chromosomes in a plant to give polyploidy. This is claimed to give tougher foliage, flowers with heavier substance, and increased plant hardiness. 'Briggs Red Starr' and 'Briggs Northern Starr' are current popular examples.

Banks' interest in the autumn crocus stemmed from his terrible sufferings from gout. "…The King is sorry to find Sir Joseph is still confined; and though it is the common mode to congratulate persons on the first fit of the Gout, He cannot join in so cruel an etiquette…" Joseph was afflicted with gout for over thirty years. He followed various regimes in the search for relief – Mr. Pittonet's ginger regime and Dr. Pitcairn's milk regime among them. This "sad companion of old age" caused Banks to write in 1797 "…I am now like a Foundered horse lame when I go out, unsound when I come in & never likely to be any more an useful animal…" Banks' formidable stamina seems to have kept him going through the next ten years. He found "getting on horseback" and an austere diet beneficial. A friend wrote "… Sir Joseph in the last three years has eat no animal food, no wine, no spirits, but lives on pudding and vegetables, and has better health for it…"

The disease was chronic and worsening in the severity of its bouts. In 1810 Banks received a bottle of a French palliative – Dr. Husson's *eau medicinale*. Banks did not tell his regular physician, Dr. Home, of this acquisition. One night Home left Banks with a pulse of 94, and gouty lesions on the great toe, ankle, heel, knee, hip, elbow, shoulder and hand – and a gloomy prognosis. Next day Home found Banks with a pulse of 62 and "all the joint pains relieved in reverse order to the sequence of their onset." "I have taken a quack medicine", Banks said. Home chastised him, whereupon Banks took a second dose which caused a slight nausea and five bowel evacuations but removed all gouty pains. Banks entered the annals of British medicine with his gouty endeavours. His physician, the skeptical Dr. Home, with insistent Banksian encouragement (he who must be obeyed) began to study *eau medicinale.* It proved to be that the autumn crocus was the crucial ingredient. In time Home evolved his own concoction using two pounds of the roots of *colchicum autumnale* in 24 ounces of sherry, brewing it for several days. Banks himself pursued the mystery of the plant 'hermodactyl' (*evidently colchicum*).He received roots from Syria with a French translation from Arabic texts. Husson's water continued to provide relief to Banks but he suffered debilitating attacks of gout that lasted for ten months of the year over his last five years. All of this is recorded – complete with charts – in Harold B. Carter's "Sir Joseph Banks", which was commissioned by the British Museum and published in 1988.

I have no idea if colchicum is still used in pharmacology. It would be interesting if some of our medical members could add a comment. There are many, many ways in which those matters that were of concern to Sir Joseph have impact on our lives. Many regard him with disgust due to his support for the penal colonies of Australia and the use of his entrepreneurial talents in fostering slavery. However, no one comes any better as a botanist.

F is for *Fortunei*
March, 2001

There is a hoary, lichen-covered story about a rhododendron gardener reminiscing on his long past experiences. He sighs: 'I don't remember the name of the town; I don't remember the name of the wine; I don't even remember the name of the girl. But the tree we sat under was *R. fortunei.*'

No doubt in our reminiscer's memory, it was the heady, sweet aroma that was stimulating his synapses.

121

However, *fortunei* is prized for more than its fragrance. It has the stature of a small tree; it is Clintonesquely hardy and has been used extensively in hybridizing, being one of the parents of such beauties as the 'Loderis'. It has a big truss.

The name commemorates Robert Fortune, a man who broke a lacuna of horticultural exploration in south-east Asia, and particularly China, in the early-to-mid 1800's. This lack of activity was due, in part, to the death of Joseph Banks in 1820 and the consequent loss of his aggressive leadership at Kew. The first Opium War of 1839-42, despite its floral origins, did not help in the peaceful study of Chinese plants. Then, with the signing of the Treaty of Nanking in 1842, Hong Kong was ceded to Great Britain and the Royal Horticultural Society woke up to the huge potential of the Chinese flora. Accordingly, Fortune, a gardener with the Royal Botanic Garden at Edinburgh and the Horticultural Society's Gardens at Chiswick was appointed as the Society's "Collector in China".

His travels extended over nineteen years. His instructions for his first expedition were extensive. Of primary interest were "the peaches of Pekin", and tea. Far down on the list was a reference to "The azalea from Lo-fou-shan, a mountain in the province of Canton". His salary was 100 pounds a year. He experienced many difficulties, including being beset by pirates on several occasions. Once he had to strafe an attacking junk with his big double-barreled fowling piece. On another occasion he relates: "From their manner I suspected that their intentions were not good...My poor plants were flying about in all directions... I felt there was no denying we were in dangerous company".

He traveled disguised as a native "from a distant province". I find it difficult to believe the Chinese were duped by his mimicry but then he seems to have been totally devoid of humour and was completely obsessed by his sense of mission. A large part of his time was spent on tea plants and getting them to India. His contention that green and black tea came from the same plant (a fact) did not seem to have been accepted by his superiors. One of the biggest ironies in his struggles to get tea established in India is that few of Fortune's Chinese plants survive there. The tea plants that were later found native in Assam are the source of modern crops.

However, returning to the matter of *fortunei* and recalling its 1855 discovery, Fortune writes: "In a romantic glen through which we passed on our journey I came upon a remarkably fine-looking rhododendron... All the Chinese in that part agreed in stating that the flowers of this species are large and beautiful, but as all rhododendrons have this character, it is impossible to predict what this one may turn out to be..." He collected a goodly amount of seed and it grew vigorously at Chiswick and was soon prized in its own right and pressed into service as a stud in Europe and latterly in Eastern North America.

Some of the seeds' progeny proved to be remarkably cold hardy. Hybridizers in the New England States, such as Dexter and Gable, found it to be a great parent. The Arnold Arboretum in Boston, along with notables like Pierre S. du Pont, used the *fortunei* hybrids to great effect in their gardens. It is still an essential genetic component of the large-flowered rhododendrons grown in the East and in our less harsh Western climate. Fragrance and stature make it an essential species in all rhododendron collections.

Nowadays, however, even to an acolyte like myself, I hesitate to recommend *fortunei* for smaller gardens. It holds its leaves for two years at most, and its height usually means that the flowers are high above the nose. In its favour, some of the recently introduced forms have intense purple petioles and bright red leaf bracts. Combined, these make a statement on their own, but cousins, *R. orbiculare* and *R. decorum* are more useable in the average garden. *Fortunei* has good kin and a majority of them are smelly. They are remarkable in their range of flowering time – from February with *oreodoxa* – to July with *R. hemsleyanum*. The newly introduced *R. glanduliferum* (1995) is causing sweaty palms among the in-group.

Robert Fortune is well remembered. He deserves to be. The linguistic purists pronounce the penultimate vowel – the 'e' – in the name of the plant. I don't think the stolid Robert Fortune would appreciate the botanical probity of pronouncing the 'e' at the end of his name. His name was 'Fortune', and if you stick an 'i' at the end that is good enough for me. And I think it would have been good enough for him.

Scotch and Water
April 2001

There are certain necessities in life that seem to need to be controlled and rationed by those who reach positions of power. The ego of our political masters overflows with smug satisfaction when a new morality can be forced on their minions and then enforced with retributive enthusiasm. The guilt of our consumer greed is assuaged by choosing some basic need, overtly ensuring that its demand continues to increase, scaremongering a crisis for its users and then placing limits on its availability. Citizens under restraint, as in wartime, are deemed to be more servile. The common enemy – using water – must be conquered.

We could have raised the Sooke dam in plenty of time to give us an adequate supply of water for these predictable droughty years. We could have had an adequate supply for topping up visiting cruise ships and for building mains to new housing (with green lawns and rhododendrons), hanging baskets, washing cars and flushing toilets – even the low volume ones that need to be done twice – if the modern day inquisitors had not held sway. Emerson said that his civilization had built a coach and lost the use of its feet. That was a long time ago but we are no different. We can build $1.4 billion highways and fast ferries – after a fashion – and worldwide webs but have trouble with a $14 million dam to store water in a region where more falls from the sky than evaporates back up.

Most of the plants that we get pleasure from are exotics – what the Newfies call "come from aways". Half of them are from China. Generally, these fancy foreigners are brought up knowing dryish winters and summer monsoons. We can grow these beauties well, provided we supplement the water that nature gives them in summer with some that we have stored, for that purpose among others, in our lakes and aquifers.

Rhododendrons, in particular, are not overly thirsty, but they are shallow rooted; they don't know how to probe deeply for water like their cousin, the arbutus does; they do not like to dry out. If the garden is small and the gardener limber enough to lug hoses around like a firefighter, then hand watering is not a very onerous matter. One inch of water per week will keep a one meter (the water police dislike serfs who mix up units) tall rhododendron in top condition. This translates to one minute's worth of water from a half-inch (12.5mm) hose per week. A stopwatch is not currently required but Stage 4 or Level 4 – whatever it's called – of the Water Board's Regulations will require its use. Better for the rhododendron would be 30 seconds twice a week. If you are growing some of our comely natives, such as Shooting Stars and Flowering Current and Menzies's Dogwood, be sure that not a drop of supplementary water is wasted on them.

In nature, rhododendron plants build up a nice mulch over the years from their old leaves. In waterless summertime Victoria, a rhododendron will be tempted to achieve this mulch in one year by dropping all of its leaves in a one-time valiant, but painfully suicidal, effort to conserve moisture. We can increase its chances of survival by providing an artificial mulch. This can be done with oak leaves (No 1), grass clippings (No 10), or ground bark (No 2). If the last is chosen, it should be done immediately as it is rumoured that the amount of water used to grind bark and the amount of fossil fuel needed to get bark from forest to our rhododendron is being monitored and if decreed by our neo-Covenanters (my Scottish ancestors were Covenanters and they were all for proscribing whisky use too) then its use in gardens will be banned. A couple of inches (5cm) are about right. Just make sure that there is no mulch touching the trunk of the bush and that the two inches is at the drip-line (i.e. where the water drops off the plant in winter). It should taper down from the drip-line to the trunk.

In our society the most popular recreational activity is gardening. Recreation is a good word. It implies enlivening, making new – and therapy and healing. I can't quote figures but I am sure that our medical costs, if we went gardenless, would soar. One would think that economists would love gardening as it is largely concerned with growth. To be successful these days one must have growth. Why has there not been an outcry from the critically wounded horticultural industry? When the automobile or the fiber optic industry, or the NHL (Owners of Canadian Hockey Clubs Unite!) hit hard times there are screams for help. Gardeners are silent, gentle people. We now need a crusade. Gardeners of the World Unite!

I've had an evil, nefarious thought that with some trepidation I will share with you. Could it be possible that some eager, snooping cub reporter would investigate the personal financial affairs of the members of the Water Board and discover that at least one of them has an interest in a company selling bottled water or better still pistol-grip hose nozzles? The current national fixation with Chretien's Shawinigate would evaporate like water from a kiddie's wading pool and we would have a truly Canadian Watergate.

Go and have a wee dram – but neat – no water – someone might be watching.

What's in a Name?
April 2001

In my copy of the Oxford Dictionary of Quotations there are 110 listings for roses and none for rhododendrons. In the main part, I suppose that this is due to roses having been known from classical times. It is probably because most roses are fragrant and their name has only one syllable and four letters. Lumbered with a name that has twelve letters and four syllables and was not at all well known until a century and a half ago, it is perhaps excusable that our favourite flower has had short shrift from the literary world.

In the past couple of days I've come face to face with a small posy of poets. They assure me that this is not a serious life threatening experience. One of them, Patrick Lane, was kind enough to send me a copy of Al Purdy's poem '*Arctic Rhododendrons*' which is the only poem known to Patrick 'on such flowers'. Here it is:

They are small purple surprises
In the river's white racket
And after you've seen them
a number of times
in water-places
where the silence seems
related to river-thunder
you think of them as 'noisy flowers'
Years ago
It may have been
that lovers came this way
stopped at the outdoor hotel
to watch the water floorshow
and lying prone together
where the purged green
boils to a white heat
and the shore trembles
like a stone song
with bodies touching
flowers were their conversation
and love the sound of a colour
that lasts two weeks in August
and then dies
except for the three or four
I pressed in this letter
And sent whispering to you
Pangnirtung

Perhaps the American Rhododendron Society should attempt to correct the imbalance between roses and rhododendrons, exercising some poetic justice, by sponsoring a show of verse along with those of trusses and photographs. Inasmuch as poets are such a rare breed, and while their affliction is certainly not at all contagious, most of us could no more write a poem than explain photosynthesis, still I think our club could help the literary world a little by coming up with a collective word for rhododendrons. If a group of curs can be recognized with a collective – "cowardice", and ladies with "bevy" and rooks with "parliament", then groups of rhododendrons should be accorded similar status. I will offer a prize of a rare rhododendron (small) – one of the Taliensia subsection – as a prize to the entry deemed, by our editor, to be the most evocative.

Life's Chosen Few
October 2001

Do you recall your years in high school and your sometime strivings for academic and social success? In my recollection, at any rate, it seems that one or two of my contemporaries managed to take everything in stride; they understood the tricks of trigonometry intuitively, could recite Shakespeare's sonnets after one scanning and never double faulted at tennis. These people, perhaps you were one of them, were destined, it seemed, to be leaders, to flourish, and live beautiful lives.

There are a few rhododendrons that seem to have these same secrets to happy survival stamped into their genetic code. They grow and bloom and look contented and well composed year after year. 'Nancy Evans' is one such happy camper. She is a good looker and although of modest stature, wins beauty contests at all the shows. She is consistent in her performance and manages on an every day diet, being neither bulimic nor anorexic. She is at home in almost any garden in these parts. Her equanimity assures her acceptance by the rest of the rhododendron group. Her comportment equates to harmony, a harmony that extends to her being one of the most prolific and nurturing parents in the rhododendron community.

I would also place 'Rosamundi' in this easygoing, congenial group. 'Rosamundi' will not be the garden's valedictorian, or medal winner, but will shine in her season and move on smoothly from year to year. I would guess that because she starts to bloom so early in the season and is so popular and ubiquitous, she gets more notice than almost any other rhododendron. I have observed that even visitors to our part of the world who come from inhospitable places (in a horticultural sense I mean) – like Ottawa or Flin Flon – want to know who is this modest but radiant beauty, blooming in January. Furthermore, she enjoys blooming so much that she does it for three or four months. She is always modestly unassuming and unobtrusive but thoroughly reliable.

I also recall from schooldays the new arrival bursting onto the scene and taking the place by storm. A big and brassy and invincible sports jock idolized by half and feared by the rest. You could certainly claim that 'Point Defiance' and 'Horizon Monarch' fit this caricature. If they were human they would be sent for drug testing. Their stature and strength are suspiciously enhanced. By what? They ask for no special favours. Compare the behaviours of, say, *R. fargessi*. *Fargessi* whimpers at the slightest threat of thirst, rolling its leaves in premature pique. It can barely bear to breed as it may die if its swelling seedpods are not removed. I have noticed the same defect in 'Chief Paulina'. If the seed capsules are not detached – difficult procedures with the Chief as she is particularly loathe to part with them – it is probable that the twig bearing the pods will die. It has to be admitted that our super heroes 'Point Defiance' and 'Horizon Monarch' also have the rachis pretty well secured to the end of the branch but a quick snap at the right spot removes the spent blossom and I'm sure it does not hurt all that much. These two giants will grow more than a foot a year and once

129

they start to get hair on their chins they blossom profusely every year. I could speculate that the breeders of corn will be looking at how to use their genes to give metre-long corncobs. But perhaps the cobs would be on five metre corn plants and therefore hard to harvest.

Another, get-it-right-first-time, shiner is 'Blaney's Blue'. He could be the show-off of the class. What a power bloomer! I don't think that in my garden 'Blaney' will ever be deadheaded. It's a life's career to tackle a full deadhead. But it doesn't make any difference. There is that old chestnut about an English gardener, Lord 'So-and-So', observing that deadheading is a foolish practice – it just makes the job more onerous the next year. This does not apply to 'Blaney's Blue'. The creature will carry on showing off with thousands of blossoms no matter how it is neglected. Also, have you noticed that often when someone is not very gifted academically she will be at the top of the heap by having a keen sense of humour? "In her attire doth show her wit, it doth so well become her." I am thinking of 'Paprika Spiced'. Here is a seriously freckled blond who stops her audience by evoking simultaneously, mirth and sympathy. She may even elicit a therapeutic response, as she appears to have an advanced case of chickenpox. 'Paprika Spiced' is surely a comic but she is also a cunning commercial success.

Being born with a deformity can be exploited to advantage if it is not too debilitating to one's health. 'Linearifolium' is among the most admired and all because of her genes being really messed up. I suppose some of her popularity could be due to her striking similarity to marijuana and the resulting hop headed response of rhododendron illiterates. 'Linearifolium's' flower is not at all striking; it has been described as strappy. The message here, I suppose, is to use what God-given features one has to the full advantage and bask demurely in the attention generated.

Some of us react very negatively to another's B.O., especially so when squeezed in a crowd, shoulder to shoulder, or more accurately, armpit to armpit. However, this is the way I like to grow my rhododendrons and in particular the ones that exude smells. I personally like the B.O. of almost all rhododendrons and we should remember it is there because it gives some evolutionary advantage. Stripping the leaves of *R. russatum* when doing cuttings releases an odor that I hope will be present in the afterworld. *R. charitopes* has a fruity sweet aroma; it will please the nose of an oenophile. I used to have a plant of *R. kongboense* (now on the most wanted list) and it was fun to ask little ones to crush a leaf and tell what it smelled of. "Toothpaste", "Bubblegum", "Kool Aid" were some of the responses.

Most of us, of course, are not endowed with film star looks or stratospheric IQs. Rhododendrons, as with people, are unable to defy the laws of statistics. Most are right in the middle of the great giant bell curve. So the 'Anna Kruschkes' and the 'Percy Wisemans' and the 'Dora Amateis' will survive, as will we, contributing our two bits and being content to be among the great silent majority of the populace, paying our taxes and keeping out of trouble. We are with honour but not singularly honoured. We cut the mustard but don't leave a burning sensation. I think O. Henry had it right when he wrote: "I'm not headlined in the bills but I'm the mustard in the salad just the same."

The PEDON – A Soiled Subject
December 2001

The unit of classification for soils is called the PEDON. Since soils do not occur as discrete entities, this unit of measurement is not an obvious one and I have only the vaguest appreciation of its significance. I do, however, know what a Pedon means in terms of impact. Recently, my disrobed two-year-old grandson rushed out, anticipating his bath, and aimed perfectly at my left leg, sock and slipper. I felt the warm gush of affection. A soil Pedon usually has a vertical dimension of one meter and the affected extent of this human Pedon was approximately the same.

131

The practice of returning organic matter to the soil has been recognized as being beneficial since the beginnings of agriculture. This recent experience suggests that some distribution methods are more desirable and effective than others. Still, it is hugely significant that almost all of the energy in the world's terrestrial ecosystems is supported, contained and dissipated in the tiny layer we know as soil.

There are certain platitudes that I find myself repeating, almost to the point of self-disgust. One such adage is 'a $50 hole for a $5 plant'. I hope it is obvious that it is what goes **in** the hole that is important. Recently, I found myself in trouble with a landscaper. I had been emphasizing to some gardeners (including it turned out, the landscaper's client) the importance of creating an enticing rooting environment for new rhododendrons. I also stressed the need to expose the roots of the new plants to the garden soil by teasing out the roots of the plants – especially if they had been container grown. I have been told that over half of potted rhododendrons planted in North America die in the first year – mainly because the roots do not leave the original root mass and never do extend into the surrounding soil. The landscaper had recently planted some 'balled and burlapped' rhododendrons, leaving the loosened burlap around the root ball. This is a standard practice. However, the client wanted the roots to be roughened and exposed and insisted that the landscaper return and do just that. The landscaper agreed to go back and tease out the roots.

I recommend digging in a lot of bark mulch to garden soil – 50% – to give a depth of 30 cm. This gives the air the roots need (20% of the soil's volume) and gives a fairly safe assurance that the acidity will be about right. A pH of 5.5 is generally considered ideal for most rhododendrons.

Rhododendron growers know that if the soil pH is high, this generally means a calcareous soil and the plants will not thrive. There are acres of paper warning gardeners that rhodos and lime are like chalk and cheese. In our part of the world most soils are acidic and so getting a suitable pH is not of great concern or difficulty. It is, therefore, something of a diversion to discuss rhododendrons growing on limestone. However, as it occurs quite infrequently, it is an interesting and revealing diversion, especially when we realize that no one can yet explain how rhododendrons grow so happily in these heretical conditions.

There were, or are, a number of commonly touted theories as to how rhododendrons grow on limestone. The main ones are: (1) They grow in pockets of organic material out of contact with the limestone; (2) they grow on dolomitic limestone; (3) The limestone is hard and more or less insoluble; (4) The heavy rain of monsoons washes any dissolved limestone out of the soil. Professor Rankine of the University of Edinburgh has written about these theories in the ARS Journal and elsewhere. He studied rhododendrons growing on limestone in Yunnan, China, measuring the chemistry of the soils (examining many Pedons) in which the plants were growing, and measuring the chemistry of the plant tissue. He showed that none of the foregoing hypotheses held water. He is not very definite about the physiological processes that do allow the rhododendrons to thrive in such limey soils. These interactions are very complex but he suggests that manganese is of great consequence. We gardeners usually think only of a plant's need for nitrogen, phosphorous and potassium. In occasional lapses of inspiration, we may also think of iron, perhaps sulphur and magnesium (we all know to give our roses Epsom Salts) but only scientists think of manganese. I recall consulting a doctor about a medical problem. "What is the cause of my problem?" I asked. With studied professionalism and ponderous severity, he replied, "It's multifactorial." – which was underwhelmingly reassuring. And that, I'm afraid, is where we have to leave the case of the lime-loving rhododendrons – at least for the time being – no one as yet understands all the processes.

A more common problem with local soils is clay. Clay soils are generally fertile soils but are not good for rhododendrons and other fine rooted plants that prefer an open, airy soil. To correct a clay soil one needs to add enough coarse mineral material to give the desirable, open consistency. In practice, this means adding a third to a half of sand to the depth of soil being amended. This depth need not be over 30cm for rhododendrons, provided there is good drainage below the new soil. Ted Irving faced the clay problem at the Horticultural Centre of the Pacific. He lifted all the rhododendrons, dug in 15cm of coarse sand and then 15 cm of leaf mould, and replanted the rhododendrons, which are now resplendently thriving. Ted emphasizes that applying gypsum to clays to improve texture is, at best, a very short-lived palliative.

For an amateur to say much about soils is a very stupid and risky business – the subject is complex in the extreme. One wonders how plants grow so well when they know so little of all the machinations, animate and inanimate, going on around their roots. That's why doctors resort to gross generalities – they are the safest – when asked to explain the physiology of our bodies. It is also probably why a lot of us rely on folk remedies.

There is a great deal of concern in our society these days about toxic and contaminated soils. Large chunks of public and private money are being spent on testing, removing and treating soils that are shown, or deemed, to be contaminated. There is a thriving business proving that such soils cannot support happy and thrifty human or vegetative populations. The future is never really predictable but what is predictable is that there will always be a demand for soil experts. This non-growing business is growing. Another field where demand for expertise is sure to grow is constitutional law. I am torn between these as the preferred career choice for my grandson. Currently, I am favouring the soil business because he already knows what a Pedon is.

A **Pedon** is defined as a 3-dimensional sampling unit of soil, with depth to the parent material and lateral dimensions great enough to allow the study of all horizontal shapes and intergrades below the surface.

134

What's Your Name? Specifically
January 2001

In 1778, Gilbert White wrote: "the standing objection to botany has always been, that it is a pursuit that amuses the fancy and exercises the memory without improving the mind or advancing any real knowledge; and where science is carried no further than a mere systematic classification, the charge is but too true." He then goes on to say that these aspersions can be mitigated, recommending that the "botanist" "should examine the powers and virtues of efficacious herbs, should promote their cultivation, and graft the gardener, the planter, and the husbandman, on to the phytologist." Ouch.

The word 'phytologist' does not seem to be in use any more. It literally means 'one who studies plants' which to us would be a 'botanist'. White, however, is clearly talking about those who are concerned with the classification of plants – "taxonomists". He is recommending that we gardeners be grafted – sounds quite surgical – onto those who dream up (and then keep changing) these complicated Latin names for the plants we grow.

About twenty years ago I sat in on the Fourth International Rhododendron Species Symposium. There were about 300 people in attendance and most of them were academics. That is an amazing number when one reflects that most of these were what White calls phytologists and that most attendees were being supported by the public purse in some fashion. Twenty years ago many of the significant technological advances that have been made in the study of plants at the cellular level and particularly in genetics were yet to come. Still, the *avant garde* were deliriously excited about the chemistry of plants and were advocating its use for deciding what constitutes a 'good' species. The old timers vigorously maintained that the morphology – the appearance and structure of a plant – was the primary determinant. The arguments grew heated and there was an anxious, almost belligerent, tension in the crowd; the debate was getting out

135

of control. If I remember correctly, the Chairman was Britt Smith and he thumped his gavel and said, "Ladies and gentlemen, this is indeed a serious subject – but not important". Order was restored.

One can't have science without classification and people with tidy logical minds are driven crazy when they can't make what is observed in nature fit a system of their own devising. They make good arguments that this plant is different from this other plant because of this factor and that factor but more often they say that the examined characteristics do not justify a separate moniker and lump together two plants that to most gardeners look completely different. Gardeners are then driven crazy when a name that has taken half a lifetime to learn is now to be known as something else and when they do the arithmetic and realize they have only two half life times, they rebel. I'm all for spouses retaining the name they were given at birth; I still stumble over my daughter's married name. *Rhododendron yakushimanum* will never be called *degronianum* ssp. *yakushimanum* by me – except, maybe, in very polite company. Nor will *R. concatenans* be cursed with the undignified burden of *r. cinnabarinum* ssp. *xanthocodon,* Concatenans Group. No wonder the flowers of *concatenans* droop. Further, one would think that modern day phytologists could coin a better word than 'Group' for a distinctive entity like *concatenans*. Even recognizing it as a sub-sub species would be better. It seems to me ironic that those – the old fashioned phytologists – who are imposing the systematics (I almost wrote systemics) on plants and generally lumping names together – have not applied the same strictures to their own genre. The biology discipline has been split into all sorts of specialties like taxonomy, genetics, ecology, and mycology without having to conform to a methodology that insists that they be ranked as species or sub species or variety, or God forbid for those affected, Group. Imagine trying to get tenure if you were classified as meriting merely the Group designation.

136

Let's look at a couple of well known native trees – the Arbutus and the Douglas Fir – to see how well White's strictures have been followed.

My favourite native tree is the arbutus. In these parts the common name is the same as the Latin name arbutus (*arbutus menziesii*) – which is good. Strangely, it has not been changed since it was christened. (Bailey in the "Cyclopedia of American Horticulture" 4th Edition, 1906 notes it having been named as arbutus *procera*, Dougl. in the Botanical Register but that appears not to have been legitimate.) It took thirty years for that christening to take place (another long but interesting story) from the time of Archibald Menzies' discovery and description of the arbutus in 1792. Menzies was the doctor and botanist with Captain George Vancouver on his famous voyage of discovery. However, Menzies was not the first European to record having become acquainted with the Pacific arbutus. In 1769, a Spanish priest, Father Juan Crespi, trekking up the coast from San Diego wrote that he encountered "many madronos, though with smaller fruit than the Spanish." If the Spanish had not been so fearful of letting others know of the new riches they had found and published their discoveries openly, our arbutus would most likely be called *arbutus crespii*. The name arbutus evidently was given to the Strawberry tree of the Mediterranean (*arbutus unedo*). This is Crespi's madrono and incidentally is the tree that figures in the coat of arms of Madrid. Arbutus was the name the Romans gave the Strawberry tree and it is appropriate that Linnaeus chose it for the genus in his *Species plantarum* in 1753. For an informative account of Menzies' meeting with the arbutus for the first time, have a read of Clive Justice's book "Mr. Menzies' Garden Legacy". A copy is in our library. For a captivating, whimsical and provoking read of Menzies' stormy relationship with his captain, George Vancouver, and the latter's torrid but diplomatically successful relationship with Juan Francisco de la Bodega y Quadra, see George Bowering's "Burning Water".

Many people are surprised that arbutus is first cousin of rhododendron. Both belong to the Heather family – the *ericacaea*. The tallest rhododendron has been reported as being 30 metres in height. Allen J. Coombes in "Trees" gives the maximum height of *arbutus menziesii* as 40 metres. The largest I have seen was in Christchurch, New Zealand. The arbutus can justifiably lay claim to being the tallest of the heathers. I suggest it can also lay claim to having a good name and sticking to it.

The rules for giving scientific names to plants are contained in the International Code of Botanical Nomenclature. I like the *arbutus menziesii* name because the first name has been around for a very long time and the second one is commemorative. The Code says, however, that such commemorative coinages '…notwithstanding their undeniable importance, are relatively accessory…' One has to wonder, therefore, about the scientific name for our Douglas fir – *pseudotsuga menzesii*. How come David Douglas loses out to Archibald Menzies when the name goes from English (really Scottish, as both of them spoke with a brogue) to Latin? Complaining about changes to the names of some of our favourite rhododendrons pales when compared to the nomenclatular gymnastics that have befallen our most important commercial tree. Arthur Kruckeberg says it would take a botanical lawyer to trace the intricate history of its nominal peregrinations. At various times it has been a pine, a spruce, a hemlock and a fir. It is now a false (*pseudo)* hemlock (*tsugu* is Japanese for hemlock). This name was given to it only 50 years ago so the story may not yet be over. Here is a case where Gilbert White's early concerns have been substantiated.

Initial encounters with Latin names are usually pretty stressful and when these often elocutionary challenging names change, we tend to blame those responsible for making the changes. We think of the perpetrators of the changes as not leading particularly stressful lives and secretly accuse them of gleefully making them up to give their academic monotony a little zip. To be fair the Botanical Code makes sense. Its first purpose is to avoid confusion and to make sure that everyone is talking about the same plant. I suppose we have to take the long view and hope young gardeners will grow up with the new names at their fingertips. We must remember that:

> The proper skill in expertise
> Is to arrange the premises
> So that the most foregone conclusion
> Can fit therein without confusion.
> Pity it did not happen with the Douglas fir.

But to be fair, common names also suffer arbitrary changes. A comely member of the sunflower family was suddenly about-faced from 'Venus Paint Brush' to 'Devil's Paint Brush' when it turned out to be a thuggish weed.

White was a clergyman and naturalist who was the curate at Selborne, Hampshire, England. Evidently he lived uneventfully there keeping a journal on his garden – "The Natural History and Antiquities of Selborne" – which, I believe, is still in print.

T is for *Triflora*
March 2002

The easiest thing to do is make a lumpy white sauce. The second easiest thing to do is to grow *Triflora* rhododendrons. The third easiest thing to do is to ignore the *Triflora* rhododendrons.

The *Triflora* (three flowers) has been a neglected Section of the *Rhododendron* genus in most gardens on Vancouver Island. The best known of the group is *R. augustinii*. Still, it is not a plant that one can find in the average nursery. A potential buyer of a rhododendron will trip over a slew of 'Unique' and 'Jean Marie' without sighting one species of the *Triflora*.

139

The *Triflora Subsection* of the scaly leafed rhododendrons (Lepidotes) is a large and important group that is centered in Western China. Most get to be quite tall and, with their smaller narrow leaves, have a slender, willowy look. Many of them have flowers, not only at the end of the branches, but also in the axils of the topmost leaves, so they put on a big show when in bloom. Interestingly, many of the *Triflora* have more than the basic number of chromosomes. This is termed polyploidy. Some have twice the normal 26 chromosomes and some three times. Cox says this limits the amount of hybridization that can take place among those with different counts.

I warm to some plants in the garden in no small part because of their association with where I got the plant, or who gave it to me, or because of the plant's history of discovery and introduction. *R. augustinii* commemorates Augustine Henry. There are reports that Dr. Henry may not have been the wittiest of plantsmen, (the spouse of one weekend host of Henry's always found excuses to be absent from his endless, boring botanical litanies), but he knew his stuff. Trained as a medical doctor, initially in his native Ireland and then at Edinburgh, he joined the Chinese Maritime Customs. After a year at Shanghai, he was sent to Ichang (Yichang) on the Yangtze as assistant medical officer where for long periods of time he was bored out of his wits. "Oh, if you knew the weariness of the exile's life. I have become a great collector of plants, and after exhausting the neighbourhood I thought of going into the mountains, so I spent six months in two journeys into the interior."

Probably the greatest of Henry's legacies was the introduction of the handkerchief tree (*Davidia involucrata*). Henry didn't collect plants; he preserved herbarium specimens (5000 species) and after following up the French missionary Pere David's original discovery of the handkerchief tree, it was his specimens that stimulated the English nursery Veitch to send out Ernest Henry Wilson to bring it back to England and subsequently to North America.

Henry, on retiring from the Orient, took up the position of Professor of Forestry at Dublin and had a second career, which testifies to his intellect and industry. So I like *augustinii.* (There is also a *R. henry* which is said not to be in cultivation. It is related to *R. latoucheae,* which was recently introduced by Peter Wharton). To me, the plant *augustinii* fills one's senses with more than a flowing cascade of "blue".

The colour of *augustinii* ranges from white to wine. The "blue" forms of *augustinii* are not seen as frequently in gardens as they should be but the other shades are downright rare. I have a clone called 'Burgundy' and that will bloom for me for the first time this year. 'Marine' is the most popular of the *augustiniis* being quite deep coloured, almost purple but I like the paler ones every bit as much. There are a couple of very good specimens in the University Gardens.

There is no doubt that the colour of *augustinii* varies from garden to garden. Ernie Lythgoe experienced this sensitivity many years ago. He admired a plant of *augustinii* in Vern Ahyers' garden. Carefully he nurtured a cutting to flowering size only to be disappointed in the muddiness of the blue. Soil has a big effect.

Similarly, the books say, has temperature. The colder the winter, it is claimed, the more red in the blue. After several years of casual, unscientific observation, I decided that the "blueness" had more to do with then Prime Minister Mulroney's standing in the opinion polls than winter temperature.

The first of the *Triflora* to bloom in spring – in February – is the yellow-flowered *R. lutescens.* Under-plant *lutescens* with the dark purple form of *Helleborus orientalis* and the green flowered *Helleborus foetidus* and some of the early flowering daffodils and perhaps a few primulas and call for Van Gogh. Then, next to *lutescens,* plant its cousin, the pink March blooming *R. davidsonianum.* The clone 'Ruth Lyons' has no markings in her throat – regarded by some connoisseurs as a mark of purity – but I like the ones with the jewels on their throats just as well. Continuing this theme of tall, willowy exclamation marks, plant the April flowering *augustinii* and the white flowering *R. rigidum* side by side. There is a very good form of the latter that I got from Greers. This has a tennis ball sized truss of 6 or 8 snowy flowers, (thus stretching the name *Triflora,* even for a taxonomist) and dark chocolate anthers.

This resplendence of rhododendrons is not complete without the inclusion of the latest of the *Triflora* to bloom – *R. tricanthum.* I think the best forms of *tricanthum* are the deep purple ones. This extends the floral show to mid June. With five plants, one can have a five-month succession of colour. Since expense is not a consideration in this imagery, let's add around the perimeter of the grouping a clump of each of the smallest of the *Triflora* – *R. hanceanum* and *R. keiskei. Hanceanum* makes a great border plant, seldom getting more than 30 cm in height but twice as wide. Its April creamy flowers are openly out-facing and numerous. These match the bronzy new foliage so well that even Oak Bay gardeners cannot complain of any tonal disharmony. The tiny form of *keiskei* 'Yaku Fairy' is the best known and is certainly a gem but there are other larger forms which might be more suited to our *Triflora* extravaganza. As an aside, I was told that the way to grow *keiskei* 'Yaku Fairy' is in a pot. Every year knock the plant out and put another 2cm of soil in the pot. "Yaku Fairy' will spill over the rim of the pot, cascading down the sides to form a splendid wig.

For those with space and who like to develop a theme to its most replete, one of the easiest to please of all the Triflora is *R. yunnanense.* Reportedly it has a very wide geographical distribution and a large altitudinal range. It varies in flower from white through pink to pale purple. I think the form with white flowers and coral markings is probably the best. I find that *yunnanense* is one of these shrubs that is taken for granted like some conifers or spireas. It is an essential element in the landscape but assumes a kind of complementary demeanour.

The collector can add the whimsically named *R. ambiguum* – an easy doer with soft yellow flowers in April/May. There is also an interesting multi-coloured form of the type species *R. triflorum*. The cream flowers are suffused with red and pink and green. At this point I have to add that probably the least garden worthy of all rhododendrons in my garden is a form of *triflorum*. Its flowers are the same insipid colour as the leaves; it is an aesthetic disaster. The reason I keep this plant is not for any horticultural or botanical interest, but for human interest. If any visitor notices the flowers she is immediately elected to my Growers' Hall of Fame. However, this plant is the exception – most are fully worthy of the space they occupy.

For recreating the landscape, or for the new gardener, but especially for the gardener who has had some unsatisfactory experiences with rhododendrons, there are plants out there that deserve your attention.

'Tis a lesson you should heed:
Try, try again.
If at first you don't succeed,
TRIFLORA.

From Bad Sex to Worse
February 2002

About a year ago I wrote complaining about the shabby treatment the literary community had afforded our favourite genus. Despite a plea for some enrichment of rhododendron in literature (it did stimulate one of our members, Margaret de Weese, to find the muse and pen a poem and a sensitive one at that) and despite our endorsement of a collective noun for rhododendrons, I have to report that matters are now very much worse.

In the Globe and Mail on 19 January 2002 there was an article "Stallions and Rising Sap" by Sandra Martin, which set out to find the worst written sex scene in Canadian literature. To help her with this dubious task she enlisted the prejudices of Susan Swan, an author and university professor, and she included on her jury a man – a publisher – Sam Hiyate.

143

In pseudo-academic fashion they began by defining their terms of reference. The task was to "ferret out pretentious, clichéd, implausible and boring descriptions of sexual intimacy." I have no strong feelings on their selections – but can you believe Leonard Cohen (yes), Hugh MacLennan and Margaret Laurence as the winners? The standard by which these authors were measured was their proclivity to use "Rhododendron Language." This for the uninitiated is *"lush, florid and pretentious."* Notice how attracted they are to the word "pretentious", which I understand to mean, "making an excessive claim to great merit or importance".

Well, maybe some of the sex scenes in the novels are pretentious – I suspect one or other of the copulating participants has felt the word could properly be used more often than is politic to admit – but to label my *R. yakushimanum* pretentious stretches the boundaries of any and all poetic license. We rhododendron growers are the first to acknowledge that not all our plants can lay claim to great merit or importance and that is why we rate our plants. We are the critics of the artistry of nature in rhododendrons. We use a standard that is subjective in the extreme but does not slight any other living group (only a few of the hybridizers would disagree with this), nor do we rate our rhodos against roses or tulips or boudoir gymnastics.

Therefore, I suggest that the professional critics of literature develop a rating system which has defensible terms of reference or standards. Throwing down the gauntlet, hoping for some genuine appreciation of judicious seeding, (tennis not botany), let's suggest that we give the first number for "Originality", the second for "Plot" and the third for "Language" and then, acknowledging that literature is more complex than rhododendrons, we will allot them a fourth rating for "Sex Scenes". 5 means 'excellent' and 1 means 'not worth reading'. Mordecai Richler's *The Apprenticeship of Duddy Kravitz* might get a 3/4/4/4. Margaret Atwood's *The Handmaid's Tale* might get a 5/4/5/3; Michael Ondaatje's *The English Patient* 5/4/4/4 *and* Wayne

Johnston's *The Colony of Unrequited Dreams* (about Joey Smallwood) 3/4/4/0.

I may now be prompted to read Susan Swan to measure her against her own use of "rhododendron language". My somewhat dated source of information records that she has written three novels, *"The Biggest Modern Woman in the World"*, *"The Last of the Golden Girls"*, and *"The Wives of Bath"* and published two collections of short stories, *"Unfit for Paradise"* and *"Stupid Boys are Good to Relax With"*. I do admit I am now a little prejudiced.

> Pretentious and florid and lush
> For sex scenes, Swan says they make mush.
> She claims they're for rhodos
> Not stirring libidos.
> Too bad all her taste's in her tush.

B Is For *Boothia*
September 2002

Micromeres means "with small parts" and *leptocarpum* means "having small fruits". How is a plant having names like these able to hold its head up? Well, it can't. But I can – just a little ways anyway. You see, there I was vacantly deadheading a *R. charitopes* with thoughts of what might be for supper or something else equally profound, when I noticed these small yellow discs on the neighbouring plant. At first I thought they were the calyces of dying flowers but on looking more closely I saw they were whole flowers. They were flat, pansy-shaped, about a half inch across with petals of a gossamer thin waxy texture, poised on the end of very long arching pedicels, a sheaf of brown tipped stigmas protruding provocatively. I have seen more authentic looking artificial flowers. I had no idea what it might be.

The leaves were similar to its neighbour, *charitopes*. It had peeling mahogany brown bark just like *charitopes* and white undersides to the leaves but it had these odd two inch spikes with fake looking flowers at their tips – most still unopened – and it was the end of June. A quick browse through Coxes' 'Encyclopedia' was not conclusive and it was not until John Hawkins took his specs off and examined a flower and a leaf with a magnifying glass that it was pronounced to be *R. leptocarpum*. If the flowers happened on a saxifrage, it would be a winner – with an Award of Merit, a First Class Certificate, the whole array of awards. It would be a horticultural "must have". On a rhododendron it gets short shrift. "Tends to be of little horticultural merit as the flowers are generally rather small". So the book says.

Still, this surprise of a plant has given me a lift – despite all the pejoratively diminishing vocabulary associated with its name. I am delighted it is there. By the stature of the plant, it must have been there for about 20 years. It may not have bloomed before. It may just have been overlooked – with its 'small parts'. It used to be called micromeres and it used to be in the subsection *Glauca* until Dr. Cullen decided it should be in with the *Boothia* and changed its name to *leptocarpum*. Davidian has it in the *Genestierianum* Subseries, with *genestierianum* as its only partner. Greer describes neither *leptocarpum* nor *micromeres* in "Available Rhododendrons" but does list *micromeres* under the *Boothia* in the list of species. One could conclude from this that it is not worth describing. What fun we have with the kinship of rhododendrons. It is more complicated than the lineage of the European royalty.

George Forrest first discovered this species in 1922 in southeastern Tibet. It has since been found to have a wide distribution – from Yunnan to Bhutan. Kingdon Ward said it was the most common epiphytic species in the mixed forests of Assam. *Leptocarpum's* new siblings in the Boothia are few – *boothii, chrysodoron, leucaspis, megeratum* and *sulfureum*. *Leucaspis* and *megeratum* are the most commonly seen. *Leucaspis* (meaning White Shield), blooming here in February, often has its flowers browned by frost. But it is a dainty fuzzy white mound. I remember when I first saw it in bloom in the Lammle's garden. The Lammles ran Rhodoland nursery on the Pat Bay Highway, some time ago. When I noticed *leucaspis* in bloom there, I remarked on it to another customer. She clearly was looking for a hybrid with cabbage sized flowers and was totally underwhelmed at my enthusiasm over *leucaspis*. Its hybrid, 'Snow Lady' – with *ciliatum* as its mate – is a very popular choice for West Coast gardens with Bruce Maycock being El Presidento of the fan club.

Local gardeners boast of growing two forms of *megeratum*. One with tiny leaves, known as the Bodnant form is a true dwarf. At home in a rock garden, it is not often seen but is in the connoisseur's class. The more common form has larger leaves although they are still smaller than those of *leucaspis*. The flowers are brassy yellow. It has its best expression in the plant in Dora Kreiss's garden. Steve Hootman of the Rhododendron Species Foundation said that Dora's plant was the best *megeratum* he had ever seen. Everyone who knows *megeratum* seems to know that the authorities say it does well growing in an old tree stump (Dora's certainly does). Say the word *megeratum* and "rotten tree stump" will follow as surely as Jeff follows Mutt. The *Boothia* grow epiphytically as well as terrestrially and hence appreciate an open, well-drained, acidic medium.

Judy Gordon has a stunningly beautifully canary yellow flowered *R. chrysodoron*. *Chrysodoron* has the most striking blossoms of the group. It is nearly always epiphytic and so demands perfect drainage. It is also reported to be the most tender of the group. I lost my plant in the notorious freeze of February '89. Not being a large plant, it would be a good candidate for a container. It blooms early in the year – before our usual show time. If it could be held back it would certainly win a trophy.

Don Whittle has a good specimen of *sulfureum* but bemoans the fact that slugs rate it very highly also. 'Yellow Hammer' is the best-known *sulfureum* hybrid. Playfair Park is the place to see a large planting of these. 'Yellow Hammer' was probably created close to 100 years ago and until Peter Cox and Warren Berg started hybridizing for small yellow flowered lepidotes, it was about the only small flowered yellow hybrid available and was very popular. Nowadays, one rarely sees it in a nursery. It blooms reliably in the fall and many consider this a bonus.

I don't recall ever having seen *boothii*. It gets a 2/2/2 rating so perhaps that is why it is scarce. Or again, it may be just like my *leptocarpum* and is frequently overlooked.

In any event I am planning to propagate *leptocarpum* and list it as a rare species and charge an appropriate price. For those wishing to have the plant but avoid an Antiques Road Show evaluation of worth it would be worth making one. The plant has lots of cutting material and members are welcome to try to get one started. We should have a competition. This would have two components – (1) getting the plant to bloom and (2) noticing the plant when it is in bloom.

F Is For Favourites
November 2002

If I were choosing twelve rhododendrons for a city-sized new garden blessed with a couple of established trees to give summer shade, what would they be? With a choice from over 2000 or 3000 obtainable hybrids and from the 400 or so species that can be grown here, the selection is indeed difficult. There are a lot of variables to sift through; yet it does not involve a huge amount of risk, as there are so many good doers. In the end, it just comes down to personal taste – or prejudice.

The tallest rhododendron that one can get is about 2 meters high when ten years old. One must remember that rhododendrons live longer than we do and they keep growing. However, for most gardeners their vision does not stretch beyond ten years and neither does their patience. My first choice therefore is guaranteed not to bloom until at least it is twenty. We probably have room for only one or two tree-like rhododendrons (actually I end up with three biggies and that is why gardeners are usually classed as collectors rather than landscapers), so we have to pick ones that we will want to look at each and every day and ones that will impress the sophisticatedly superior visitors to our garden. So to start, I would opt for *R. macabeanum*. Its leaves are 20/25 cm long and half as wide and they have whitish indumentum on the undersides. It is effective, therefore, to plant it where, in time, we can walk under the foliage. The tops of the leaves are dark green and shiny. The flowers vary from cream to a strong yellow. In one of Peter Cox's books he advises that the paler forms should be avoided. This is, by and large, a gratuitously useless bit of advice as most plants of *macabeanum* that are available in nurseries are grown from seed and it is very seldom that a blooming sized plant is available. If such a plant were available, it would be a sizeable one and would involve the physical difficulty of moving the plant and the painful financial difficulty of moving the buyer's funds to the grower's. The best one can do is to get a known clone that is cutting grown or grafted or, more likely, seedlings that have been hand pollinated. *Macabeanum* blooms in March and we must remember that when choosing the next eleven.

I really do think we have to have two more big rhododendrons. Having three statuesque specimens gives us vertical structure in the landscape and leaves room for incorporating all the choice underplanting that will give complementary colour and texture all year round. In this idyllic setting there are no deer, or if there are, they are either concrete or have been to Jenny Craig's.

The other two Rhodos that I would pick would be 'Lem's Monarch' and the pink form of *R. auriculatum*. This latter plant has large long somewhat fuzzy leaves that in themselves make a statement. *Auriculatum* blooms in August. Our garden will be without rhododendron bloom for a maximum of only three months if we make the appropriate choices, as we will see. "Lem's Monarch' is a May/June bloomer. The large flowers are soft pink with a darker pink picotee rim. We have to have a bloom in July and I would pick the red hybrid 'Good News'. It is not too large, will take some sun and will look good with light coloured annuals.

To start the rhododendron season I don't think you can better 'Lee's Scarlet'. The most popular early bloomer is 'Rosamundi'. Why 'Lee's Scarlet' does not hold this honour I have never understood. It probably has the same parents as 'Rosamundi' but has a deeper coloured flower and better meets our cultural need for Ho Ho Ho hues at Christmas. 'Lee's Scarlet will give us that – not in great amount as it blooms for close to four months – from November to March – with a succession of opening blossoms rather than in one big splurge.

Our garden during the short sombre days of the early year will be brimming with colour. There will be snowdrops and daffodils and tulips (no deer), hellebores and primroses and witch hazel and cyclamen. In one of the sunnier spots, one that we see or pass by every day, I would place a 'Snow Lady'. In the shade it will be leggy but with good light it becomes an igloo – a white mound on which nary a leaf will be seen. 'Snow Lady', being a lepidote, does not have large trusses but often has three or even four flower clusters at each branch terminal. The chocolate coloured anthers give a startling contrast. Close to 'Snow Lady' I would put a 'Razorbill' – my wife's favourite rhododendron. In fact, I would put three 'Razorbills'; it is small. It has the most unusual tubular pink firecrackers, borne in profusion. This is a special plant for me as I brought it back from Scotland many years ago and propagated a few that fortunately went to better homes. I lost the original plant but got a little one back, an offspring of my offspring.

Now we are at the spring equinox and the choices are virtually unlimited. I think we have to go with the masses and choose the most popular of the reds – 'Taurus'. Great dark shiny tough foliage, beetroot buds and pure primary red flowers with not the slightest hint of blue. But because it is a big plant and we are running out of space, I may have to veto it and go for the more modest sized 'Rubicon'. It has the same flower colour and has the kind of dark rugose foliage that meets the criteria of the growers of perennial herbaceous plants.

You will note that this chosen baker's dozen has no evergreen or deciduous azaleas. I'm afraid that this exercise is just like a Prime Minister choosing a cabinet; someone has to be left out and the political wrath of those not represented will have to be faced, although never mollified. Probably over represented (cf Prince Edward Island) are the lepidotes and my next five choices are of this ilk. These are 'Ginny Gee', 'Blaney's Blue', *R. rigidum, R. hanceanum,* and *R. campylogynum.* 'Ginny Gee' is certainly one of the best small rhododendrons to grace our gardens. Draped over a big rock or wedged between two big rocks, it is a complete synthesis of realism and abstraction. Pink and white, inside and out, it is a profusion of contentment. *Hanceanum* is more subdued but if anything a neater plant then 'Ginny Gee', and after its show of smallish pansy-like cream flowers it gives a rich ambience to its locale with its bronzy new leaves.

We bemoan the lack of a true gentian blue in the genus rhododendron but we will cavil less when we see a four or five foot 'Blaney's Blue' in flower – a potential deadheading nightmare. Alongside this place the blue leafed form of *rigidum* is selected – the one with globs of white flowers and chocolate anthers, in contemporary landscaping parlance, 'colour echoing' our earlier 'Snow Lady'.

The last little gem of a lepidote is *campylogynum.* This species comes in the tiniest of forms and ranges from 20 cm to those that may get to a meter tall. I don't care which form is chosen. They are all choice. Just make sure it has perfect drainage, never dries out and never even catches a glimpse of granular fertilizer. Use a little Alaska Fish fertilizer, and put it in a sunny spot.

I suppose it would be like having a missing front tooth if we did not have a stereotypical medium sized May blooming full trussed pink show off. There are hundreds that would fill the bill. I give my vote to 'Fantastica'. There is colour gradation in the flower; it is a dependable bloomer, is not weevil fodder and does not fade too badly. I could be easily persuaded to go for other varieties and I may pass this one on when it reaches its late teens to another compulsive fanatic who has more space.

We also must have a really good yellow and without question my choice is 'Nancy Evans'. Not too big, wider than tall and as reliable a bloomer as the nefarious 'Herb Robert'. Its buds are brick red opening to a hot yellow. Nancy is a rent payer if ever there was one.

There we are – selection is made. Only the companions – the lilies and the hostas and the roses and clematis need to be chosen. Our dozen has stretched to 14 but is that not the way of the world? We always have to squeeze in just a couple more than we originally planned for and no doubt a home will still have to be found for the odd impulse purchase and all those countless indigents we win in raffles. I hate it when the server in a restaurant admonishes me to 'Enjoy'. But how else can I conclude than with that admonition?

M is for *Maddenii*
December 2002

"Until you understand a writer's ignorance, presume yourself understanding of his ignorance." Wise words. The ones that follow come from a not well-experienced grower of the group of rhododendrons known as *R. maddeniis*. Nevertheless, I will now go charging off in all directions.

There does not appear to be much known about Lt. Col. E. Madden, apart from dying in 1856. He was what Davidian calls "a traveller in India." However, he has left his name to, perhaps, the most taxonomically confusing tribe of rhododendrons in the whole genus. For example, when botanists made the first stab at classification (Hutchison at Kew in the 1920's), there were 30 species in one of the *Maddenii* groups. That was reduced to 12 in 1980 and it looks like it may be decided in the next little while that there are only two or three species. These wild plants vary considerably but in a seemingly even and continuous flux.

The *Maddeniis* are mostly open, rangy, straggly shrubs that grow quite often epiphytically on other rhododendrons or associated trees. As a group they prefer semi-tropical areas. The only one I ever saw growing wild was right on the north-eastern border of Thailand and Myanmar at 1800 metres where the lowest temperature ever recorded was 5°C. They are not very cold hardy but there are a few that we can grow almost with impunity in the Victoria area.

Let's list these first and then mention some of the more flamboyant, tenderer ones: *R. burmanicum, R. ciliatum, R. fletcherianum, R. johnstoneanum,* and *R. valentinianum.* All of these, I grow outside without any real difficulty, although I have lost plants in exposed situations and in long cold windy periods (1989). Good drainage is vital.

Cox now says that what we have been growing as *burmanicum* 'Glendoick' (named for his nursery/estate in Scotland) is a hybrid. For the purist this is not a very good start, but 'Glendoick' is said to be a better yellow and a hardier plant than the true species so I choose not to examine its passport too closely.

In appearance *ciliatum* looks a lot like *R. moupinense* – with hairier leaves. They are closely related but *moupinense* is in its own subsection. I would not be surprised that when DNA profiling is done, *ciliatum* will prove to be closer to *moupinense* than to some of the larger plants in the Maddenia. In any event it is a choice, small, softly pink early bloomer that needs a nice sheltered spot. *Fletcherianum* is a low grower with thick bristly leaves and significant yellow flowers and appears in the lineage of many hybrids. I still call it *fletcherianum.* Some drop the 'i' but I first knew it with that vowel included and old habits die hard and besides it's most likely correct. *Johnstoneanum* can get quite large. There is a double form called 'Double Diamond', that is in the connoisseur's class, with flowers like gardenias but it is considerably less hardy than the white to cream trumpeted one we see more commonly in local gardens. *Valentinianum* has interesting peeling bark and pleasing yellow flowers. It blooms in January/February so it must not be in a frost pocket. It also has lots of progeny.

Now, we come to the show-offs – a characterization that some envious onlookers often ascribe to their growers. *R. Lindleyi* have large trumpets of lily-like flowers, often only two or three in the truss. The ones with whitish flowers are usually powerfully fragrant. The ones with yellowish flowers are usually scentless.

On the subject of scent, I recall a caution that I have long wanted to put to the test. Unfortunately, I have never had more than two in bloom at any one time. The cautioner had a very refined nose and warned that the combined aroma of many different varieties blooming simultaneously resulted in the 'smell of horse piss'.

I always have a smile to myself when *R. lindleyi* is mentioned. About 20 years ago, on a pilgrimage that is now ritual, a group from the club was in Daphne Gibson's (Ken's mother) garden in Tofino. One of our senior members – senior both in age and professional reputation – was Ernie Lythgoe. Ernie was crouched down, lecturing in his best Oak Bay High teacher manner, on the finer points of *lindleyi*. In particular we were to note the 'potter's thumb marks' at the base of the corolla. Maybe the fragrance really went to his head but he pulled the flower right off the plant. Silence. In any event *lindleyi* is a fine thing to have – even if only for a short while.

A close relative of *lindleyi* is *R. nuttallii*. Here the flowers are not only 12 cm long but equally wide. 'Hamish Robertson' is a *nuttallii* cross and was registered under that name by our late member, Hamish Robertson. It is a spectacular plant. The flowers are huge with a blending of white, purple, yellow and pink. The new foliage is violet. Some of our members are trying to increase its availability.

Maddenii ssp. *Maddenii*, in the best forms, has a pink/purple base to the trumpets on the outside and a yellow throat on the inside. The spectacular flowers are up to 12 cm.

154

(5 in.) long. The hardier subspecies *R. crassum*, we can grow outside, and being a June bloomer it is a good choice for even the small garden. It will get to be quite tall but can be kept to an upright shape so the area it needs is relatively small. *R. odoriferum* and *R. manipurense* were species under the old classification but are now reduced in rank to forms of *crassum*. I still like to keep the old names and grow plants with these labels on them. They have not bloomed for me yet.

One of the most surprising and crowd stopping flowers on a rhododendron belongs to *R. rhabdotum*, now classified as a variety of *R. dalhousiae*. This plant should be the mascot of a military regiment or a police force as the flowers have a broad red stripe running down the middle of each corolla lobe from petal tip to calyx – or from belt to boot strap. And it blooms in July! We once had a big plant of this gem. It got to be over two metres (6 feet) high and moving its huge pot to shelter every winter became a very onerous business. One winter it died from hypothermia.

One of the most satisfactory plants I grow as a pot plant is *R. taronense*. This name is now sunk under the name *R. dendricola*. Gary Hadfield gave me this plant six or seven years ago. As I write, I can look out the window and see it boasting a flower bud at every tip. The plant is about a metre wide and high. The leaves are "bullate", i.e. having a puckered appearance. The flowers are pleasantly smelly, white, of respectable size but not huge. You may recall that our latest winter occurred last March. We had several nights of below freezing temperatures, one night going to -6°C. *Taronense* came through this with only a few flower buds damaged.

A larger plant, with even more bullate foliage and with one of the most pleasing smells of all the *Maddenia* is *R. edgeworthii*. I am back in my childhood days spooning my mother's nutmeg redolent egg custard when in the presence of the flowering *edgeworthii*. I think if I were on a desert island and could have only one rhododendron it would be *edgeworthii*.

There are others worthy of mention but both the reader's patience and mine are reaching exhaustion. I should, however, mention that the *Maddeniis* were popular with the Victorian gentry in Britain where they were grown as conservatory plants. Many hybrids were created. Some are lost but some are still grown and have become widely sought after. Many will know or recognize 'Fragrantissimum', 'Lady Alice Fitzwilliams', 'Countess of Haddington', 'Forsterianum'. These can all be used to contribute to the aromatic mélange. You have been warned. And there are newer ones of great merit – 'Else Frye' and 'Mi Amor', for example, and watch for some of the New Zealand plants that are becoming available. One of the most interesting blooms in our garden last year was 'Felicity Fair'– probably only half a maddenii – but its peach trumpets and bold shiny foliage make it "a good thing".

Our new $1000 per month Poet Laureate, George Bowering may be thought by some to be irreverent, by others irrelevant, but I am looking forward to what he has to say. He already said something that encouraged me to write this. He observed that those who stick to only what they know never learn anything.

Pride and Prejudice
January 2003

When the *Endeavour* reached Australia on Cook's epic first voyage, Joseph Banks, the biologist, was dutifully recording in his journal the ship's approach to this almost unknown land. The expectations of the crew about the natives had been conditioned by the sketchy reports of the two or three occasions of prior contact. In particular, the travelogue of William Dampier, a privateer, which was part of the *Endeavour's* library, contained very disparaging commentary on the Aborigines. They were "enormously black", Dampier wrote. Banks, a more discerning observer noted, "So far did the prejudices which we had built on the

Dampiers account influence us that we fancied we could see their Colour when we could scarce distinguish whether or not they were men." On the same day, he also noted, that while he and a few others still dreamed of finding a southern continent, "...the rest begin to sigh for roast beef." The *Endeavour* had been away from England for 18 months. Prejudgment and nostalgia.

It is true that often we are conditioned to expect some result or sensual impact before we have actually experienced it – some even start to cry before the onion is cut – and most of us yearn for the old standbys, taking pride in the things that are most familiar to us.

When we were first planting a few ornamentals in this patch of bush that we now inflatedly call a garden – I had an *Endeavour's* prejudice about purple foliage. This had resulted from association with a landscape architect who must have eaten some rotten beets as a youngster because he hated all things purple with a passion. Purples created black holes in the landscape – and the West Coast was a landscape, in large, already replete with black from the unlit foliage of cedar and fir. Purple was out – gold brightened up the vista – and gold was in. Also, we knew gold well as we had had a couple of Golden Pfritzer junipers that lurked under the snow at our house in Ottawa. There is no doubt we thought of golden junipers as the roast beef of suburban gardens.

There were a few rhododendrons that I was preconditioned not to like. 'Vulcan' and 'Ernie Dee' come to mind. My prejudice has since been on trial and in both these examples I have come around. 'Vulcan' is a rent paying user-friendly plant. It is a June bloomer and it is dense, well foliaged, floriferous and is certainly one of the easiest rhododendrons to grow. 'Ernie Dee', a small flowered lepidote, blooms for three months in the fall and two months in the spring. Its great sin is that its flowers are mauvey-lilac. Every gardener with a British background knows to despise the colour mauve – especially on a rhododendron. This aversion is instilled most probably because of the ubiquity of *R. ponticum*. Its mauve flowers are therefore, in the minds of the elite horticultural opinion moulders, definitely non-U. (There, I have really dated myself). *Ponticum* is linked to the proliferation of the proletariat and absence of refinement in breeding. It is ironic that the pinkish mauve of the common heather is quite acceptable. Heather provides good honey and cover for game birds. Therein the irony of the no mauve movement is further compounded when it is remembered that *ponticum* was introduced to provide just that very thing – cover for game. As I said, I have seen the light and have discarded the canon Law of Mauve Proscription. 'Ernie Dee' is now as welcome as the flowers in November. 'Ernie's' happy face beams on its neighbours for four or five months and I have never seen a bird chased away by it. And, although it is not choice deer fodder, I have disturbed a doe asleep cozied up to its aromatic foliage.

My early mentors in rhododendron growing were certainly people of taste and learning. Among them were Albert de Mezey, Clive Justice, Ernie Lythgoe, Stewart Holland and Peggy Abkhazi. I had long listenings with Clive on his retracing the rhododendron-strewn path in Sikkim taken by Joseph Hooker in 1848-49; Stewart Holland's normally studious eyes glazed over when he talked about *R. augustinii* and *R. thomsonii*; Ernie Lythgoe drove up to our place one day with a six foot wide rhododendron on his trailer. Would we like to naturalize it? He had grown it from seed as that most sought after rhododendron, *R. yakushimanum* and clearly the bees had interfered. Not to belittle Ernie's generosity but he was not going to grow an unrated hybrid in his garden. It's actually a fine plant and is now addressed as 'Lythgoe's Legacy'. Albert de Mezey spent considerable sums importing the F.C.C. and A.M. forms of species from nurseries like Reuthes of England. From these he made hybrids which in their creator's eyes had superior status. In the Abkhazi garden, the rhododendron alpha and omega were the January *R. dauricum* and the August *R. auriculatum*. I learned that those who knew, grew species. The assumption was that what nature had taken 60 million years to perfect could never be equaled by tampering from humans – except in a few individual cases. Hybrids, by and large, were for parking lots and industrial estates.

I probably misheard their message, a message amplified by not being able to find any species rhododendrons in local nurseries. I probably thought that the hybrids that were available were merely *ponticums* with more pronounceable names. Perhaps if I had known Dave Dougan at that early stage I would have had a more open mind. Dave always stresses that he doesn't give a hoot (Dave sometimes says it more forcefully than that) whether a plant is a species or a hybrid, and I have to repeat his declaration that he would rather grow spinach than *R. proteoides*. It is more rewarding.

Nowadays, I think I am very open-minded and completely without prejudice and admit to just a little pride. If you want to listen I will bend your ear off with endless advice on what should be in your garden. There is a quote in the new book on Peggy Abkhazi, "A Curious Life" by Katherine Gordon, which is appropriate. Princess Abkhazi wrote, "There are some odd facets to life, and one runs into the oddest characters – knowing all the time that one's own character is just as odd."

Don't forget the roast beef.

The Tube of Toothpaste
November 2003

I wish that there were more things in life that were like a tube of toothpaste. Routinely, I go to the ever-growing grocery list on the side of the fridge and add "toothpaste". Two weeks later, I am still getting another squeeze out of the old tube. There are very few things in this consumer-driven society of ours that keep on giving a little more the way the tube of toothpaste does. Someone said that a frugal cook squeezes a lemon until the pips squeak but it's easy to feel frugal with the tube of toothpaste.

159

Families and friends are notable givers of the extra squeeze. Pets often give good returns on emotional investment, but in the inert category it's hard to think of many things that give that little bit more than expected.

I think gardens can be likened to the tube of toothpaste. At any rate, in my experience, the garden's rate of return increases with time. Time, helped a little by our labour, usually results in the returns getting bigger and better each year. I know a time will come when things are just too big and cramped and overgrown but even after more than a quarter century, my garden hasn't reached that stage yet and my personal 'best before' date will surely come, if it's not already reached, before that of the garden's.

You often hear it said, "There is no such thing as an instant garden". In my opinion that's a very happy situation. An instant garden implies constancy – it has already achieved its limit. There will never be that pleasant raising of eyebrows when that extra, unexpected extrusion is laid on the toothbrush.

I would classify some plants as being of the toothpaste tube genre. The English primrose (*primula vulgaris*) always surprises me with its bountiful giving. It shows a bloom for the six darkest months of the year. *Cyclamen hederifolium* (*neapolitanum*) is a ten-month plant. Its heart shaped leaves have silver markings – as individual as our fingerprints – and they persist for 10 months. It flowers for over three months – from August to November. *Potentilla fruticosa* blooms from May until October as do many of the *cistus*.

Among rhododendrons, I would put 'Ernie Dee' in the toothpaste class. He blooms for five months – half in the fall and half in the spring. 'Lee's Scarlet' is another plant that seems to give that unexpected extra, blooming for five months over the winter. 'Noyo Brave' always surprises me with its polished decorum. It is as nattily dressed as a behind-the-bench NHL head coach. I would pick 'Dreamland' as the female equivalent in sartorial refinement. 'Nancy Evans' always gives more than she gets. I don't know who 'Nancy Evans' is in human terms, but I would surely like to give her

160

a big squeeze for all the surplus squeezes she has given me. (Note: I now know she was the wife of the Governor of Washington State.)

Arbutus trees keep on giving – leaves and bark and berries and even branches – but this is not a true gift like that bonus from the toothpaste tube. It takes considerable effort to blow all of this detritus onto the neighbours' property. It does, however, make good mulch.

On the other hand, some things are always taking. Have you noticed how much it now costs to let the bank use your money? Service charges are bigger than interest payments. Banks are more like vacuum cleaners than toothpaste tubes. And for some strange reason, the dues we pay to get this newsletter seem to keep sucking in more of our hard earned cash. Thank goodness most of us think the interest we get from being a member is still worth the annual investment.

Still, it's probably best to concentrate on the things and events that perk us up with their surprising generosity rather than mope on the leech-like cupidity of our contemporary culture. "The little things are great to a little man."

A Gardener's Diary
February 2003

January

Happy New Year. My resolution is that I will have a happier garden this year. It's a bit inclement to do much about it right now but as soon as the days start to lengthen I'm really going to get on top of things. One rule will be 'No Weeds' – especially in the gravel driveway. I wish someone had given me another hoe for Christmas. A hoe is a gardener's best friend. One year's seeds are seven years' weeds. There is going to be some genetic cleansing around here. 'Herb Robert' is to be exterminated. Most geraniums are thugs. That darn ivy that we planted 20 years ago and is now 80 feet high in the Douglas fir will be exterminated. And all that is needed for that dry area where we lost a few rhododendrons last year is a simple extension on the irrigation line – half a day's work and less than a hundred bucks. I'll scare the bejabbers out of that half acre of lamium – make things a lot tidier. I must get a new pruning saw – that old one wouldn't cut tofu. It's crazy having these fruit trees and so little fruit. I'll continue this list later and keep it posted on the fridge but I hear the call that dinner is ready.

April

Some parts of the garden are truly spectacular – as good as Butchart's. I just need to get on top of those weeds – unfortunately some have already seeded. I'll go and buy three hoes and leave them at strategic places where I can wield them savagely whenever I see a weed. However, some of the hellebores and snowdrops and cyclamen seed themselves so one has to be a little restrained with the hoe. The lecture last week by that imitation Martha Stewart paragon gave me some good ideas. She really was a show-off, although quite modest about it; and she doesn't have deer. She did say she had fenced her place but she must have a pile of money. And she said she usually bought only one of any new plant and propagated it tout suite. I've got to get some order in that greenhouse of ours. It's too bad that erythronium take so long from seed. I could divide these English primroses. They do bloom for a long time and cover quite a bit of ground. My soil is pretty poor though. What I need is more humus. Still some of these Alpines seem to grow on nothing. Pity we have so much shade.

July

It's pretty hot and there is still a lot of deadheading to do. Still, they say that rhododendron seed production does not take up much energy. Deadheading sure does. If only we could get a good downpour – not a drop of rain for three weeks. These cutesy weather forecasters on TV make me sick. They are merely flunkies for the Tourist Bureau. A

162

cloud in the sky is as welcome as the West Nile virus. They don't seem to realize that the hanging baskets need watering twice a day in this hot touristy weather. I forgot to fertilize them last week. Too bad I spilt all the fish fertilizer at the back door – quite a stink although the weeds loved it. I'll need to get some more fertilizer. The humming bird feeders are just crawling with ants and I see quite a lot of wasps. It's going to be a bad year for them. No one will say anything about wasps until the Saanichton Fair – most of the tourists are gone by then. Too bad I broke the handle on the hoe. I could hear the weeds laughing at me. I really don't know why people put benches out in their gardens. I don't think I've ever sat on the one under the arbutus. It took two weeks to do all that stonework to make it an attractive place to meditate and admire the glory of the garden and now it needs a coat of urethane. There was a guy on the radio talking about low maintenance gardening. He was just like all these financial advisers. If they knew how to make money they wouldn't need to be writing books or taking a fee to talk about it on the radio. I hate having to lug hoses all over the place. I was blaming the deer for the missing flower heads on the geraniums but I now think it happened when I yanked that hose across the bed.

October

I must put a few cuttings in the propagator. Some years I've had roots on them by now. Still as dry as the Gobi desert. I spend all my time at the end of a hose. I'll need to get some new ones. With all these leaks only half the water comes out the nozzle. Too late for this year but I'll look out for sales. There seems to be a new crop of weeds every week. I wonder why the deer eat prickly things like roses and poisonous things like kalmia but they don't touch 'Herb Robert'. I notice they have had a go at my big *euphorbia mellifera*. Their tongues must be glued to their lips with latex. If I so much as touch it, I break out in an agony of a rash. I sure miss my trusty scuffle hoe. A shovel is not nearly as wieldy. The Himalayan blackberries have canes as

163

thick as the shovel handle and if I don't get them dug out we will soon not be able to get up the driveway. Still, blackberries with brown sugar with the morning cereal is pretty good fodder. Canada is certainly multicultural and I know why we are such a great melting pot. Plants and people just take root here. Scotch broom and English Ivy and Himalayan blackberries think this is paradise. There is all this push on to grow native plants but I can't keep *cornus canadensis* alive for more than a year. Maybe I should give up gardening and become an advisor.

January

Pity it's not gardening weather. My son dressed up in a Santa Claus suit on Christmas Day and marched in with a staff in each hand each covered with a shopping bag and a red ribbon. He shouted, "Hoe, hoe." And that is what they were. Pity there were not three of them. "Hoe, Hoe, Hoe." sounds better.

P is For *Pontica* (Part I)
April 2003

A basic belief, instilled in every Scot of my generation, was that our race could survive in any clime, in any regime, in any soil. Given the slightest opportunity a Scot would put his roots down anywhere.

The *Pontica* subsection of the Rhododendron genus is a bit like a Scot. More properly, it should perhaps be phrased the other way round. There are members of the *Pontica* all over the map. Almost anywhere a rhododendron will grow, *Pontica* will have a settlement. Such a sweeping biogeographical claim will be instantly challenged by those of different national origins, who will point out that no member of the *Pontica* is known in that great centre of rhododendron diversity – the Sino-Himalayan region. To this, a Scot would reply that the economic incentive – the promise of a bawbee or two – wasn't very great in that part of the world in the

164

heyday of migration – and if it had only been known that the Gurkhas of Nepal wore kilts, the Scots would have been over there as fast as they could down a dram – or two.

Why there are no *Pontica* in these high regions (Ted Irving calls them "the regions of extreme relief") is a complex matter. It is a subject that may be addressed by speakers at our upcoming 2005 convention. Dr. Ben Hall from the University of Washington will be talking about the latest studies of DNA in rhododendrons. The analysis of DNA is proving to be a great new tool in helping to solve the mysteries of plant evolution and distribution.

It is not easy for plebs like me, who think in time intervals of hours, days, years or, at most, generations, to grasp intervals of millions of years. When we think of current and past biogeography we have to make the effort to imagine these huge time spans. Rhododendron fossils date back about 55 million years – to just about the time the dinosaurs became extinct. A lot has happened to our planet in 55 million years. Rhododendrons have mutated, moved around, been sexually promiscuous, flourished and perished. They currently inhabit our globe in about 1000 different sorts. These, we call species. In the last 200 years – not even a blip in this evolutionary time scale – we humans have been presumptuously monkeying around with these 1000, producing a much larger number of hybrids. These we are now growing with wanton abandon.

About 14 of the 1000 species have been grouped together by our taxonomists to form a subsection of the genus Rhododendron called the *Pontica*. Of all the subsections this one has the widest geographical distribution – western and eastern North America, northeastern Asia, Asia Minor, Siberia, Japan and Taiwan.

The *Pontica* subsection takes its name from the species *R. ponticum*, a name known to everyone who has ever lived in or visited Scotland, England, Ireland or Wales. Once when visiting the latter, I noticed an advertisement in a local paper calling for the application of herbicide to *ponticum* – a pernicious weed. *Ponticum* was introduced to the British

165

Isles to provide cover for game birds so that the landed gentry could have better shooting. If the gentry had not cut down all the trees that covered the land there would have been no need to try to recover it. Anyway, the immigrant *ponticum* was so successful in covering up bare land that eradication had to be practiced once again. Readers who questioned the opening analogy of Scots and *ponticum* may now be in full agreement with its appropriateness.

The provenance of *ponticum* is the Caucasus and northern Turkey. David Leach wrote a fascinating article entitled "The Two Thousand Year Curse of the Rhododendron". One section of this article features *ponticum* as the villain. In 401 B.C. the Greek military commander Xenophone was retreating from Babylon. Near Trebizond, on the coast of the Black Sea, his pursued army came across "great quantities of beehives." Xenophone wrote, "All the soldiers who ate of the honeycombs lost their senses, and were seized with vomiting and purging, none of them being able to stand on their legs. Those who ate but a little were like men drunk, and those who ate much, like madmen, and some like dying persons. In this condition great numbers lay on the ground, as if there had been a defeat, and the sorrow was general. The next day, none of them died, but recovered their senses about the same hour they were seized; and the third and fourth day they got up as if they had taken a strong potion." Fortunately for Xenophone, his pursuers did not find him or his horizontally heaving army and he successfully completed his retreat.

Three hundred and thirty five years later, three Roman armies under Pompey camped at almost the precise spot that Xenophone had. This time the antagonist, the King of Pontus, with his army, massacred the prostrated Romans. Caveat *ponticum*.

Ponticum has such a bad reputation that it is seldom planted nowadays apart from the variegated leaf forms which are proving to be quite popular. However, in the Victoria area and elsewhere, *ponticum* (see below for an alert) is ubiquitous. Most of the rhododendrons imported to this area prior to WWII were grafted plants. The understock was usually *ponticum*. The reasons for choosing *ponticum* for understock were its ease of rooting as a cutting and its eagerness to grow from seed. This vigour is such that it has subsequently overwhelmed the desired grafted material and *ponticum* flourishes with its mauve flowers held just as high as the head of the King of Pontus.

Holding *ponticum* as the "mother of evil plants" has recently taken a bit of a hit. Perhaps the "mother" connotation may be acceptable but there could also be a "father" involved. David Chamberlain of the Royal Botanic Garden, Edinburgh, gave a talk at the 1999 International Rhododendron Species Symposium in which he cited some studies that had been done by a doctoral student at St. Andrews University in Scotland. It had been long known that plants from the Turkish population of *ponticum* did not do well in the British Isles. The Turkish *ponticum* is, in fact, quite a tender plant. How then were the introductions that were made in the 1800's so successful? These earlier introductions had come from what were thought to be populations of *ponticum* growing on the Iberian Peninsula that reach as far south as Gibraltar. Comparing the DNA of the British weed plants with the DNA of Turkish plants and with the DNA of other members of the subsection showed that the weeds were hybrids with the paternal DNA coming from *R. catawbiense* – a native of eastern North America! What was thought to be *ponticum* was the result of the mating of these two closely related species. *R. catawbiense* is famous for its gift of extreme hardiness to its hybrids. In the early days of hybridization it, and its close cousin *R. caucasicum*, gave rise to a group of hybrids known as 'The Ironclads', some of which are still popular today. The addition of *catawbiense* to *ponticum* gives an outstanding example of what is known as "hybrid vigour". Caveat *ponticum* x *catawbiense*.

The species *catawbiense* in its more compact forms is a much better garden plant than the heretofore-named *ponticum*. Two forms are common in cultivation –

167

catawbiense 'Album' and *catawbiense* 'Boursault', the latter having lilac-purple flowers. Some suggest these are hybrids too, but they still go under the specific name. A plant known as 'Roseum Elegans' may also be a form of *catawbiense*. Joseph Gable of Pennsylvania raised 'Catalga' from the seed of the wild white form and it is credited with being the most attractive of all. These plants are particularly useful for having a latish blooming time – late May into June. One of the toughest and easiest to grow of all rhododendrons is 'Cunningham's White'. This is a cross between *caucasicum* and *ponticum* and is now used extensively as understock for grafting, particularly in Europe. A plant with 'Cunningham's White' roots is claimed to be more cold hardy, less prone to root rot and have more intense colour in the flower.

In North Carolina the hills are a mass of *catawbiense*. One writer claims that the *catawbiense* bloom is the finest floral display in all of North America, the entire vista becoming a billowing ocean of mauve rhododendrons.

P Is For *Pontica* (Part II)
May 2003

Around these parts, *R. caucasicum* is rarely seen. David Leach says it is most often found in the filing cases of herbariums. Its importance in our gardens is, however, huge. It is a parent of our best early blooming hybrids. My crusade to have our gardens populated with winter blooming rhododendrons was boosted this past winter by the outstanding performance of 'Nobleanum Coccineum', 'Lee's Scarlet' and 'Rosamundi'. The first named opened its first bloom on the 15th October, the second named on the 15th November and 'Rosamundi' just before Christmas. There were still blooms on all of them in early March. Any shrub that blooms for over three months in wintertime deserves prime garden space. It is true that 2002-3 has been one of the mildest winters ever and not one of the flowers in our garden suffered browning from frost.

The true *caucasicum* has thinly textured pale yellow flowers and is seldom more than a metre high. Its yellow genes are recessive but it passes on its compactness, hardiness and some indumentum to its progeny.

Closely related to *caucasicum* is *R. aureum. Aureum* is a very successful plant in inhospitable parts of the world. It covers great stretches of the steppes and hillsides of Siberia, northern China and northern Japan. I find it hard to grow, probably because it scorns the cushiness of our conditions. Its creeping, mounding habit has evolved to suit its Spartan homelands.

Another member of the *Pontica* that can only be called a "collector's plant" in most temperate gardens is *R. brachycarpum. Brachycarpum* lays claim to being the most cold hardy of all rhododendrons. In the last 25 years it has received great exposure in rhododendron literature due to the successful developmental efforts of Dr. Tigerstedt of Helsinki, Finland. He has raised countless thousands of seedlings of this species and crosses them with other hardy varieties. These he plants out and lets the severe Finnish winter cull out the weaklings. Few succeed but the survivors have given a whole new dimension to gardens with continentally cold winters. Dr. Tigerstedt was awarded the Gold Medal by our society. Gardeners in Edmonton and Winnipeg are certain there has never been a more worthy winner of the Gold Medal. With us, *brachycarpum* survives and flowers well enough but it does everything in a great hurry; the flowers open as the new growth is being made and the display is, as a consequence, demurely hidden. It quickly sets seed and then wants to go to sleep for six or seven months and our climate keeps waking it up, causing sleep deprivation.

The taxonomical wanderings of the next species have no doubt been necessary but for most gardeners the changes have caused utter confusion, excessively long plant labels and widespread denial. Most of us continue to call our plants *R. yakushimanum, R. degronianum*, and *R. metternichii*. The classifiers insist that the first is a subspecies of the second and

169

the last name should not exist. *Metternichii* is synonymous with *degronianum*, but just to keep us hopping and buying books, *degronianum* is awarded another subspecies – *heptamerum* – (a word I have yet to use, although what I still call *metternichii* should probably be called *heptamerum* Var. *heptamerum*). If you are confused, please refer to Coxes' "Encyclopedia of Rhododendrons", and if you can work it all out and relabel your plants correctly, then you are most sincerely urged to volunteer to go through every other member's garden and do the same for them.

I'll give long odds that *yakushimanum* will still be known as that in 20 years. After all, very few plants are so loved that they have shortened nicknames. *Chrysanthemum* affectionately becomes 'Mum' and I have heard some people call *narcissi* 'Daffs', but everyone calls *yakushimanum* 'Yak'. This species stormed the horticultural scene immediately after WW2 when Lionel de Rothschild of Exbury showed it at the Royal Horticultural Society. He had obtained in the late thirties three plants (Davidian says he had only two) of this newly discovered plant from Koichiro Wada, the famous Japanese botanist. One would think that in an ancient culture like Japan the native plants would have been known and described long, long ago but here was *yakushimanum*, claimed by many to be the crème de la crème of all rhododendrons, growing on this one island, Yaku Shima, (Shima means island) at the southern end of the Japanese archipelago in unknown splendour – until the 1930s. The characteristics that make *yakushimanum* so desirable are its dense compact shape, (those coming from the peak of the island being dwarf, 18 inches at maturity, reaching four or five times that size at lower elevations), its ease of flowering, pink in bud maturing to white (the symbolism of this being cherished by gardeners), its thick, disease and bug resistant indumentum and its surprising cold hardiness. Still lower down it melds into *degronianum*, – at lower elevations the plant becomes larger – which is common on Honshu and first described in 1869 so the older name has precedence.

What I grow as *degronianum* has longer leaves and more stature but of such regular shape that it looks as if sheared. The flowers are darker pink than what I call *yakushimanum* but that is academic, as of the two 30 year old plants we have, one has never flowered and the other has had, at most, half a dozen blooms.

What I grow as *metternichii* blooms well after reaching about ten years of age. *Metternichii* has seven lobes in its corolla, *degronianum* five, but according to the taxonomists that is not of enough importance to give *metternichii* specific or even subspecific status. The indumentum on this plant is not woolly like *yakushimanum's* but looks as if it has been plated with bronze or gold.

Probably the second most sought after member of the *Pontica* tribe is *R. makinoi*. This is a rare plant in cultivation as it is very hard to propagate from cuttings and is not easy to keep in a thrifty, unchlorotic state in our gardens. The leaves of makinoi are the narrowest of the genus. (*roxianum* var. *oreonastes* might dispute this). It blooms in late May with acceptable pink flowers but it is the exotic spikiness of this smallish shrub that makes it so desirable.

With a similar spiky habit, *R. hyperythrum* from Taiwan is a good candidate for a prominent spot. This plant is free flowering when it comes of age (10 or so). I have not seen enough of it to judge for myself but most writers claim the whitest forms are the best. (I sometimes wonder if some of the more recent authors merely copy what has been said before). The form I grow has a tinge of pink in the opening flowers. I think I should claim this as a sought after feature and say it is the best form. *Hyperythrum* likes an open situation – more than mine currently has. It is claimed it will do well in hotter summers than ours and colder winters than ours. As it roots from cuttings fairly easily I do wonder why it is not seen more often.

The latest blooming member of the Pontica is *R. ungernii* – opening in July. This grows in the same geographic area as *ponticum*. One can tell they are related but it is easily identified with its white indumented underwear. It gets to be two or more metres high. The flowers are almost white with a trace of yellow and perhaps pink.

Another member of the Pontica coming from this same part of the world is what I call the "vodka" rhododendron – *R. smirnowii*. About the same size as *ungernii* it has an indumentum as thick as *yakushimanum's*. The flowers are a strong pink. It is a good garden plant. David Leach produced a hybrid of *smirnowii* with *yakushimanum*, which he named 'Crete'. In my opinion this is one of the best Yak hybrids ever.

The penultimate plant to be described is our own *R. macrophyllum*. It is one of the great ironies of horticulture that a plant that grows wild 50 miles from here is so reluctant to pay taxes in Victoria. I despair of this plant. Dora Kreiss grows it well at Sooke, Brian Saunders grows it well at Cowichan Lake. It survived for a few years at the University Gardens. John Dickman grows the rare, choice, white form at the side of his lake at Metchosin. With me it is evanescent. When one sees the abandon with which it grows in Washington State along the Hood Canal and on the littoral sands of salt-sprayed Oregon, one would think it would thrive with the TLC it gets in the City Of Gardens. It seems that that is just what it does not want; it revels in neglect.

The first Westerner to note *macrophyllum* was Archibald Menzies. Menzies was the doctor and botanist on Vancouver's ship *Discovery* and he recorded and collected *macrophyllum* on May 4, 1792. *Macrophyllum* means 'big leaf' and so it was Menzies nomenclature – as none of the Asiatic rhododendrons were known at that time. It is at its northern limit with us on Vancouver Island. Its southern extreme is Monterey County in California. It was not described adequately enough for Menzies to get his name after the plant. (Thank goodness he got his kudos with the *arbutus*). Subsequently, Joseph Hooker published an account of the plant under the name *R. californicum*, which was subsequently officially sunk although it does crop up from time to time.

There has been more written about *macrophyllum*, I think, than any other rhododendron so I will say no more than urge anyone who has not seen the plants at Rhododendron Lake, south of Parksville, to do so.

The last of the Pontica to be mentioned is *R. maximum*. To eastern North Americans this is the most familiar of all rhododendrons. I believe it is indigenous in Nova Scotia and Quebec; that is its northern limit. It becomes a much larger plant as it goes south and in Georgia reaches 40 feet. It is often referred to as the 'Rosebay Rhododendron'. The pink to white flowers are relatively small and appear after the new growth has developed. Easterners love it but it is seldom seen in our gardens.

One last thought. The Scots may have overstayed their welcome in some parts and some of the Pontica may only be of botanical interest but there are some real gems in the Subsection and by intermarrying with everything it could get close to, it has contributed most generously to the splendour of our gardens. Caveat emptor but do go after the good ones.

Tour De Force
September 2003

I've been watching on television the cycling classic – the Tour de France. This is a voluntary masochistic ordeal in which about 200 males profess to enjoy having their feet constantly orbit at about 100 times every minute so that they can leave a long trail of sweat on the encircling roads of France. The participants do this for four or five or six hours a day for three weeks and after traveling about 3400 kilometers, the fastest one arrives in Paris at the finishing line a few seconds before the disappointed runner-up.

The average rider loses around 9% of his body weight on each stage of the race despite imbibing about 20 liters of liquid while streaking unseeing through some of the most breathtaking scenery in the world. For the cyclists, it's not the scenery that takes the breath away. For them, the touring experience consists simply of flat bits, bits that go up and bits that go down, all of which have fiendishly contrived twists and bends along the way so the pedalers' eyes never see the ripening wheat, the sloping vineyards, the snowy peaks or the turquoise waters. The winner's rewards are a few Euros, three pecks on the cheek from each of a couple of statuesque demoiselles, a bunch of flowers and a stuffed lion (a big boy's teddy bear).

After watching this madness on television I go outside into my rocks and slopes and trees and soil and what I see is a troupe of rhododendrons, called a peloton in the lingo of the Tour de France. These, in the blazing July sun, have also lost 9% of their body weight from dehydration. So I have to give each of them 20 liters of water. Unfortunately, I miss out on the smooches from the misses but there are lots of bunches of flowers to fill my arms and my 'Leo' and 'Teddy Bear' are real, actively alive and thankful for my ministrations.

The competitors in the Tour de France are supported by dedicated experts in human physiology who know all about calorific intake, blood sugar levels and all the complex chemical and physical reactions that go in to driving the species homo sapiens on a bicycle at a sustained speed of nearly 50 kilometers an hour. Incidentally, the daily calorific intake of a competitor in the Tour de France is about 8000. For comparison, if my assumptions and arithmetic are correct (they were checked and amended by a friend), to drive a car at the same speed over the same distance takes up to twice as many calories per unit of weight as does cycling.

I know as little of these human machinations as I do about the ones taking place in our rhododendrons. What I do know, however, is that rhodos quickly show signs of stress if their roots either don't get enough, or can't pump enough water to keep the cells turgid so that photosynthesis and all the related and necessary cellular and intercellular combinations and divisions can carry on.

Of course, in their own habitat, the wild ones are more or less quite well looked after by nature. I lecture people that if we do only one thing to keep our plants happy, it should be to ensure that they never dry out. If I suspect the lecturee might enjoy the odd tipple, my sermon goes, "If rhodos were alcoholics and water were booze, then they would be in a dipsomaniac's paradise as they would never need to worry about where the next drink was coming from." That said, they are not really water hogs. Give a one-metre tall rhodo two to three centimeters (1 inch) of water per week and it will flourish. If you water by hand from a regular garden hose this translates to about one minute per week. It really is much easier to keep a rhododendron in top form than it is to keep a cyclist competing in the Tour de France. By and large, most of my plants probably do not get quite as much as they would like. Despite automated irrigation systems, a lot of plants still need to be watered by hand and as the summer goes on I seem to spend more time (resentfully) at the end of a hose.

One only needs to visit the Gibsons' garden at Tofino to appreciate what lots of water will do for growth and bloom. At the wholesale nursery where I buy plants the water table is about three metres below ground. They have recently dug another large well and give their plants more water than in the past. The owners claim the growth is appreciably stronger. Some people claim to give very little supplemental water and mysteriously their plants survive. There is no doubt rhododendrons will suffer a lot of stress from water deprivation before dying of dehydration. But in these situations I really think it would be more satisfactory, and kinder, to grow *cistus* or *ceanothus*.

I saw some seriously chlorotic, stunted rhododendrons in a garden that was very well cared for in the sense of fertilizer application, weed control – good husbandry all around – except for supplemental water. Had the use of fertilizer been less, the plants would have fared better. What was happening was that because there was more moisture in the plants than in the soil and a higher content of salts (nutrients) in the soil than in the plants, osmosis was drawing water from the plants back into the soil. The plants were trying to water the soil.

The winner of this year's Tour de France had already won the race four times previously. He clearly is a very fine athlete. However, a few years ago he had a serious cancer that was rampant and spreading. He was given a 40% chance of survival. What a survivor!

I was recently given a lovely big specimen of 'Mi Amor'. This rhododendron is only marginally cold hardy in Victoria gardens. Cold, however, was not the problem. The plant had been given a hot treatment by being taken for an automobile drive in temperatures of over 30 °C. The leaves looked like cured tobacco. The branches were cut back, then cut back again, and cut back once more. All that was left were two green leaves at the base. I did not give it a 20% chance of survival. Nevertheless, with these poor odds I gave the stump lots to drink.

Within a month the dormant buds showed a hint of green. Currently, there are 23 small branches on this floral Phoenix and I am going to have the bushiest, best-shaped 'Mi Amor' ever seen. It is being coddled and I plan to exhibit it in due course at our annual show. Who knows, it may even win the best in the show. It may even do that five times. Even if it doesn't win, I will give it three pecks on each of its topmost leaves.

Rhododendron anhwiense. A Conspiracy?
February 2004

Every time I walk past *R. anhwiense* I stop and admire it and say some nice words to it hoping to boost its self-esteem. It does not look to be in any great need of counselling but I'm sure it must know what people are saying about it. David Leach in Rhododendrons of the World doesn't say anything at all. He doesn't even list it in his index. Under the British Quality ratings it gets no stars – not one. Whether this is because they feel it does not merit any or just because nobody knows it is a mystery. Davidian in his stolid, robotic, standardized, unemotional style admits *anhwiense* gives a 'fine display' but is uncommon in cultivation. In the Cox's Encyclopedia, *anhwiense* is summarily dismissed with "…a very free-flowering and tough species but the foliage is rather uninteresting and tends to look pale and yellowish."

Well, on the basis of the two plants in my garden I wish I could invite all these experts to come and, without prejudice, record their impressions. Then I would like them to hold a branch of the plant and speak their thoughts aloud. Harold Greer evidently grows and knows it better than the previously mentioned authorities, as he says the "…medium sized oblong or ovate leaves are bright, shiny and waxy." So it would be nice to have Harold here to lead off with the recitations.

I have just been out looking at the older plant. It is nearly three meters across and two high. Previously, when I was taking some cuttings it was hard to find a shoot without a flower bud. I am sure if it were in bloom at the time of the annual Victoria flower count – which it isn't – it would give a space-shot boost to this spurious statistic. So I am quite glad it does not bloom until April.

Now here's a contentious comparison I'm prepared to defend. The floral impact of *anhwiense* is greater than that of *R. yakushimanum*. It has the same – perhaps not quite so intense, two-tone apple blossom pink and white elegance as *yakushimanum* but the flowers are longer lasting and as the plant is bigger it is more of a cloud than an igloo.

The province of Anwei (Anhui) in Eastern China is one of the smaller provinces and until fairly recent times was one of the least developed and poorest. It seems to have been largely bypassed by western collectors. Even in contemporary times it receives little mention. Roy Lancaster in his compendious and florally fascinating book "Travels in China, A Plantsman's Paradise" does not include plants from Anwei and yet the name means "beautiful place".

The introduction of *anhwiense* to western horticulture seems not to have been well recorded. Davidian notes that it was first collected by H.K. Ip in August 1923 but I can't find out anything about Mr. Ip. I wonder: had it been collected by Forrest or Wilson or Rock or Kingdon Ward, would it be more highly thought of? It did get an Award of Merit from the Royal Horticultural Society in 1976. Not to detract from this distinction, a sizeable proportion of all rhododendron species has been similarly honoured.

Anhwiense is currently placed in the 'Maculifera Subsection'. This Subsection contains such prized species as *R. morii, R. pachysanthum, R. pseudochrysanthum,* and *R. strigillosum.* Davidian had placed it in his 'Irroratum Series'. Chamberlain, in his 1982 revision of the classification of the genus, did not even rate it as a full species – only a subspecies of *R. maculiferum.* This latter species is found in Sichuan, Guizhou and Hubei provinces, so there is at least 10 degrees of separation of longitude between the habitats of *maculiferum* and *anhwiense.* The province of Anwei does not have a large number of endemic rhododendrons. Notable neighbours, however, are *R. fortunei* and *R. discolor.* It is unfortunate that the fossil record of rhododendrons is so sparse – mainly due to the small size of the seed and the fact that there are only very small differences in seed morphology. No doubt DNA work will shed more light on how close the relationships are between those plants to which we currently assign specific or subspecific rank.

I would not make a good taxonomist. Because I like *anhwiense*, I want it to be a full species. The plant of *maculiferum* that we have is quite large, probably four meters by four meters. It blooms in March and is useful for that early bloom. Still, it does not inspire the gasps of admiration that *anhwiense* does. If the differences between *anhwiense* and *maculiferum* are as insignificant as Chamberlain details them to be, then for my druthers, I would make *maculiferum* a subspecies of *anhwiense.*

One of the nice aspects of writing about rhododendrons is that one is afforded much more liberty to be prejudiced than if one were writing, for example, about affairs of state. That said, I would still like all the experts, past and

178

present to meet in my garden, assess *anhwiense*, dismiss their prejudices and record their thoughts on what they observe.

Oh Deer, Deer Deer
March 2004

For browsing animals the palatability of plant tissues is learnt and not instinctive. Once bitten twice shy is the way fawns learn. Young inexperienced deer are far more numerous now than they were when we first lived here. My guess is that we have about triple the number of savouring deer than we were punished with 27 years ago.

Charles Darwin made an interesting observation in his diary 'The Voyage of the Beagle'. He writes... "..*Cervus campestrus*... is exceedingly abundant, often in small herds, throughout the countries bordering the Plata and in Northern Patagonia. If a person crawling close along the ground, slowly advances towards a herd, the deer frequently, out of curiosity, approach to reconnoiter him. I have by this means, killed from one spot, three out of the same herd. Although so tame and inquisitive, yet when approached on horseback, they are exceedingly wary. In this country nobody goes on foot, and the deer knows man as its enemy only when he is mounted and armed with the bolas." Darwin subsequently concludes that it takes only a few generations to adapt instinctively to potentially dangerous situations.

Twenty-seven years ago we were not really punished too badly by deer. We even had an unfenced vegetable garden and for a couple of years we managed to get a few feeds of peas and beans. The deer quickly learned there was good foraging where the vegetables were and soon started harvesting as soon as green shoots appeared. Nowadays, the young, poorly brought-up fawns browse on all growies including our rhododendrons until they get an ache in one of their four stomachs. Currently we hear and read a lot of commentary on how serious the problem of obesity is in western society. A consoling thought is to theorize on how much worse it would be if we had four stomachs.

It is pretty evident that deer do not like rhododendrons as they only browse along paths and driveways where they don't need to get their feet dirty by wandering from the beaten path. Evergreen azaleas have always been deer caviar and occasionally the deciduous azaleas would be nibbled when pushing out new growth, but the big thick leathery indumented varieties were never touched. I think that mother knew that they would need a shot of antacid if they ate andromedatoxin-laden rhododendron leaves and would pass them by and the young would follow. These days, with their population explosion, the competition for food is so great that mother's preoccupation is to fill her own stomachs first, and she pays less attention to her offspring.

My wife claims that our Blacktail Deer are first cousins of the kangaroo. We often see them bouncing around on their hind hooves to reach precious branches higher up. Last year I planted out in a new bed a magnolia 'Galaxy' that I had grown from a cutting and a *sorbus hupehensis* grown from a seed. Both were about two and a half meters high and were well protected by a circle of chicken wire. Both were snapped off at about half height by rear-bipeded deer bouncing around like kangaroos.

Talking of bouncing, anyone with a Scottish background will know the word 'stot'. To 'stot a ba' is to bounce a ball and to be 'stotting drunk' is to be seriously over the 0.08. I had not realized until recently that this is the correct word to describe a deer's bounding gait. In open country, deer just run but in rough plant-covered terrain they stot. They can change direction much more adroitly than their only real predators – cougars and wolves – and are thus often able to escape.

Readers may be thinking that the solution to deer being the predators of our plants, which have no ability to stot, is to build a fence. I have gone as far as costing out installing a fence. The U.S. of A. may be able to run a half trillion-dollar deficit. I, unfortunately, am not in a similar position.

Still, I cannot expect any sympathy. The deer were here first and clearly they like cohabiting with us very much. They are, however, taking an awfully large chunk out of my paycheque. They are as expensive to keep as our own adult offspring. I recall a conversation with an extremely irate lady resident of the Queenswood area of our Saanich municipality. Her exquisite garden had been largely digested by deer. She told me she was petitioning our municipal leaders to have the deer trapped and moved out to the north end of the municipality. She probably did not know that we live right on the boundary.

The lady did have a point. Reports are that the deer population at the northern end of Vancouver Island has diminished significantly, much to the chagrin of local hunters. I would think that with good organization the northern hunters could arrange to trap our Saanich deer and move them to Port Hardy. Let's encourage them.

Taxonomy – A Taxing Topic
October 2004

As a grower and a small time merchant of rhododendrons, who has had no formal training in subjects to do with plants or indeed anything to do with living things, I am often at a loss to understand why there is so much fuss about what to call a wild plant. There is no mercy spared, as was by another more famous merchant, by those concerned with assigning plants' names on the users of improper names. To keep themselves in business and keep the nomenclatural brew boiling they keep changing the plants' names.

People who give living things names are called taxonomists. Here are a couple of examples of the writings of a rhododendron taxonomist: "Inflorescence terminal, 1- or sometimes 2-3 flowered…" and "…with closely or widely scattered dark brown scales." The uninitiated might think that whether a plant had one or three flowers would be important. And the novice might think that describing the spacing of the scales on a leaf, as being 'close' or 'wide' would cover every possibility that could exist and be of absolutely no help in differentiating one scaly leafed plant from another. Being a good taxonomist requires the special skill of being accurately vague.

Professor David Rankin of the University of Edinburgh says in an ideal world we would have taxonomy machines. "Into one end we would feed bits of plants, and at the other end we would be presented with a few Latin words, as well as small amounts of compost." However, this Garden of Eden that we live in is not completely ideal. No matter how elegantly discriminating the classification system devised by taxonomists becomes, nature is in flux and there is a continuum in the differences between living things. Darwin famously wrote about the origin of species and brought to our notice the fact that the survival of the fittest relied on changes in living things — an ongoing process — making individual taxons moving targets.

At the 2005 convention, which we will host, we will hear about some of the work being done to make the differences between what we call species (taxons) more precise. It is doubtful, however, if the distinctions will make it any more clear to a gardener why he has to make a new plant tag.

In the early day of the science of taxonomy, it was thought that the shapes, sexual function and numbers of different parts of a plant would be sufficient to distinguish one kind of plant from another. For example, if a flower had five petals on one plant, that would make it a different kind from another plant that had seven petals on its flowers. I would intuitively think the number of lobes or petals on a flower would be an important characteristic. My plant of *R. ririei* is an example showing this is not the case. (I know it is *ririei* because that is the name that was on the label when I acquired that plant.) Some of the flowers have five lobes on each corolla, some have seven. Consequently, I can accept that the number of lobes is not a good measure.

The classification experts have grouped some species together into Sections and Subsections. Plants are grouped like this because they have similar features. *Ririei* is placed in Subsection 'Argyrophylla'. *Ririei* has prominent nectaries. *Ririei* is the only one in this Subsection that has nectaries. Intuitively, I would think that would be a significant distinction but evidently it is not. I am now waiting for some expert to say my plant is not *ririei* at all; or to be told that its closest relatives are not in Subsection 'Argyrophylla' and it should be slotted into some other part of the genus's spectrum; or even worse, the experts could decide that it is not a species at all but a hybrid.

I think it's important to recognize that the main reason for trying to place plants into tidy slots is so we can communicate. For this same reason, we use a universal Latin-like language. It's all about being able to talk to each other. It's also important to remember that speciation is one of the fundamental processes in evolution. A very general definition of what makes a species a species is that the members included are able to breed among themselves but generally not easily with others. There are well known examples of hybrids, i.e. inter-specific crosses, like the mule – the offspring of a horse and a donkey. But we all know how easily large numbers of species in the genus rhododendron behave promiscuously and mate with every Tom, Dick, Sally and Sue to produce hybrids. Unlike the mule, these are most often not sterile. As a result, the majority of the rhododendron plants we grow in our gardens are, in fact, hybrids.

Over 30,000 hybrids are considered by someone, somewhere to be worthy of a birth certificate and be registered with the botanical authorities at Wisley, England. Unlike species, once a hybrid's name has been entered into the record it cannot be changed. 'Hoppy' – one of the Seven Dwarfs – should be 'Happy' but was incorrectly spelt on registration and no deed poll can change that.

Jane Brown, in a new (2004) book on rhododendrons, 'Tales of the Rose Tree', writes that, "Rhododendron taxonomy is a path to lonely sainthood, pursued in chilly garrets and overheated laboratories." And, "Taxonomy is a rolling sea of knowledge, entered at great peril; the lists and classifications are the bulk tankers of the rhododendron world, necessary but ugly and best left to go about their business unheeded." I'm not quite comfortable with this tanker analogy but it does highlight the facts that only Master Mariners can command them, that classifications keep moving and that they are very unwieldy.

Despite all the difficulties of getting the right name on your plants, the effort involved in trying to determine that correct name is really a worthwhile exercise – better not left unheeded – and can add significantly to the enjoyment of growing a plant. But don't take it too seriously. The late Mrs. Berry of Washington State had a large collection of rhododendrons, many of which were grown from seed. She would be visited every year by a succession of the world's plant experts and would ask, label in hand, each expert to identify her plants. At the end of the year she would have six or eight names on a plant. Come the New Year she would clear off all the tags and begin again.

History's Distinguished Plant Persons
January 2005

This is the first in a series of short articles on small, often trivial, events in the lives of people who were of consequence in matters of interest to our Society. We call the people who went out into the wilds to find plants for our gardens "The Plant Hunters". Most of us recognize their names and we have all heard talks or read books about their pursuits. Looking them up in an encyclopedia will give the broad course of their lives but reading their more detailed biographies often reveals an incident or discovery that seems particularly important in perhaps a parochial way, or is somewhat relevant to contemporary events. Sometimes they may even be comical or whimsical.

Joseph Banks and Newfoundland 1766

Joseph Banks had an omnifarious mind. His curiosity and energy spurred him to become intensely involved in so many of the great contemporary issues that one needs a catalogue to list them. He is known best for having been the botanist on Cook's first voyage (1768-71); for holding the presidency of the Royal Society for 41 years; for being the principal drive behind the establishment of Kew Gardens; for the founding of New South Wales and for the introduction, from Tahiti, of the breadfruit tree to the Caribbean. These latter events have led to his being held in disrepute by some because of strong connections to the transportation of criminals and for the establishment of slavery. He has also been pejoratively characterized as being a Gentleman Amateur of Science. He certainly did not earn his livelihood from practicing science – he didn't need to; he was a wealthy man. But neither did Charles Darwin. Banks wrote '...a man is never so well Employ'd, as when he is labouring for the advantage of the Public; without the Expectation, the Hope or Even a wish to derive advantage of any Kind from the Result of his exertions.'

Most of the information for this article comes from Dr. Averil Lysaght's compendious book "Joseph Banks in Newfoundland and Labrador, 1766: His Diary, Manuscripts and Collections". In the book's foreword, Joey Smallwood (Premier of Newfoundland and Labrador, 1949-71) rates it as one of the dozen greatest works about Newfoundland. Averil Lysaght was subsequently and consequently given an honorary DLitt from Memorial University. (Incidentally, as a 15 year old in New Zealand, Lysaght discovered a new species of moth on Mt Egmont/Taranaki, which was named melanchra averillia in her honour. The world famous rhododendron garden, Pukieiti flourishes on the western slope of Mt. Taranaki).

The movie "Master and Commander" was awarded two Oscars in 2003. The events in the filmed version bore little resemblance to the book. Personally, I thought it not such a good movie and certainly not as enjoyable as the books. Its author, Patrick O'Brian, wrote another nineteen in a series of 19th century naval action stories. He also wrote an excellent, well researched, easily read biography of Joseph Banks – more easily understood than some of the naval manoeuvres in the Master and Commander books. In O'Brian's biography, he includes Banks's entire Newfoundland journal. In contrast, H. B. Carter's "Sir Joseph Banks", published by the British Museum and supposedly the authoritative biography, devotes about three (of 671) pages to Banks's trip to Newfoundland.

Constantine John Phipps had gone to Eton with Banks. Phipps had left school early to go to sea on HMS Monmouth. His uncle was her captain. Part of the great attraction the navy had for upper class English youth was the possibility of prize money. This could be of staggering proportions. Phipps, recently promoted to lieutenant, got £2,000 for serving under his uncle, equivalent to about thirty years pay. An admiral could receive about forty times that – an amount that in today's terms would make Conrad Black, when at his best, a relative pauper. Compared to Phipps's £2,000, a seaman got £3 14s 9p.

Thereafter, in 1766, Phipps was without a ship and on half pay. Like Banks, he had excellent connections and was conveniently given a 'naval mission' to Newfoundland on HMS Niger captained by their friend Sir Thomas Adams. The Grand Banks (the fishing area, not the man) was the scene of constant rivalry and hostility among the British, French, Spanish and Portuguese fishermen, as it still is 250 years later. Banks too was able to pull influential strings to allow him to go with Phipps. Phipps was also a keen naturalist, although more interested in animals than plants. He was the first to describe the polar bear scientifically.

The "Niger" spent four and a half months in Newfoundland and Labrador. I have been in St Johns only once. I thought it full of interest and friendliness. Here is what Banks thought, as recorded in his journal, "It is very difficult to Compare one town with another tho that Probably is the Best way of Conveying the Idea St Johns however Cannot be Compared to any I have seen it is Built upon the side of a hill facing the Harbour Containing two or three hundred houses & near as many fish Flakes interspersed which in summer time must Cause a stench scarce to be supported thank heaven we were only there spring & fall before the fish were come to the Ground & after they were gone off For dirt & filth of all kinds St Johns may in my opinion Reign unrivaled ...."

Banks returned with a collection of specimens, many of them never before seen in Europe. These specimens provided an important building block for his famous herbarium. Banks had recognized the Swede Carolus Linnaeus' plant classification system as detailed in his "Systema naturae" (1753) and subsequent writings. Its principal proselytizer in Britain was Daniel Carl Solander, a favourite pupil of Linnaeus. Solander, in 1766, was working at the fledgling British Museum. At this time he and Banks were socially conversant. This quickly developed into their deep friendship, which led to their partnership on the first great voyage of then Lieutenant James Cook on the "Endeavour" in 1768. In 1782 Solander suffered a stroke while breakfasting at Banks' house and did not recover. The ever stoical Banks subsequently unveiled himself a little when he wrote, "Suffice is to say that few men howsoever Exalted their pursuits were ever more feelingly miss'd either in the paths of Science or of Friendship."

The Linnaean system was based on the sexual arrangement of the flowers' parts. Banks' botanical descriptions of his Newfoundland finds – 340 of them – followed the Linnaean prescriptions using botanical Latin. An example of an entry in Banks' Plant Catalogue (translated) is, "Husbands live with wives in the same house, but have different beds": i.e. male and female flowers on the same plant. Another is, "nuptials are celebrated privately." i.e. flowers are concealed within the fruit. Such openly sexual language aroused anger in many of Linnaeus' critics.

187

But Linnaeus often had the last laugh by naming the most noxious weeds after his most vocal objectors. On the other hand he named many genera for his pupils and friends by adding an 'ia' to their names, e.g. Kalm, Lagerström, Alströmer, Thunberg, Magnol, Dahl and Garden.

Banks was diligent in collecting everything he could find – flowering plants, ferns, mosses, seaweed, birds, mammals and insects. Whether some of the plants were truly indigenous or were the result of naturalization after being introduced accidentally by earlier European visitors caused much debate which in some instances is still ongoing. Banks did find three species of rhododendron; R. *canadense*, R. *lapponicum* and R. *groenlandicum*. The first of these he introduced into cultivation.

I will close this fragmental snippet on Banks's life by noting, apropos of nothing that has gone before, that he should be regarded, at the very least, as being an honourary Canadian. Pierre Berton's recent death has reminded me of his defining a Canadian as one who could make love in a canoe. In Caroline Alexander's 2003 "The Bounty" (a good read), she comments on Banks's boundless curiosity into all aspects of living things this way:

"With his zeal for new experiences, he had thrown himself into Tahitian life, learning its language, attending burials and sacrifices and dances, endearing himself to its people, even having himself discreetly tattooed. The happy promiscuity of the Tahitian women was already well known … and Banks's adventures on this front provided additional spice. Outstanding among the stories that made the rounds of London social circles was the tale of the theft of Mr. Banks's fine waistcoat with its splendid silver frogging, stolen, along with his shoes and pistol, while he lay sleeping with his "old Friend Oberea" in her canoe: (Oberea was a Tahitian queen.)

"Didst thou not, crafty, subtle sunburnt strum
Steal the silk breeches from his tawny bum?
Calls't thouself a Queen? And thus couldst use
And rob thy Swain of breeches and his shoes?"

George Forrest, Mr. Bulley and Professor Balfour
April 2005

"And flowers azure, black and streaked with gold,
Fairer than any wakened eyes behold."
Shelley.

No doubt flowers figured larger in the psyches of
Isaac Bayley Balfour and George Forrest than did gold but
that sometimes-noble element was instrumental in bringing
these two disparate men together. George Forrest, (*R.
forrestii*) who was probably the greatest plant collector of all
time, had spent ten of his oat-sowing, formative years
roughing it in Australia. He had grown up in Scotland. He
was the youngest of thirteen children, only eight of whom
made it to adulthood. In 1903, George, at age 30, was back in
Scotland living with his widowed mother and fairly desperate
for work. The gold connection followed from a previous one
concerning bones.

George had a huge curiosity about the natural world
and spent most of his time outdoors. He was keen on fishing
and shooting and knew all the plants and birds of his
neighbourhood. On one outing he noticed an unusual stone
protruding from an eroded bank. His careful scraping
uncovered more of the stone, which proved to be a lid for a
coffin. There were bones inside.

George took some of the bones to the Keeper of the
Museum of National Antiquities in Edinburgh. They proved
to be about 1500 years old. The Curator of the museum was
impressed by this stalky, intelligent, independent and
ambitious young man and took it upon himself to write to the
Regius Keeper of the Royal Botanic Garden Edinburgh, Isaac
Bayley Balfour and (*R. balfourianum*), asking if he knew of
anyone looking for a botanical collector. In his short letter he
noted that Forrest had "...some experience roughing it as a
gold digger...." Balfour, who was twenty years older than
Forrest, had also done some plant exploring but perhaps,
more importantly, had a trace of gold fever in his system. He

had been induced by a friend's "...flakes of gold as big as a man's hand...slicing it off with cold chisels. By jingo it's more like Arabian nights than modern gold mining," and had invested £100 in a mining venture in Queensland. He felt disposed to offer Forrest a job in the RBG's herbarium at 10 shillings a week. In those days there was no Minimum Wage. Balfour's offer was probably about the very least that could be offered. Nevertheless, Forrest jumped at it. So began a relationship that was deep, sincere and enriching – not in terms of gold – but in their shared knowledge of the natural world. Most of the gold went into the pockets of others. One who so profited was Arthur Kilpin Bulley.

A. K. Bulley was a complex man. He was a wealthy cotton broker whose legacy now lives on in the Ness Gardens at Liverpool, England. His mother had 14 children all of whom survived. He had a wonderful nose for business and a competitive but sincere love for plants. He was an atheist, and an evangelical socialist. Among his other political endeavours, he tried, unsuccessfully, as a Women's Suffrage candidate for a seat in the British House of Commons. In these days part of the uniform of the business tycoon was a bowler hat; he wore a fedora. From his reading and business contacts he knew there were undiscovered treasures – aesthetic and financial – in southwest China. He was loath to compromise his socialist principles by exploiting his love of plants and his skill at growing them for monetary gain. So at first his collecting strategy was to write everyone and anyone who was in these foreign parts (including the "Papist missionaries") soliciting seed. This did not produce many tangible results – only more mouth-watering descriptive enticements of what might be found there. Dr. Augustine Henry, when stationed in Szechwan, did send some seed to Bulley who wisely sent some of these to Isaac Bayley Balfour. Balfour had the facilities to grow plants but had no mandate or funds to sponsor a professional collector. Bulley was still merely a private gardener. Meanwhile, in the south of England, the multi-generation Veitch nursery had sponsored Henry Wilson to go to China. Wilson was instructed to bring back, among other things, seeds of Henry's discovery – the handkerchief tree (*Davidia involucrata*).

The Veitch name was on the tips of the tongues of the loftiest and wealthiest of British horticulturists. Bulley was prominent in this group but regarded by this elite with distancing reservation. Slowly, he came to realize that to have the newest and rarest plants he had to engage his own collector. Swallowing some of his socialist doctrine he decided to send a collector to Yunnan. Augustine Henry had told him, "Don't waste money on postage – send a man." He also decided to set up his own nursery, in direct competition with Veitch. He established A. K. Bees & Co. (*R. beesiana*) but to assuage his scruples he called it a cooperative with the motto, "All to Gather – all Together".

A. Henry had picked up on Yunnan's great plant wealth from Abbé Delavay's pioneering discoveries. Delavay, a French missionary, had been sending herbarium specimens and a few seeds back to Europe. China was a country on a grand scale. Three of the world's deepest gorges, the Salween, the Mekong and the Yangtze coursed through Yunnan and the variety of material growing there was breathtaking, the climatic range being so wide that conservatory gardeners and alpine plant enthusiasts were all salivating at the thought of savouring its flora. Henry proffered the menu and the Veitches and Bulley ordered the seven-course meal.

Bulley bought space for a small advertisement in the Gardeners' Chronicle. It read, "Wanted, a Young Man well up on Hardy Plants, to go out to the East and Collect, – Box 15, G.P.O., Liverpool". Balfour responded with a short letter which concluded with, "He is a strongly built fellow and seems to me to be of the right grit for a collector." Bulley wasted no time in hiring Forrest; after all Veitch had a five-year start by having sent out E. H. Wilson (later known as Chinese Wilson).

Forrest left Edinburgh on the 14th May, 1904, and was soon on board the SS Australia bound for Bombay. He traveled by train to Madras. The voyage from there to

Rangoon was ghastly on a filthy, mechanically unsound, storm tossed steamer that had to be towed into Rangoon by a rescue boat. Forrest wrote that a baby died on the ship and "was thrown overboard like a bundle of brown paper." His route through Burma to Yunnan was largely unknown to westerners. The rigours he faced were a mere foretaste of how he was to spend the next three years. Forrest thought his stay was to be for two years.

The agreement between Forrest, Bulley and Balfour seems to have been a loose, verbal one. It seems Forrest received about £600 a year to cover everything. Agreements for subsequent expeditions spelled out a salary and detailed support costs. Balfour's understanding was that he was to get all the herbarium collection; Bulley thought he was to get all the seed and photographs; Forrest thought he could keep some of the seed and duplicates of the herbarium sheets.

The disagreements arose in earnest after Forrest's return to Edinburgh. The saga of this first (there were seven) Forrest expedition is one of horrendous hardship, success, elation and the deepest despair. (In July 1906 Balfour wrote to Bulley, " ...there is little doubt that Forrest has been murdered."). This stranger than fiction tale is told in many books but the best account is in Brenda McLean's, "George Forrest Plant Hunter". Here, it is only the relationships between these three forceful personalities that are being discussed so readers are encouraged to read McLean's book; it is in our library. Each of these men was highly principled, highly intelligent and highly motivated. Each was egotistical and tenacious.

Balfour found a spot for Forrest in his old job at the herbarium of the RBG. The pay was now £2 a week. Before leaving for China, Forrest had become engaged to another herbarium worker, Clementina Traill (*R. clementinae, R. traillianum*). On his return they were married much against her mother's wishes: she was not much impressed with George's occupation. Of course, Clementina had to give up her job. George was not in good health as a consequence of his three grueling years in China and often missed work.

Working hours were inflexible and the newly married Forrests lived six miles distant from the RBG. George had always walked to work but when ill was unable to do so and the only train did not get him to work in time. Balfour was an understanding man but had to administer a large staff and couldn't make exceptions. Forrest's immediate supervisor was not at all sympathetic.

Forrest thought he owned one set of the herbarium specimens. Balfour thought otherwise and sent a truck to collect them. Bulley thought he had complete ownership of all seed and Forrest had kept some, which he was selling. Forrest felt compelled to offer his resignation and Balfour accepted it. Would a modern high priced contract lawyer have prevented this outcome by having the three signatures duly witnessed on a 20-page document?

Forrest did keep in touch with Balfour and was still sending him plant identification lists – the result of long hours of work – but their relationship was icily strained. Forrest wrote to Balfour, "Any indebtedness which may have been due to the Garden by me I consider to be more than repaid by the collections I have already presented." At heart, Balfour still considered Forrest his protégé and was a man of reasoned compassion. He invited Forrest to come and have a free and open discussion of the difficulties. They ended up shaking hands. Forrest never forgot how understanding and avuncularly supportive Balfour had been. His respect for Balfour never wavered again. Simultaneously, Bulley and Balfour became the closest of friends and remained so. Balfour always seemed to be able to build friendships on individuals' strengths, ignoring their weaknesses.

Forrest could not do that and his respect for Bulley had changed to wariness. Forrest had not forgotten that Bulley had insisted that Forrest take a camera with him as an essential item in his kit. In the early 1900's, photographs were taken on plates in a large box mounted on a tripod. Imagine trying to scale the precipitous chasms lugging a camera to photograph a two-inch primula. The first set of plates that Forrest took with him was ruined. The precautions needed to protect the plates in such an inhospitable climate had to be learned the hard way. Bulley demurred at the cost of replacing them, refused to provide paper and developing material. Forrest wrote, "Mr. Bulley ...said there was no necessity to take photos. This after telling me to take a camera with me. He is a rather peculiar individual."

Forrest seems to have been constantly fretful of not being able to meet Bulley's expectations. He wrote, "I might as well be scuppered as go home a failure." Bulley seems to have been unable to give his collector the encouragement and reassurance that he needed although he was loudly praising Forrest's discoveries to others. It was a feudal master-servant relationship and the collector's free spirit was compromised.

Forrest, following his resignation from RBG Edinburgh, was in limbo. He wanted to go back to his old hunting grounds; he had learned the local language; he had trained some of the local people to collect and had gained their respect and loyalty. Bulley, however, was lukewarm despite having promised never to let Forrest "sink into the ranks of the out of work." A little later, he wrote, "But the simple facts are that I can't see it costing less than £600 a year, and ...I am a comparatively poor man."

Twelve days after Forrest quit the RBG, his mentor, Balfour, wrote him to tell him that Professor Sargent from America had visited him and was looking for someone to go to China. Sargent was Director of the Arnold Arboretum of Harvard University. Forrest and Sargent met at the Veitch nursery. The American wanted plants for New England; he wanted hardier stuff than Forrest had collected in Yunnan. Forrest was loath to go further north; he was sure there were still great riches in the Mekong-Salween divide. Balfour encouraged Forrest to accept Sargent's offer of £300 a year plus expenses. Forrest asked for time to consider and stalled, mainly because Clementina was pregnant with their first child. He missed his opportunity.

In the meantime, some of Forrest's seeds were germinating for Bulley. *Primula malacoides*, (an "arable weed" to some observers; however, J.C. Williams, one of

Forrest's later sponsors, did call it "an unfailing delight") was selling at 7s 6d a plant. Bulley was advertising, somewhat untruthfully, "During the past five years or so we have spent large sums of money in sending out collectors to China. We now have an enormous stock of new plants on trial in our nursery. These we shall exhibit and offer for sale, as they prove of merit..." *Primula bulleyana* had been named and it too was fetching high prices. (Bulley preferred the name *beesiana*. But he wrote, "However I am indifferent. Beesi, Beesorum, Beesensis, Beesium, Beesica, Beesiana, anything which brings the name in...") There were 22 species named after Bulley from Forrest's first expedition. He did think that *Gentiana veitchiorum* sounded hideous. Bulley's 'beastly money' became less beastly, and knowing Forrest had not agreed to Sargent's demand that he leave before the birth of his child offered him £200 plus expenses to go back to Yunnan. Forrest, having been present for the birth of his son, was now in no position to refuse and left for China in January 1910.

As soon as he arrived in Rangoon, he was within a hair's breadth of returning home. Bulley had failed to send the money for equipping the expedition. Forrest had to beg the ship's captain to let him stay on board until Bulley had cabled £150. Bulley's unapologetic explanation was that there had been a mix-up in Bee's office. Forrest was now sorely angered and disillusioned. Further delays in payment followed; it seems inexplicable that a man of Bulley's business acumen would let his collector go without resources. Forrest decided in Rangoon that he could not work again for such an employer but he would honour his contract and see it out. He let it be known that Bulley was a "cad of the first order." He had a hate on for nurserymen, particularly English nurserymen. "There is a lot said about the meanness of the Scotch but in my time I have met more stingy English than Scotch, and Bulley and Veitch, the great Sir Harry, are types, extreme types." Bulley called Forrest's bluff and wrote him, "I shall not want any formal notice of your desire to go." Forrest did finish his term, introducing many of our most treasured garden plants. Bulley's one-inch thick catalogue listed 67 species of Asiatic primula. His business was prospering and he offered Forrest a two-year extension to his contract. This was immediately turned down,

This story is, of course, incomplete. It is just a glimpse into the lives and affairs of three men who played immensely important roles in British horticulture. Sir Isaac Bayley Balfour was the scientist and the statesman. His classification system for rhododendrons was used for the best part of a century. He, himself, knew it was only an expedient but I, like most older gardeners, still use it. Forrest undertook another five successful expeditions. He died of a heart attack, suddenly, in January 1932 while out collecting bird specimens with three of his Chinese employees. During his first two expeditions he had developed a great love for rhododendrons. We, who grow them, should toast his memory.

K. C. Bulley had little time for rhododendrons and had in fact sold all the rhododendron seed from the second expedition to J.C. Williams of Cornwall. Fortunately, Forrest developed the same kind of rewarding relationship with Williams as he had with Balfour. Bulley continued to sponsor plant hunters in the Sino-Himalaya. He was hugely instrumental, not only in introducing new plant material, but also in making it available to everyone. His one-penny seed packages were designed for those with only a windowsill of space. Although he was an uncommon man, his second great love was for the common man and woman. Bulley died in 1942 after 44 years at Ness. His widow wanted his epitaph to read "Bulley, his fortunes and misfortunes." His daughter, Lois, presented the whole Ness estate, along with a large endowment, to Liverpool University.

Looking Backward – and Forward
October 2005

Robert Louis Stevenson remarked, "I've a fine memory for forgetting." I'm sure mine is worse but looking over the raffle plants at our last meeting, I was struck with their number, variety and quality. I had a flash of recollection to our early meetings, over 26 years ago. We've always had a raffle and in those early days I think there might have been three or four plants on display. These were often somewhat scrawny plants but they were proudly arrayed on the table in front of the chalkboard in David Ballantyne's classroom at U Vic. A big change since then has been making the huge technological leap to duplicate pre-numbered tickets. The first plantings at the University Gardens – not yet called the Finnerty Gardens – had just taken place with plants from the Lake Cowichan, Buchanan-Simpson bequest. Some of these were to my lustful mind, truly exotic. Almost none was available in any Island nursery. In fact – and my mind is clear on this – in the few years prior to our club's existence I could find only one species rhododendron for sale. That was *R. impeditum*. Subsequently we found *R. keleticum* and then the fairly uncommon *R. searsiae* at Tony Walner's Cedar Hill nursery.

We knew, of course, from listening to the tales of Albert de Mezey, Peggy Abkhazi, Ernie Lythgoe and Stewart Holland about the treasures that had been available in the past from the Greigs' at Royston and Layritz's on Wilkinson Road. In those days *R. yakushimanum* was as rare as a Tom Thomson painting. Cuttings of *yakushimanum* were reputed to cost $200. Albert de Mezey glowed and gloated with satisfaction recalling how there was one show-off plant of *yakushimanum* prominently placed outside the Layritz office, and when the nursery was folding down and the stock being sold off he offered to buy "that rhododendron". The person in charge of the sale called it 'Bow Bells' and sold it to Albert for a few dollars. Albert's visitors approached this with silent reverence. It had a prime site in front of his grotto.

In the early seventies, the Lammlies started Rhodoland on the Pat Bay Highway. Bill and Olga would make an annual buying pilgrimage to Washington and Oregon nurseries and one year (probably 1976) came back with a couple of dozen *yakushimanum* and *R. pseudochrysanthum* among other rhesplendencies. I was able to purchase ten one-gallon plants of each for the University. These were planted out along the pathway in what was then known as 'Phase One'. There were two of the first and three of the second still there after a week. Clearly there was a demand for the choice varieties of rhododendron and Victoria was calling out for some organization that could meet that demand less furtively and more honestly.

Still on the subject of the portability and mobility of rhododendrons, it was perhaps ten years later that the last plants from Mary Greig's garden were dug up and donated to public gardens. The University was favoured by being given a 25 or 30-year-old plant of *R. proteioides*. This is still one of the most meagerly available collectibles. The donated trophy-plant was a perfect hemisphere of about 30cm. diameter. Despite advice that such a rare plant should not be planted out in the Gardens but should be planted in a specially-built window planter outside the President's office, it was planted out in the gardens and it didn't take very long for it to disappear. Inasmuch as *proteoides* is not an immediately obvious plant (Dave Dougan's famous quip about preferring to grow spinach should be recalled) the thief was obviously one of the cognoscenti. I'm sure most of us don't want to live in a society where one is always in red alert mode but there is a cautionary lesson in this for us gardeners.

One of the main changes that has come about since the formation of our Society, 26 years ago, is the increase in the availability and variety of plants. The choices are greater than at any previous time. Harry Wright in his book lists the rhododendrons grown on Vancouver Island. He names over 4000. Another change for the better is that many more people are propagating rhododendrons so I would guess that at least one half of the plants listed by Harry can be found locally by a diligent searcher.

I can think of two respects in which we are less well served than we were in the last 20 years. Les Clay's nursery pioneered tissue culture in Canada. Sadly, it has passed into history. At its zenith, Clays' had an impressive catalogue of rhododendrons. These were readily available as liners at a very reasonable price. Les was always putting another variety in the test tube. He had a rare talent for being able to activate the meristemic process in his ultra-clean laboratory. The second recent loss of choice rhododendron plant material on the Island is due to Clint Smith's abandonment of the rhododendron propagation scene. I have often claimed that Clint could propagate a broom handle. He could root the most stubborn – the *R. proteioides*, the *R. roxianums*, the *R. flinkiis* and the 'Lem's Cameos. At the peak of his productivity he was supplying almost every nursery on the Island. Still, when one assesses the plants that are available through our club—in the raffle, on the Bargain Table and at our Show and Sale—the gardener is hugely better off than was the case 30 years ago.

During this same time span Victorians interested in rhododendrons have been able to see mature specimens of many that previously could only be read about. Finnerty Gardens is now assuming that hoary status that accompanies longevity and rarity. The Horticultural Centre of the Pacific is beginning to live up to its pretentious title. The Weesjes' garden rivals some of the best-known British gardens. And many of our members' gardens are of a noteworthy class. Beauty, in gardens, as in wines and violins, is almost always a function of age.

We have hosted two conventions in our fairly short lifetime; (I am reminded of Woody Allen's observation, " I recently turned sixty. Practically a third of my life is over.") We can be proud of how good our conventions were. One consequence of staging a convention is that it hastens the maturation process of a Society. It is even more effective as a catalyst in the maturation of a Society's members. I recall thinking when it was decided to host the 2005 event that I had a pretty good chance of it not being a personal concern. Being now much closer to Woody Allen's expected lifespan, I'm certain that I'll need to go to a venue other than Victoria if I want to attend another rhododendron convention. However, some of you should be putting that 'Bring Forward' tab in your memory in order to start the convention machinations one more time.

One of the stellar achievements of our group is the monthly newsletter. It is certainly one of the best of any chapter of the ARS. We have been truly blest in having our present editors and in our previous one – the late Alec McCarter. These people provide our societal cement. It wasn't always so. When we started, the newsletter was all of a one-sided page. I undertook to do that for the first few years. It was always a challenge to get enough material to fill that one page. Fortunately, I had access to typing skills. Back then there were no easy-to-use word processors. I recall one month when I had to try to type the newsletter myself. It looked like a two year old's finger painting. An entire bottle of Whiteout was used on that one page. We have come a long way. James and Pat Fuller still need material to keep up the standard of the past few years. Everyone has a story to tell – one paragraph or thirty. Send it in.

A Society that is dedicated to one genus of plants is constrained by its own prescribed boundaries. One advantage that a rhododendron club has is the size of the genus and the promiscuity of its members (i.e. the plants). True, the Orchid Society has us well and truly trounced on this score but with over 30,000 registered rhododendron hybrids – a number growing by hundreds every year – we are not going to run out of choices for our gardens. Assuming our rainfall stays much the same and we have some stored water available for summer irrigation the future looks promising, even with global warming. Many of us are now risking the *Maddenia* outside and if temperatures get even warmer we have almost half the genus in the *Vireya* still untapped.

The quality of our annual show has attained an enviable status. Not one of us readily wants to admit to being a trophy hunter but it is satisfying to have one's name inscribed on a piece of silver. Every garden has at least one truss or spray worth putting in the show. Some year you may hear the comment, "The show is a bit thin this year but the quality is high." This is a real danger sign. The show needs quantity as well as quality. That first impression of a hall full of exhibits is the most important and lasting. When one has only one or two blooms on a plant it is not easy to make the decision to use the clippers. I have sometimes resorted to a 'pleasure factor' to help make the choice. If the truss remains in the garden it might get a total appreciation time of 15 days x 2 minutes x 3 people = 90 people minutes. At the show it will likely be looked at by 400 people for one minute = 400 people minutes. Perhaps the flower would choose the latter.

I have recently read "Collapse" by Jared Diamond. This examines the factors that make societies fail or succeed. I found this book a disquieting read in terms of our global society (Woody Allen again: "More than any other time in history, mankind faces a crossroad. One path leads to despair and utter hopelessness. The other, to total extinction. Let us pray we have the wisdom to choose correctly"). I found the book had some messages of reassurance in relation to our Rhododendron Society. There is no way we are going to cut down the last tree and become modern day Easter Islanders. We have lived one generation as a group and aren't limited by having a finite number of generations ahead of us. We can do better than Woody Allen. Make a vow to bring in a new younger member – someone under the age of, say, eighty – and make sure we copy Johnny Walker; "just keep on going".

Hall's DNA
December 2005

I recently received a copy of Dr. Ben Hall's [University of Washington] latest paper on his findings on the inner secrets of rhododendron DNA. It is the formal statement of what he told us at the spring convention. I must give you the title but don't let it stop you reading what follows. The paper is called The Molecular Systematics of Rhododendron (Ericaceae): A Phylogeny Based Upon RPB2 Gene Sequences. Loretta Goetsch, Andrew J. Eckert, and Benjamin D. Hall are the authors and the paper was published in the journal of Systematic Biology.

Many of you will remember Ben Hall's talk at our convention. It dealt with the taxonomy – the classification of the genus rhododendron. Fundamentalist believers in Intelligent Design may experience some difficulty with fitting this kind of evolutionary evidence into their theory. It is hard to logically deny the existence of the evolutionary process. Ted Irving and Richard Hebda, at the same conference, gave us some insight into the geophysical and climatic conditions giving rise to the creation of new species of rhododendron and magnolia. This was a follow-up to the paper they gave at our 1989 conference on the origin and distribution of rhododendrons.

Science always tries to sort what is found in nature into an orderly arrangement. Living things are notoriously difficult to fit into neat and tidy slots. Neat and tidy slots imply that matters are static. Living things are not static; they are changing and evolving. Consequently the 'system' that the classifying scientists come up with is not perfect and can almost always be improved. The analysis of DNA is a new and powerful improving tool for describing how one organism differs from another and by how much. It helps to fine tune earlier classifications.

About 25 years ago I attended an international conference on the classification of rhododendrons in Kent, Washington. It was attended by about 300 people most of whom were professionally involved in trying to put rhododendrons into some logical order of kinship. DNA analysis was unknown at the time of this conference. Most systematizers were using the classical technique of minutely examining a plant's morphology – the number and shapes of the flowers, leaves, seed, etc. (i.e. the physically visible characteristics). The cutting-edge scientists at that time were using analyses of the chemistry of the plants.

I was told that this was the first international conference on rhododendrons that the Chinese had attended. Inasmuch as a large percentage of the genus rhododendron is native to China, what they had to say was of very real consequence if there was to be international agreement on a classification. The Chinese had carried out meticulous measurements on the spacing, shape and size of scales on the leaves, flowers and twigs among other things. The results of the more esoteric analyses did not always quite agree with the more classically derived results. The Orientals and the Occidentals got into a fairly steamy argument. I recall the chairman calling for order and saying, "Ladies and gentlemen, please remember that this is a serious subject but not that important." Things quietened down.

It is perhaps worth observing that the Irving/Hebda approach involves processes on the macro scale – ice ages, mountain building, and continental collisions while that of Hall works in the micro-sphere, looking at the molecular variations within a small part of the DNA strand. The first explains the causal forces for the evolution of new species; the second records the microchemistry of the mutations that have taken place over long periods of time.

The most important of Hall's recent findings upsets the basic division that we gardeners have been using to divide the genus. We have recognized four main types. We first of all divide those with scales from those without (i.e. lepidotes from elepidotes). We can easily distinguish an *augustinii* from a *fortunei* and we know that these two types have evolved so differently that they will not mate with each other. The non-scaly (i.e. elepidote) rhododendrons we have split into three groups – the larger leaved ones, the deciduous azaleas and the evergreen azaleas. This is the grouping that Chamberlain, Cullen et al follow. Many of us use the 'Encyclopedia of Rhododendrons' by father and son, Peter and Kenneth Cox, as our basic reference. It divides the genus Rhododendron into these four main subgenera – the lepidotes are called sub-genus Rhododendron, the larger leaved ones are called sub-genus Hymenanthes, the deciduous azaleas are subgenus Pentanthera and the evergreen azaleas, Tsutsutsi. There are five other subgenera but most of us can forget about them as they each contain only one or a few species, the botanical curiosities, and are seldom seen in gardens.

One of the most important empirical factors supporting this subdivision is that members in each subgenus, while sexually profligate amongst themselves, almost never produce offspring with members of the other subgenera. However, the DNA results obtained by Ben Hall do not support Pentanthera being a subgenus. He proposes that it now become part of Hymenanthes. The genetic differences are not significant enough to warrant sub generic rank. The ranking below Subgenus is Section. Hall proposes that Pentanthera be given a Section ranking. He proposes other changes in the other smaller subgenera but as most of us are not familiar with the species involved, these will not be detailed here. I can provide a photocopy to those who would like to have one.

Dr. Hall is clearly excited about these results. In a separate communication he says, "Regarding Subsection Pontica", not all the dust has settled as yet but I see these getting scattered in three or four directions. First, eliminate *R. hyperythrum*; it never should have been separated from *R. pachysanthum* and *R. pseudochrysanthum*." He says the most derived and cohesive cluster in the Pontica Section is *R. macrophyllum, R. caucasicum, R. aureum* and *R. catawbiense*. He also says that there appear to be several interesting clusters in the non-Section Pontica of the subgenus Hymenanthes. It is to these that his next efforts will be directed.

I recall a remark made by one of my mathematics professors at university. He had just explained some esoteric problem and he said, "If this does not give you a thrill, you are not a mathematician." My memory of his saying this is clear but I have not the slightest idea what the thrilling problem was. Remember too the words of Conan Doyle. "It has always been an axiom of mine that the little things are infinitely the most important".

The Birds and the Bees
February 2006

At the American Rhododendron Society convention held in Victoria this last spring two of the world's great rhododendron gurus participated in a short but significant ritual. Peter Cox, plant explorer, author, hybridizer had traveled from the UK to present the Royal Horticultural Society's Loder Rhododendron Cup to Warren Berg of Washington State, plant explorer and hybridizer.

Both men have made outstanding contributions to the knowledge of the Asian flora and to the cultivation of Asian plants in Western gardens. For many gardeners it is the creation of new hybrid rhododendrons that ensures their lasting renown. For a hybrid to be a success it must be significantly better or markedly different from its parents. There are now in excess of 30,000 registered rhododendron hybrids. It is probably safe to say that a mere 10% of that number meets these two criteria.

Both Cox and Berg have demonstrated a ruthless scrutiny in the protracted assessment of the new progeny of their hybridizing efforts. A hybrid from Cox or Berg is almost always worth growing. Cox is the creator of a series of hybrids of small stature to which he gave the names of birds. Berg's most well known hybrids contain a 'Bee' in their bonnet. There are more Birds than there are Bees. Several of these plants have been around for about 25 years but it is not easy to find commercial sources for some of them. They are more easily available in British nurseries than they are in British Columbia and consequently are seen in more gardens over there. I recall admiring several of the Birds in a plot that was probably not more than 100 square feet behind the iron railing of a Georgian terrace house on a busy street in the center of Glasgow. It was a tasteful tribute to Peter Cox's efforts.

Here are the names of the Birds known to me, 'Chiffchaff', 'Chikor', 'Curlew', 'Egret', 'Eider', 'Grouse', 'Merganser', 'Phalarope', 'Pipit' (a natural hybrid), 'Razorbill', 'Snipe', 'Wigeon' and 'Wren'. These are all lepidote rhododendrons, (i.e. the undersides of the leaves and often other parts of the plants have scales). Whether a rhododendron has scales or not is an important factor in determining its botanical classification. Berg's Bees are comprised of both lepidote and elepidote rhododendrons. Here are the names of the Bees that I know, 'Ginny Gee', 'Golden Bee', 'Honey Bee', 'Jan Bee', 'King Bee', 'Patty Bee', 'Too Bee', 'Wanna Bee' and 'Wee Bee'. I grow a plant called 'Queen Bee'; however, I suspect someone preferred the title Queen to King (maybe an ardent feminist) because the Queen and the King are to my eye identical. Furthermore, the name 'Queen Bee' is officially given to a plant that was registered by another hybridizer in 1962 and I am sure that Warren Berg would not endorse a name, even in a casual way, which was already taken. ('Queen Bee' is in fact an authentic name.)

A small area would accommodate all of the above for a period of say 20 years. If my memory is correct there is a bank in the Cox garden/nursery at Glendoick, Scotland, with some, or maybe all, of the original Birds and some of these plants are now taller than a human. I have a plant of 'Egret' that is over 30 years old and it is almost shoulder height. Albert de Mezey, of local horticultural fame, and recently deceased at the age of 102, once advised me, "to grow rhododendrons one needs a physical age of 30 and a longevity of 300." This is true but one also needs a garden that is ever expanding as the darn things can become quite big during that period of time.

It is always satisfying to give one's prejudiced opinions an airing, so I offer some comments on the worthiness of some of these plants. In this age of governance by opinion poll one cannot ignore the preference of the buying public. The winner is without doubt 'Patty Bee'. 'Patty Bee' is a cross between *R. keiskei* 'Yaku Fairy' and *R. fletcherianum*. It passes the test of being better than either parent in several characteristics – although I would not like to be without either. 'Patty Bee' is more floriferous and reliably so from an early age; it is easier to please; the yellow flowers are of deeper intensity and of greater substance. Given a well drained but never dry, fairly open location, it will flourish and not outgrow a 75cm space for many years. The runner-up in the sales department is 'Ginny Gee'. I can hear the protests already; "this is not a Bee". Warren Berg introduced both hybrids about the same time (1970's). I suspect he had not settled on a line of Bees at that time and perhaps now he wishes he had perfect continuity. But perhaps not: 'Ginny Gee' is clearly a commemorative name and for that reason is cherished both by Warren and the chosen honouree. It grows in the same fashion as 'Patty Bee'. Its leaves are not so glossy and the flowers are pale pink and white. They both bloom in April. Having dwarf narcissus or other bulbs as companions solaces the sensibilities, even of those with acutely refined tastes.

My personal favourite is 'Razorbill'. Peter Cox writes that this is a chance seedling of *R. spinuliferum*. Imagine being so fortunate as unexpectedly discovering such a treasure! The flowers on 'Razorbill' are most unusual being up-facing tubes of rosy pink grouped in sizeable clusters. They are produced in profusion in March.

Cox's most famous dwarf is probably 'Curlew'. This won the Cory Cup at the Royal Horticultural Society for the best hybrid of any genus (1980?). It has proportionately very large flowers for the size of the leaf. It is surprisingly robust given the miffiness of both parents, *R. ludlowii* and *fletcherianum*. I have seen the first parent only at the Cox nursery and brought back two plants to Victoria. One I gave to a much better grower than I but neither of us was able to satisfy its temperamental needs. 'Curlew's flowers are a bright yellow with deeper shading and greenish brown spotting. Its bark is attractive and it has a somewhat open but interesting architecture. It does not like a hot site and resents too much fertilizer.

'Chikor' is a tiny bushy plant with soft yellow flowers in profusion – if well grown. This is one plant that certainly does better in the cooler Scottish summers. Gardeners who like the challenge of growing the higher elevation Asiatic primulas will enjoy 'Chikor'. 'Chikor' is a partridge-like Asian bird.

I really like Berg's 'Wee Bee'. It is very similar to 'Too Bee', being a sister seedling. Warren tried to register it as 'Not Too Bee' but evidently this was not allowed. The flower buds of 'Wee Bee' are of quite a dark hue; some call the colour turkey red. They open to a rose pink on the outside and pale yellow on the inside. If I had space for only one plant I would choose 'Wee Bee' over 'Ginny Gee'. Thank goodness they are dwarfs so this seldom becomes a gut wrenching decision.

Most of these plants are described in "Greer's Guidebook to Available Rhododendrons", third edition. This book is recommended as an inexpensive reference. However, the best reference is to see thrifty plants in a local garden. The easy ones pay their rent every month; the more difficult ones boost the ego and give a muted reward when a whimsical name like 'Too Bee' or 'Wanna Bee' rolls subtly off the tongue of a showing off gardener.

"Demons in Eden"
Book Review by Norman Todd
March 2006

This is a book I recommend you read. I found it fascinating and frightening. Jonathan Silvertown is a professor of ecology who, in this book, attempts to give some explanation for the Darwinian paradox that if evolution is driven by the survival of the fittest why, in the plant world, at any rate, are there about 400,000 species? Further, is there, to use his phrase, a 'Darwinian Demon' — a super-organism — waiting to swamp and conquer these 400,000 species? Our species, *Homo sapiens*, has caused major changes to occur in about 40% of the world's land surface. Have we become the 'Darwinian Devil'?

Silvertown is the author or editor of a number of previous books and I found it eerily significant that he states in his preface that finding a publisher for "Demons in Eden" was an "endurance test requiring the tenacity of a hardy perennial". This book is certainly a call to arms but Silvertown's approach is not just a tree hugger's tirade. I was persuaded by the logic of his observations and his adherence to scientific standards. The environment is being degraded incrementally. So what if another one or two, largely unknown, plants disappear every day? No one person or group or nation is responsible and it is not only 'economy versus environment' that is causal; it is our own perceived need for survival – on an ever-increasingly consumptive scale. A similar problem exists with human-generated emissions to the atmosphere. There is near unanimity in the scientific world that calamitous climate change is happening and we are causing it but the message is not being heard in any practical sense and, worse, is being denied and largely ignored.

Silvertown starts out with a current account of the green part of the "Tree of Life". The concept of showing the evolution of life-forms in the shape of a tree is a Darwinian one. In fact the only diagram in "The Origin of Species" is a schematic 'tree'. A particular part of Darwin's 1859 tree has now been redrawn using the molecular systematics of DNA. This part of the book describes the relationships among the flowering plants – the angiosperms. (The 2006 winter edition of our JARS has an article showing how Ben Hall and some of his students used this powerful kind of analysis to show the relationship of the various groups of *R. macrophyllum* growing on the west coast of our continent). The 'Tree of Life' story, as told by Silvertown, is short but complex. It has resulted from the collaborative work of forty-two scientists. Would you like to know the name of the plant at the base of the tree? It is *Amborella trichopoda*, an almost extinct tree from New Caledonia. Two surprises for me were that the division between dicotyledons (like oaks and rhododendrons) and monocotyledons (like grasses) did not occur at the base of the tree but up quite a way on one branch, and that the second oldest group of plants was the water lilies.

I had never heard of Barro Colorado Island. This is an island of fifteen square kilometers in the Panama Canal on the man-made Gatun Lake. Since 1923 an inventory of every growing shoot has been maintained. On the island there are 365 species of tree, 116 shrubs, 265 climbing plants and 466 herbaceous species. Their life cycles have been traced for over eighty years. Where are the demons? It is true that if you randomly chose one precise spot on the island there is a fifty percent chance of it being occupied by one species of tree. But there are rare plants and they continue to exist. Is rarity a survival mechanism in that it is not worth a predator's effort to evolve an appetite to use it as a food source? Can there be 1212 different niches that 1212 different plants can exploit? Silvertown quotes Dr. Seuss. I think it is worth repeating:

And NUH is the letter I use to spell Nutches
Who live in small caves, known as Nitches, for hutches.
These Nutches have trouble, the biggest of which is

The fact that there are many more Nutches than
Nitches.
Each Nutch in a Nitch knows that some other Nutch
Would like to move into his Nitch very much.
So each Nutch in a Nitch has to watch that small Nitch
Or Nutches who haven't got Nitches will snitch.

There is a chapter on how small these nitches can be.
Near Brighton in the south of England is Castle Hill
National Nature Reserve. It is an unremarkable – to the
uninitiated – stretch of grassland. Yet typically one square
foot of turf will contain thirty different species of flowering
plants. Here is the paradox. How can somehow similar
species compete with one another and yet coexist? There are
still many unanswered questions but you will be rewarded
with a better understanding of nitches on reading the book. I
was left feeling uneasy about how we grow our
rhododendrons. By and large we say, "Give them an acid,
humusy soil, lots of water and the ones with the bigger leaves
more shade." Still, despite being ruthless in exterminating
rhododendrons' obvious competition we have many
casualties. Read the book; it won't give you answers but will
certainly provide some excuses.
      There are other chapters: on the flora of the Canary
Islands; on a demon mountain in Japan, (should we be getting
a message from the demon bamboo that has learned that you
can't exhaust yourself in procreation and expect not to die in
the process?); on the rampant success of demons in Florida
and on pros and cons for genetically modified plants. I was
astonished to learn that North America is ten times more
welcoming to alien demons than Europe. However,
Silvertown cites the devilish success of "Rhododendron
ponticum" in Britain. The name is in quotation marks
because it is not *R. ponticum* any longer. The plants of
ponticum that were introduced to the U.K. quickly hybridized
with *R. catawbiense*. The latter is a very cold/heat hardy
plant. The vigour of the new hybrid was truly demonic and it
has laid claim to a nitch as aggressively as broom has here.

"Demons in Eden" is not a big book; it is only 147 pages but every one of these pages is disturbingly and challengingly provocative. I am about to take a swab from my mouth and send it off to the National Geographic Society. This organization has partnered with IBM in a genographic project. They will analyze my DNA and tell me where I fit on the humanoid "Tree of Life". I am going to receive confirmation of my monkey ancestry – a "Darwinian Demon"?

Jonathan Silvertown, "Demons in Eden" (The University of Chicago Press, 2005. ISBN:0-226-75771-4).

Bounty of *Basilicum*
May 2006

Some things are truly worth the wait. I sowed some seed of the big-leaf *R. basilicum* thirty-three years ago. The one remaining plant is now four metres high and is planted, unfortunately, too close to the driveway. The arching branches so annoyed the garbage collector that he would take purposeful aim at these big paddles of leaves, using his truck as a mobile macerator while dervishly screaming unprintable descriptions of the offending owner and the innocent basilicum. It had to be pruned and tied back.

I cherished the plant but it never bloomed. Every time I passed it I would coo encouraging words and tell it that I was not going to croak until it showed me a blossom. It has bloomed for the last three years. Now, as I pass it I am somewhat trepidatious and have changed my message to one of praise for its beauty and how it is adding to my longevity.

This year it opened its first bloom at the start of February and two months later it is still resplendent. The first flush of colour is a soft salmon cream. Inside, the corolla is a dark purple blotch. The substance of the flower is of a heavy, waxy, vellum-like texture. As they age the flowers lose the warmer tones and become a cool cream. There are sixteen

212

stamens. The flowers were not harmed by the frost we had in March when it got down to -3°C. Some of the thinner substance blooms like 'Snow Lady', 'Airy Fairy', and *R. ririei* went brown. The rhododendrons that bloom early do last longer than the later flowering ones but I can't think of another rhododendron where the flowers last for two months. In fairness, I do have to mention 'Lee's Scarlet' and 'Nobleanum Coccineum' for length of bloom. The latter opened its first flower in October, the last in March. 'Lee's Scarlet' had colour for 14 or 15 weeks. However, these plants open their blooms in a succession; each individual truss lasting three or four weeks. Still, the vital question is, dare I take selfish, ominous comfort from the longevity of the blooms on *basilicum*?

Basilicum (meaning 'royal') is in the Falconera Subsection in the Subgenus Hymenanthes. Its closest relatives are *R. arizelum* and *R. rothschildii*. I read, fairly recently, that the true *basilicum* is rare in cultivation. I hope, for snobby reasons, that mine is correctly named. No one has contradicted its appellation but not many of the authorities have had a chance to cast judgment. I was ecstatic when about two weeks ago two passing municipal workers who were looking for potholes to fill came into the nursery and one wanted to buy that "tall plant with the pale yellow flowers". The potential buyer was less than ecstatic when I told him it was not for sale.

In a woodland setting there are no better plants for early season impact than the large-leaf rhododendron. The big drawback is their slowness in reaching the age of puberty. One can rationalize about this characteristic by reminding oneself that one must treat rhododendrons as foliage plants; as a bonus they occasionally have flowers. Now that there are one or two that indulge themselves (and me) in an annual floral extravaganza, I consider the twenty or thirty or more years waiting to see a bloom, time to be well spent; yet there can be no denying the obvious truth that, in modern times, when the average person will not buy a green banana, the large-leaf rhododendrons are merely botanical curiosities.

Some authorities claim that a flower lasts for as long as it takes to get the job done, (i.e. to effect pollination). I am not expert enough to be able to say if *basilicum* is one of the plants that does not ever self-pollinate. There are other rhododendrons blooming close enough to *basilicum* that would probably have compatible pollen. So this year I will leave the spent flowers on the plant and determine if any seed have formed. I then plan to sow these seed. I may have time to find out if the seed will germinate but....

We are now at the end of the last weeks of April and the first flowers are still adorning the driveway. I will not remove them. I will indulge the garbage collector and let him press them with his heavily laden tires. Plants give pleasure in so many ways. *Basilicum* deserves a few bravos and olés. "Large was his bounty and his soul sincere."

Postscript. Not fifteen minutes after I typed the word "sincere" above, the garbage truck was here and deftly put a gouge in my wife's car. I must exonerate the driver. This was his first time here (not the usual driver) and he came in the wrong way. He had not seen *basilicum* at that point. He was still able to crush the flowers on the way out.

Memories of a Salesman
August 2006

Ernest Hemmingway said that all you have to do to get going in writing an article was write the truest sentence you know. The rest came easy. A true sentence that I know is "I enjoy selling rhododendrons." Another is, "Time makes most memories pleasant." I'm not at all sure that the rest will come easily but it worked for him so I'll give it a try.

Often one memory leads to another. Pajamas link the first two. Both occurred about twenty years ago. It's always a lot of work to select, gather, price and load plants for the sales the rhododendron clubs hold each year. I have always had a small truck and stacking as many plants as possible into the limited available space is an acquired skill.

Come the Saturday, I set off for Courtney or Campbell River, I've forgotten which, in the pre-dawn stillness. The salivary glands were becoming over stimulated as I passed the still closed cafes. Seven o'clock found me at Bowser when I saw the 'Closed' sign being flipped to 'Open' on a homey looking roadside eatery. The proprietress gave a friendly 'Good Morning', rubbing her still sleep filled eyes while putting on the coffee. Two or three locals ambled in. We sat in a row and watched our hostess grease the grill and start our breakfasts. During conversation, as I was being quizzed about what brought me to these parts, I said that I was on my way to a sale of rhododendrons and that my down-by-the-stern truck parked at the front door was jam-packed with choice plants. I know the lady owner used the phone but the local Bowser communication system worked more quickly than B.C. Tel could possibly have, and soon a sizeable proportion of Bowser's population, many clad in their pajamas, was milling around my truck. I could only reach the plants that an opened canopy door would allow but it didn't really matter. In a very short time I had sold 17 plants and was on my way with a contented stomach and a lighter truck.

Sleepwear figured in another rhododendron sale. I had a visit from a lady asking if I could come and look at a site where she wanted to plant rhododendrons. It was a south facing sloping site treed with Garry oaks, ideal for rhododendrons. The only problem was the soil was clay. It had to be amended. The lady said that that would not be a problem; she had lots of help and would attend to it right away and could I deliver the next Monday morning at eight o'clock?. It turned out that she was the sister of the Catholic Archbishop. She and her brother lived on the top floor of a fairly large three-story building. The rest of the building was occupied by the labour-supplying nuns. When I arrived on the Monday morning with a full load of plants the ample planting holes were awaiting their new inhabitants. The sisters may have forgotten the early eight o'clock start but in any event they eagerly turned out in sleeping-robe habits to place and plant the new residents. But not before we all stood with bowed heads as they were given a welcoming blessing.

A person can become fully aware of his limitations when selling. A very elegant lady came in to the nursery and wanted a very particular colour of pink rhododendron. She had a paint chip to show me precisely what was required. I started out very positively, as good salesmen do, but pointed out that the flowers of most rhododendrons changed in hue from bud to maturity but that at least for some of the time the one I was suggesting would be close to that of the displayed Cloverdale prescription. My assurances were unavailing; it had to be that precise shade. As we walked around I quickly exhausted my vocabulary of adjectives and in despair, I said, "You know, I really don't give a lot of thought to what colour goes next to what." The lady drew herself up imperiously and observed, "That is very obvious; but you are not an artist."

It's the name of a plant that is the important factor in a surprising number of cases. I often get requests for 'Golden Anniversary' and 'Golden Wedding'. I suppose with the divorce rate increasing such requests will become less frequent. There seems to be a continuing demand for 'Bambino'. One lady had just lost her pet rabbit. She had buried it in a prominent place and wanted to mark its entombment with an appropriately named rhododendron. 'Forever Yours' met all the specifications. I felt more comfortable with another burial site planting where the person being commemorated was an Inuit. Her daughter thought a planting of 'Snow Lady' was symbolically apt. The best cat we ever had was Kate. She was a silky longhaired bundle of mischievous unconditional affection. I had a vague recollection that Lionel de Rothschild had named one of his hybrids for his eldest daughter – 'Our Kate'. It is a cross of R. calophytum and R. macabeanum. It took a while to find a plant but I eventually did and it is thriving atop the beloved Kate. I should say that it was thriving. This year its big leaves have burned in the endless sunshine. At least I hope it's sunburn; it could be that Kate is paying for all her pranks in her afterlife.

One time a plant's name was its downfall. The customer owned waterfront out at Sooke. The site was exposed to the November southwest gales and he needed a tough plant. However, it had to grow to some size and have large blossoms. I had a nice blooming plant of a then fairly new hybrid that was reputed to be a vigourous survivor. The customer was enthusiastic about the suggested candidate. During conversation he mentioned that he was an important member of the Social Credit party. Bill Vander Zalm was Premier at the time. In discussion, I must have said that the plant's name was 'Solidarity'. He winced. My suggestion that he call it for his dog or his wife was to no avail: not under any circumstances would he have a plant with that name in his garden.

We laugh at it now but at the time we were aghast. One of the early sales put on by the Duncan club was held in their big shopping mall. We had our sales tables set out in the central concourse. As I recall our sales area was marked by rope strung between stanchions. As is normal the price of the plant was on a detachable label, which was removed at the time of sale. One of the potential customers was a strikingly beautiful blonde. She assiduously studied each display of plants and quizzed the avid vendors about their qualities (i.e. the plants). I remember Les Clay was totally enraptured for some time before the Duncan Duper, as she later became known, turned her charms on Gordon Pirie who as usual was helping sell at my tables. Gordon is a great salesman and in time had her shopping cart filled with about $200 worth of prime rhododendrons. The steely-nerved lady wheeled her cart straight through the checkout unchallenged. Gordon's height, or his fascination, allowed him to observe her progress and he shouted out, "That lady didn't pay!" He and another member gave chase and as she reached her truck they politely asked her if she had paid for her plants. The price tags were still obvious. She bold-facedly stated she had paid; the

217

checkout people must have forgotten to take the tags. She loaded her truck and drove off, never to be seen again.

I'll finish this with a tale I've told before. I used to have an annual visitation from a sculptor and his model/assistant/companion. I knew the lady's husband, having worked with him years back. The sculptor was clearly of an anticipatory, amatory frame of mind and indicated that he intended to buy her a rhododendron. It was early in the year and there was not a huge amount of bloom. However, 'Emasculum' was in its full glory. While the choice of plant was being considered the lady decided she needed a bag of fertilizer. To this the sculptor objected on the grounds that he did not want to risk the 25-kilo plastic bag being punctured with possible corrosive contamination of his gleaming new macho automobile. I could sense a tension. This developed in a volubly heated fashion. Breaking away, the lady returned to admire 'Emasculum'. I had explained that it was the only one I had and it was not for sale. I must have been blabbing on, as I was somewhat embarrassed at being witness to their tiff. Anyway, I pointed out that the plant was so named because it had no anthers; it had no male parts. The lady, who was continental European by birth, became very emotional and agitated and jumped up and down while exclaiming that she simply must have it. She just had to have it. They did come back the next year.

I've got a grand memory for forgetting but these are some of the memories that have stuck and they do meet the Hemmingway veracity standard.

Conference Collecting
November 2006

I suppose I must admit to being more a collector than a gardener. There is a saying that I've heard other rhododendron growers with the same problem use, "The best rhododendron is the one you don't have in your garden." With so many thousands of hybrid rhododendrons even the most addicted collector is never tempted to think, even when daydreaming, of acquiring a collection. The most ardent might try to collect every plant of one hybridizer's efforts. With species, however, if one has a bit of space there is a possibility of growing a sizable proportion of the total available plants.

My affliction is less severe than that of some others I know or have known. I restrict myself to growing only those that have a chance of surviving outside. The *Vireyas* are not an uncontrollable temptation. Even thinking about growing those species that might survive our temperate conditions is an unobtainable goal. The Rhododendron Species Foundation and The Royal Botanic Gardens do not have a complete collection.

Nevertheless, acquiring a species one does not have is a red-letter day. The law of marginal returns does not apply. So the recent conference at Harrison Hot Springs was for me a stellar affair. I latched onto eleven species not currently in the garden. I have to admit that three of them are replacements. This means there is a stimulus for greater care in having them survive. Then, to put icing on the cake, Burns Morrison gave me a *R. taggianum*, one of the *Maddenia* that was on my extensive wish list. The other events at the conference were pretty good too – the talks, the bonsai workshop, the after-banquet talk (performance is a better word) by Des Kennedy. One drawback to the weekend was that the photographs that Steve Hootman of the RSF showed at his talks accentuated the acquisitive affliction – I wouldn't say it made it much worse but it kept it very much alive.

I will now bore you with a list of the new goodies and try to defend why I want to grow them. *R. flinkii* has fabulous foliage. If you know *R. lanatum*, then deepen the luxuriance of the indumentum, put it on a plant with a better figure and you will have a good idea of its desirability. I already had a couple of these plants in the garden. These I got from Clint Smith who could root the darned thing. There is no use making excuses – they are no longer around. Carol Dancer has a magnificent specimen growing in a pot and that is what I am going to do with the new one.

I have also had *R. baileyi* before. I even had flowers on it. I don't think it is too challenging to grow; it is hardy enough for our region. I'm sure some members grow it but I can't remember seeing it. It is not a real showstopper but it is different. It has deep purple flowers, 2 to 3 cm across. What is different is that the flowers have long pedicels that spray the flowers out like a bursting firework. Cox puts it in its own Subsection while Greer includes it with the *Lepidota*. Also in its own Subsection (and one I have also owned and killed) is *R. genestierianum*. The flowers are similar to those of *baileyi* but the leaves are much longer. The plant I got at Harrison is quite small so it too will stay in a pot and have winter protection. It starts into growth very early and is not very hardy. When I do plant it out a western exposure would be advisable.

Completely unknown, with a name I have difficulty remembering, is *R. pubicostatum*. It has very handsome foliage with the underside of the leaves purple/red – the precursor of indumentum. In the Cox Encyclopedia there is a one-inch entry that notes it comes from N.E. Yunnan and that it is probably a natural hybrid of *R. bureavii*. It is definitely a keeper. *R. ochraceum* induced sweaty palms and an aggressive grab when spotted. This is evidently like a small leaved version of *R. strigillosum*. Cox writes that it may well be one of the best introductions in recent years. I will not have to wait long to see the flower; my plant is budded.

I don't recall ever seeing a plant of *R. cyanocarpum*. This could well be a difficult plant to keep happy. It is reputed to be fussy about location and susceptible to powdery mildew. It is a member of the Thomsonia, and has apple blossom pink/white flowers on a small tree early in spring.

I acquired another member of the *Thomsonia – R. stewartianum*. This is another rhododendron not often seen. It is also a challenge, as it is known for its lack of vigour in cultivation. Certainly the one specimen I had years ago whimped along for a few years, getting more and more frail before giving up the ghost. The plant I got at Harrison has an ARS seed number and may be a new introduction; I hope so, as it may be a more robust version.

This list seems without end but I have to suppress my modesty and keep on bragging. *R. jucundum* before the latest taxonomic revisions was given specific rank; now it is a subspecies of *R. selense*. It is supposed to bloom as a young plant, the flowers being bell-shaped in a rich pink truss of six or seven.

Steve Hootman showed a picture of a *R. hardyi* that confirmed my purchase was a good one. It is the white form of *R. augustinii*. To be truthful I had looked at photographs and read descriptions of this subspecies and was not overly lustful to possess it. Steve's photograph was of a plant I thought to be as good as *R. rigidum* (this plant was co-winner of the Peoples' Choice at the last show). The new plant has a single stem about 25 cm high. I was very tempted to snip its head off for a cutting but after reading it was difficult to root from a cutting I desisted and will wait until there is more propagating material.

Another treasure is *R. facetum*. I already have a plant of this but I believe the new one is a better form. *Facetum* is a red, late flowering medium sized shrub. The plant I have in the garden is leggy and open. The recent collections give promise of a neater habit. The last one (phew!) is *R. pruniflorum*. This is a plum/purple *R. glaucophyllum*. The smallish leaves are whitish underneath with very visible brown scales. It is a good leaf to demonstrate what a lepidote is. All of the plants in the *Glauca* have strongly aromatic foliage. For those who benefit from aromatherapy taking cuttings of this group is a recommended pastime.

I am writing this at Thanksgiving. One thing I like about Thanksgiving is that along with Labour Day we have not yet found an aggressively exploitive way of commercializing it. It could be that if turkeys came in different flavors or colours there could be a temptation to collect them. In some ways I equate the annual regional fall conference to a holiday. It really is a thanksgiving and now I

221

have to find a way to defend it as not having become an orgy of consumerism.

Early Bloomers
January 2008

    I was not an early bloomer but I do remember a few who stood out or sat up in my early schooldays. They sat up because the bright ones were always seated at the top of the class. They were not always the best looking but they certainly were aware of their status. Standing out right now, as I write this in mid-November is the first flower of the vibrant red 'Nobleanum Coccineum'. This champion will have some opened flowers until the end of March or even into April. Blooming all through winter has its drawbacks, as had some of the Grade 2 smarties who were often not very coordinated in the gym. The opened flowers will take -2°C or even -3°C before going brown. The unopened buds stay patiently waiting for the unwelcomed, discourteous cold snap to go back to Alberta.

    'Nobleanum Coccineum' has a pink sister with another (now disallowed) pretentious, specific sounding name, 'Nobleanum Venustum'. Both are hybrids from mid-1800's, when there were no nomenclature police to prohibit hybrids sounding like species. 'Lee's Scarlet' always blooms for Christmas and it too lasts for at least three months. We call it the "Ho, Ho, Ho, plant". 'Heatherside Beauty' – white with a pink spotted throat – is the most backward of this group, not blooming until February. They are probably all *causicum, arboreum* crosses. I have a plant called 'Jacksonii' that has, to my eyes, the same flower as 'Rosamundi', but I think over almost 200 years some plants could have been mislabeled or mixed up and one must be somewhat suspicious of what is on the tag. For example, the plant called 'Christmas Cheer', in my garden anyway, doesn't bloom until the end of March. I have read that it was so named because in the mid-nineteenth century only the wealthy were growing

222

rhododendrons and this plant could be brought into their stove houses and forced into bloom over Christmas. It is often confused with 'Rosamundi'.

The first species rhododendron to bloom for us is *R. rirei*. This is a big plant now placed in the *Argyrophylla* Subsection. Most years it blooms for New Year's Day. Last year with our earlier bitter November it decided it was not salubrious enough to risk showing its crowning glory until the 1st of February. This was a wise decision because its flowers are very frost tender. The blossoms are lilac-purple with very large dark nectarines. From these flow copious streams of nectar, like the tears from a grief stricken widow. I never see any insects tapping this bounty but perhaps with the Anna's hummingbirds now being resident all winter their hyperactive metabolism could benefit from utilizing it. I will be watching for them. There is an early blooming plant with a deeper flower colour at the University with the *rirei* name on it but it has no trace of indumentum. This makes the name doubtful. It could be a hybrid but with what? Perhaps someone knows the provenance of this plant.

In this short piece I define 'early' as "starting to bloom before the end of February". There are a number of the smaller leaf lepidotes that will meet this criterion. Thirty-five years ago when the Abkhazis were still gardening their Fairfield property there was a good dark, January blooming, purple form of *R. dauricum* . I'm not sure if it's still there. I propagated it and had a plant for quite a few years but it too is no longer. I certainly would like to replace it. *Dauricum's* deciduous cousin *R. mucronulatum* will give a great show in February. I claim that the 'Cornell Pink' form is better than any cherry, although, of course, much smaller. 'Praecox', a *mucronulatum* hybrid gives a rewarding show, as does 'Olive'. Both are old veterans.

There are two plants that I love – most of the time. When 'Airy Fairy' blooms I think it is the best plant in the garden. It's not too bad in October/November when many of the old leaves are bright red and orange but for the rest of the year it can only be described as nondescript. It is a cross of *R.*

lutescens and *mucronulatum,* and the yellow of the *lutescens* melds artfully with the clear pink of *mucronulatum.* There is a newer plant with the same parents called 'Coral Glow'. It is more deciduous than 'Airy Fairy' and in the fall months looks really scruffy. But when it blooms in February it is stunning (roses, too, look awful in winter). 'Coral Glow', although I have not grown it long enough to be on statistically solid ground has, over the last few years, bloomed for at least two months. It is a tall, narrow plant growing about 50 cm a year. It does not need much acreage and thus is good for the small garden where some height can be pleasing. *Lutescens*, the first of the *Triflora* to bloom, is a great plant. The end of February usually sees that impressive sunny mass lighting up the still short days.

There are two other end-of-February bloomers that are among the hard working infantry of our rhododendron army and must be mentioned in dispatches. No garden should be without them. They are not very large so there is room for them in every landscape. Place them side by side with at least two of one and one of the other. 'Cilpinense' has *R. ciliatum* and *R. moupinense* as parents, whereas 'Snow Lady' substitutes *R. leucaspis* for *moupinense*. 'Snow Lady' has fairly open pure white flowers with contrasting chocolate anthers. It has fuzzy, hairy foliage. 'Cilpinense's' leaves are shinier. Both are broader than tall and need good exposure to keep a tight shape. 'Cilpinense' (often mislabeled *moupinense*) has pink rims to the white centers. The pink bleeds into the white like a watercolour painting.

Earliness of bloom gives those who possess it a memory-jolting advantage over the thousands that start their blooming career in March when they are competing with so many challenging and bright good-lookers. The late bloomers lose out somewhat too, because there are so many other summer blooming rivals in the landscape.

Our local climate is really quite favourable for the earliest. Sure, they might get their noses frost-bitten once in a while but they always manage to give some show. Besides, we can play the victim when some blossoms are browned and seek commiseration from our fellow gardeners. We all love to play "Ain't it awful". It is nice, too, to tell your eastern friends and family what's blooming its head off in January.

A Spring Surprise
April 2008

I know spring is not here yet if you go by something as technical as an equinox that occurs with some precision someplace in the world, but there is a first flower on a plant that had been forgotten in the mess I call my garden and that to me means spring has arrived. The plant has the name *R. hylaeum* on it. That probably doesn't mean much to most people but that is really not so surprising as until fairly recently those who know about these things said it was doubtful if it was in cultivation.

Hylaeum means 'living on the mountain' and I can believe that is where it would show up best as it will get to be a fairly large shrub or small tree. The now dated but still regularly used Davidian's "The Rhododendron Species" with its four volumes of boilerplate prose does not even describe it other than placing it in with the Thomsonia. The Coxes say it should probably be merged with *R. faucium*. No matter, it pleases me. The one, solitary truss has a dozen rich pink flowers, bell shaped, each about 5 cm long. These are supplying an army of small ants with a Cowichan Bay smorgasbord of scrumptious sustenance. The upper lobes of the corolla are heavily spotted in purple/pink.

Now comes the dilemma. The Species Workshop starting this coming weekend (15, 16 March) will have the top North American taxonomical expert, Steve Hootman, teaching those fortunate enough to be attending how to key out the various species. This abstruse and, to most, mysterious process will be made transparent by Steve. This could confirm, or deny, the authenticity of my plant's label. But to sever that one truss would take a fair amount of courage. Then, if Steve pronounced it was merely *faucium* or,

225

still worse, a hybrid, could I accept the resulting psychological damage? I still have memories of a visit Steve made to our garden and to my deep chagrin pronounced many of my chestswelling treasures to be rogues. One characteristic of the plant gives me a little confidence; the bark is supposed to be smooth and peeling. My plant is not old enough to show this clearly but there are indications that the bark may exhibit this. I hope so. *R. barbatum* is another species with shiny purplish bark. I have a clear image in my mind of a surreal grove of century-old *barbatums* in Dunedin, New Zealand with shining ghostly trunks. My plants of *barbatum* are still just juniors at a quarter of that age, and only now does this become a feature worth remarking on.

I have a lovely yellow of low sprawling habit now blooming that I am not going to take to the Workshop. It has the name *R. valentinianum* on it. I can't remember where this plant came from. It may be it came from a now demised plant of that name that occupied what proved to be an inhospitable site. The late Herman Vaartnou decreed it to be merely a lowly hybrid called 'Quaver'. 'Quaver' is a Rothschild cross of *R. sulphureum* and *R. leucaspis*. Herman maintained that *valentinianum* should have a straight style (you can gather from this degree of exactitude how fussy these darned taxonomists can be – and very often they disagree with each other). The little that I have read on *valentinianum* does not mention a straight style as being diagnostic. The few pictures I have seen of *valentinianum* show a style much longer than the anthers – not the case in my plant – so I am resigned to having one less species and will not waste Steve's time. From a landscaper's plebian point of view, 'Quaver' is probably a more pleasing plant so I can rationalize about playing down the snobbiness.

Somewhat disappointing this year is the amount of bloom on the four or five plants I have of *R. irroratum*. The flower colour on the species is very variable; some are deep pink, some almost white and some cream. Some open in early March and others stay in tight bud until April. They all exhibit a severe case of measles. Every lobe is covered with

226

noninfectious spots that might inhibit our medical members from including *irroratum* in their gardens. Two of Victoria's local dignitaries are commemorated by what the socially conscious cognoscenti claim to be good members of the species: 'Prince Abkhazi' and 'Princess Abkhazi'. These originated from the aforementioned Herman Vaartnou's garden and were grown from open pollinated seed. The Prince, in accordance with the protocol, comes two weeks before the Princess. I would never wish to be counted among those who cast any doubt on the purity of their lineage so the plants are in the *irrorata* for sure, and I will definitely take a branch to the Workshop for forensic examination. We have a very fine watercolor by Bonnie Moro of the freckled Princess gracing a wall that one faces descending stairs, so it is always advisable to hold the banister tightly as the picture is mesmerizingly dangerous.

I will remark on one other gem that is in bloom. It may be worth having keyed out. I got it many years ago from Milton Wildfong of Mission. He called it the Exbury form of *R. strigillosum*. Most of us think of this species as being a strong primary red and I have to admit that I like the forms that stay red better. (Also they are certainly better sellers.) The Exbury form opens with deep red flowers but fairly quickly they fade to deep pink. There is a close relative called *R. pachytrichum* that has pink flowers. Ken Gibson grows a plant called *R. monosematum* that some authorities classify as a variety of *pachytrichum*. This is described as being half way between *strigillosum* and *pachytrichum*. It could be that what I call the Exbury form of *strigillosum* is this intergrade. (It turned out to be *pachytrichum*.)

I have to mention one other spring surprise. Again, I have some doubt about the correct nomenclature for this plant. It is certainly *R. oreodoxa* but is it Variety *oreodoxa* or Variety *fargesii*? The flower is a deep pink that is more typical of *fargesii*. I have another plant with that name and it is the best moisture meter in the garden. As soon as this *oreodoxa* experiences any lack of moisture the leaves curl up, long before any other rhodo shows any sign of stress. This is said to be a genetic trait of *oreodoxa*. The plant that is blooming now does not evince this habit.

One conclusion from all this is that names can become a fetish or a phobia. One should also remember that there is sometimes no clear disjoint between species. The concept of a species is a fluid one – essential for science but not at all necessary for the enjoyment of a garden. Still, I would not like to be referred to as thingimijig.